P9-BVM-450

DISCARDED

Being and Becoming in the Classroom

Recent Titles in
Issues in Curriculum Theory, Policy, and Research
Ian Westbury and Margery D. Osborne, Series Editors

The Pursuit of Curriculum: Schooling and the Public Interest
William A. Reid

In Search of More Effective Mathematics Education: Examining Data from the IEA Second
International Mathematics Study
Ian Westbury, Corinna A. Ethington, Lauren A. Sosniak et al.

Deliberation in Education and Society
J.T. Dillon

Reconceiving Mathematics Instruction: A Focus on Errors
Raffaella Borasi

Against the Odds: The Meaning of School and Relationships in the Lives of Six Young
African-American Men
Jeremy N. Price

Looking into Classrooms: Papers on Didactics
Peter Menck

Narrative Inquiry in a Multicultural Landscape: Multicultural Teaching and Learning
JoAnn Phillion

Being

— and Becoming
in the Classroom

Wolff-Michael Roth

Issues in Curriculum Theory, Policy, and Research
Ian Westbury and Margery D. Osborne, Series Editors

Ablex Publishing
Westport, Connecticut • London

Library of Congress Cataloging-in-Publication Data

Roth, Wolff-Michael, 1953–
    Being and becoming in the classroom / Wolff-Michael Roth.
        p. cm.—(Issues in curriculum theory, policy, and research)
    Includes bibliographical references (p.   ) and index.
    ISBN 1–56750–670–4 (alk. paper)
    1. Teachers—Training of. 2. Teaching. 3. Teaching teams. I. Title. II. Series.
LB1707.R68 2002
    371.1—dc21   2001053830

British Library Cataloguing in Publication Data is available.

Copyright © 2002 by Wolff-Michael Roth

All rights reserved. No portion of this book may be
reproduced, by any process or technique, without the
express written consent of the publisher.

Library of Congress Catalog Card Number: 2001053830
ISBN: 1–56750–670–4

First published in 2002

Ablex Publishing, 88 Post Road West, Westport, CT 06881
An imprint of Greenwood Publishing Group, Inc.
www.ablexbooks.com

Printed in the United States of America

The paper used in this book complies with the
Permanent Paper Standard issued by the National
Information Standards Organization (Z39.48–1984).

10 9 8 7 6 5 4 3 2 1

Contents

Acknowledgments

A project that leads to a book such as this is never possible without the help of many others, whose agency remains in the background.

I am grateful to the teachers who invited me to teach in their classrooms, an experience that was foundational for the work I am describing here. These teachers include Nadely Boyd, Charles Davis, Josette Désquin, Ken Foster, Ken Neale, Laurie Roche, Christina Schnetzler, Kenneth Tobin, Bridget Walshe, and Andrea Zimmermann. They never hesitated to have me coteach with them in their classrooms, despite differences in experience and power that could have mediated our interactions. My thanks also go to the superintendents and principals who encouraged us to work in their schools and thereby to assist some of the resident teachers to improve their praxis and learn about teaching. I am grateful to all of these individuals for allowing us to videotape coteaching lessons and cogenerative dialogue sessions, and for allowing me to use the materials in this book. Important members of my research team were Sylvie Boutonné, Michael Bowen, and Michelle McGinn, who were reliable companions in the classrooms, always prepared to videotape, transcribe, and serve as sounding boards for my budding understandings.

My special thanks go to three individuals, Daniel (Danny) Lawless, Domenico Masciotra, and Kenneth (Ken) Tobin. Through his willingness to discuss my evolving ideas, Danny allowed me to recognize my shortcomings and, by attempting to overcome them, to learn about teaching. Having traveled for some ways with me without ever beginning his Ph.D., Danny has felt the calling of the classroom. I feel a deep gratitude for his presence in my life and the joys of supervising that he has allowed me to experience. He did a tremendous job in editing some of the chapters and in assisting me in formulating several key concepts. Another individual tremendously important to my own learning and the shaping of the concepts presented here is Domenico. A highly accom-

plished practitioner of karate, his experiences and thoughts on action without reflection have been highly relevant to my thinking about teaching in a non-
rationalist manner. Ken has been a traveling companion for some time and we
have engaged in many conversations about teaching, conduct research together,
and communicate almost daily via email about our latest ideas on teaching. This
book would not have come about without Ken's continuous support and encour-
agement.

Importantly, I thank my wife, Sylvie Boutonné, because, with seemingly
infinite patience, she put up with the countless hours that I spent at the computer analyzing data, communicating with other researchers, and writing chapters.

Finally, grants from the Social Sciences and Humanities and Humanities
Council of Canada (410-96-0681 and 410-99-0021) assisted in the data collec-
tion and writing of this work. However, all opinions are my own.

Introduction

To understand the structure and dynamics of different forms of learning, whether incidental or conscious, we have to study them as parts or aspects of concrete historical activities with specifiable subjects, objects and instruments, within specifiable contexts. (Engeström 1987: 29)

This book is about being and becoming a teacher. It is also about coming to understand the lived experience of teaching, not through the objectifying gaze of an Other, but through my own experience of teaching, particularly teaching alongside one or more others. In the process of becoming a teacher, I have had to wrestle with the gap between the experience of teaching in the then-and-there of each classroom and the models of teaching that I had come across. It is not that teaching as reflective practice (Schön 1987), the distinction of teacher knowledge along content and pedagogical aspects (Shulman 1987), or any other model, for that matter, did not describe some aspect of my teacher being. Outside the classroom—or even in the classroom while my students were working independently—and while talking to others *about* what I was doing, I both engaged in reflection and could classify such models in terms of content knowledge, pedagogical content, etc. But these frameworks did not describe my experience, for example, of conducting a whole-class conversation about the forces in a pulley system. In the heat of the moment, there is no time out for reflection; there is no time to consider various aspects of content and pedagogical knowledge. In the heat of the moment, I teach the way I walk: I do not think *about* teaching, but teach in the same unreflective way that I place one foot in front of the other. For many years, I did not talk about this gap but rather attempted to repress it because the reigning hegemony of reflective practice and professional knowledge made me feel to be a lesser teacher because of it. Although I learned to talk about my teaching in terms of reflective practice and the different parts of professional knowledge (Roth 1993), I did not openly admit to the gap between my lived experience of teaching and what the existing theories of practice articulated. But I am getting ahead of myself. To understand the phenomenological project underlying this book—concerned with being and becoming in the classroom—it has to be situated and studied, historically, as Yrjö Engeström intimates in the introductory quote.

BECOMING A TEACHER

Around the age of ten, I wanted to become a teacher. One year later, however, while repeating fifth grade because of the academic problems that I was experiencing, I viewed teaching much less glamorously.

Becoming a teacher was not on my mind again until, after two years of college, I had to decide what to do with my life. Somehow, teaching art or a physics/geography combination had surged as viable career options. After weeks of agony, the choice fell in favor of the physics/geography path. However, the program advisor at my university forecast trouble. He only gave me two semesters, suggesting that I would drop out because of the lack of mathematics in my chosen program, which would lead me to failure in physics. Out of spite, I abandoned the idea of becoming a teacher and switched into a research master's degree in physics with applied mathematics as a minor. I did fail a couple of courses! But I was allowed to retake them and ultimately I passed. Thus, despite my early failures, I ended rather successfully.

During the five years in the physics program, I began to tutor high school students in physics, mathematics, and chemistry. The *Feynman Lectures in Physics* (Feynman, Leighton, and Sands 1989) had taught me that looking differently at problems changes them and allows for different solutions, which are often easier to implement . This was what I attempted to teach my tutees, with some success as their rapidly improving grades appeared to indicate. I also did a lot of mathematical exploring with my tutees rather than sticking with the problems from the textbook.

My First Classroom

Having completed my graduate degree in physics and done some contract work, I searched for employment in Montreal in the hot summer of 1980. The job market for physicists was tight. It was tight for teachers, too, and I knew of teachers with less than ten years of experience who were being laid off. But in my search for a job, I began to notice the ads for teachers in the north; they frequently did not require teacher training or a teaching certificate. I began to apply, and my second interview resulted in an opportunity: I was offered a position to teach science and mathematics in Rivière St. Paul, Quebec, a small, isolated community on the south coast of the Labrador peninsula.

There was little work—fishing was the only way to make a living besides teaching or running one of the few tiny stores. Usually, men attempted to work only for ten weeks, which was enough to qualify them for forty weeks of unemployment insurance payments. Only some of the women worked, usually in the fish plant; the others stayed at home, tending the children. There was little incentive for doing schoolwork or completing school—to go beyond ninth grade, students had to move a thousand miles away; of those who made the move, most dropped out of school within one year and returned to the village.

When I arrived, it turned out that I was not only to teach mathematics and physical science but also, over the two years that I stayed, biology, art, physical education, moral education, and sexual education. How was I going to teach science and mathematics? How was I going to teach arts and physical education? For lack of a better starting point, I considered the most enjoyable learning experiences I myself had experienced. It turned out that these were mostly associated with situations that were not formally organized: while doing contract work, while painting or shooting photographs, and while doing projects whose goals I set myself. In all of these situations, learning was rewarding, contrasting my own, rather drab experiences of learning at school. Most important, I wanted to avoid giving my students the experience of failure that I have had in the past. I promised myself to always look at students with difficulties through my own experience as a fifth grader.

After a few weeks, my physical science students began to design and conduct their own experiments with the materials that came in the kit of *Introductory Physical Science* (Haber-Schaim, Cutting, Kirksey, and Pratt 1994). Although there was no room for a lab other than an open basement with a six-foot ceiling, we never stayed in the classroom. At the beginning of each lesson, the students had to use buckets to bring water down into the basement. Each group had to huddle around the few desks that functioned as lab tables. The fire extinguishers had been out of order for years. A few 100-watt bulbs sparsely lit the scene. Despite these circumstances, students appeared to enjoy science: meeting me in the village after school, they talked about what they would do the next day. Together, we did some of the experiments that were suggested in our small textbook; but we invented many more investigations by asking questions, individually and collectively.

Other subjects asked for creative problem framing and solution finding as well. For example, the school had no art materials other than a few cans of watercolors. For years, the students had been asked to do pencil drawings; they never had had formal instruction in the arts. Having had four college art courses and being a hobby artist, I thought to change that. We collected dry driftwood and, with the tools students brought from home, made "feelies," objects that felt good in the hand. A book on Goethe's color theory inspired me to propose color experiments. I brought the cans of watercolor and a few dishes from the science kit to hold and mix small amounts of color. Choosing their favorite color, the students first painted a scale from pure color, subsequently mixed the color with water, until they used water only on the other side of the scale. Then they made a painting in monochrome. Next, before doing a picture with two colors, they constructed a scale moving from one color to another. We continued our investigations by asking, "What would be interesting to try next?" and moved to other experiments related to color contrasts, shadows, mixtures, and so forth.

The Theory-Praxis Gap

At the end of the school year, I felt good. Although what I had done could be described only as untutored experimenting in pedagogy, it turned out to be a successful year. The students overwhelmingly liked my classes; their parents wanted me to return to the village for the following year. I knew that *this* is what I really wanted—*being in* the classroom. But to be re-employed, I had to take coursework. On the free ticket my school board provided, I returned to Montreal for the summer and enrolled in a six-credit educational psychology course.

It was in this course that I first came to experience the gap between the praxis of teaching and the theories that were used to describe and explain teaching and learning. It was not that the theories were incomprehensible: they made sense in their own right, they were models that one learns to manipulate and to apply to carefully and strategically crafted materials. My problems arose when the instructor talked about applications. Being an outspoken person, I created many situations of conflict because I openly confronted theory and proposed applications with accounts of my practical experience. I often said things similar to, "This may work in *your* theory, but out in my school, it is a very different matter." The experience of *being in* the classroom and talking about it in terms of the theory at the university was very different, and sometimes incompatible. The role of *being* in the classroom (Chapter 2) appeared to me a much better place for learning to teach than the university course that I was taking. I was glad when the summer was over and I could return to the classroom.

More Gaps

After another successful year in the village and more summer courses, I moved to Newfoundland to teach science and computer science in a high school that also serviced several small neighboring fishing communities. The unemployment rate among eighteen- to twenty-four-year olds was seventy-five percent, and over forty percent of the students failed to complete high school.

It was a rough place. It was like starting all over again—not unlike what my friend Ken Tobin (2000) experienced when he returned to teach in an urban school. What I had learned as a teacher, both through experience and by taking classes did not seem to work. My principal assured me that when changing schools, even experienced teachers needed about three years before teaching became a routine activity again. Teaching skills and pedagogy do not easily transfer, he told me. I believed him because at the end of the year, two experienced teachers who were new to the school did not receive tenure. But what he said did not make sense in terms of the theories about teaching that I had learned. When you have developed pedagogical knowledge, why should it not be applicable in a new school? Why should the skills not transfer, and why did the theories not explain the difficulties experienced teachers have when they change school contexts? In the end, I felt fortunate, because I had come through a rocky year. There were only a few kids who failed to respond to what I did, and in the heat of the action, I did not seem to have sufficient room to maneuver to avoid conflict. In one situation, I became so desperate that I slapped a ninth-grade student—I did not even know I was doing it until it was all over and he started to cry. I ran out of the classroom, reported myself to the principal, and proposed to tender my resignation. Out of character, he offered to help me if I agreed to stay.

It took me almost two decades to understand such situations as the result of the special, temporal character of teaching. I now understand the dialectical relation of experience and anticipation, and the indeterminate relation between plans and situated actions arising from the *temporality* of praxis, forcing the practitioner to act without having time out to deliberate (Chapter 1). When I look at the first year in Newfoundland now, I know that some of the dispositions (which I will introduce as *habitus* in Chapter 3) that I had brought to the situation were inappropriate. Although in my previous school, I had grown to the point of having multiple ways of dealing with situations, my room to maneuver (which I will introduce as *Spielraum* in Chapter 4) had shrunk tremendously when I began teaching in the new school. In fact, when I slapped the student, I had no room to maneuver and so responded with an act of desperation.

In my second year, the tide began to turn. Fellow teachers and students overcame my non-native status in Newfoundland and began to accept me. Students spent many hours after school in science and computer science laboratories; sometimes, I drove a student home at 10 P.M. or parents picked up their kids at midnight. One of the assistant superintendents noticed what was going on; he encouraged me to get a graduate degree so that I "could have more impact on science teaching in the district." Initially, I resisted because I did not want to be subjected to more theory, taught by professors who frequently had not been in a high school classroom for decades. But there were gaps and contradictions in my everyday praxis of schooling as well, so I ultimately decided to pursue additional training. But it was only recently that I recognized the role of contradictions in everyday praxis as a site for development and growth in teaching (Chapter 9) and in the organization of teacher education (Roth and Tobin in press).

One of the central contradictions at the school and school board levels was the distance between the curriculum to be implemented and the abilities and needs of the students. For example, in the early 1980s, special classes had been created for students who were several years behind their peers in academic achievements—fifteen-year-olds reading at about a third-grade level. The students were labeled "educationally mentally retarded" not only on paper, but visible to everyone above the door to their classroom, on a small plaque containing the inscription "EMR." I was provided with a class set of workbooks on atomic theory, containing worksheets that asked students to fill in the blanks with words from the text on the preceding page. My principal and my department head had declared the students unfit to engage in science activities in one of the laboratories. I was asked to keep students busy, and therefore quiet, by making them read the texts and complete the blanks. I thought, "this might seem reasonable from their desks, in theory, but it is an unreasonable way when you work in the trenches, that is, in practice."

These expectations on the part of principal and department head made no sense to me. I had come to know some of the students quite well, especially those who had been transferred in and out of my homeroom, which was the lowest of four academically streamed ninth-grade classrooms. Outside of the school, these young men and women apparently related in normal ways to their peers in the other classes. They smoked dope with their peers and shared the "magic mushrooms" growing within sight of the school. One of the young women in a higher academic stream had gotten pregnant from her relation with an EMR student. Especially on the weekends, the male students worked on the boats with their fathers and siblings. Yet at school, they were reduced to lesser beings, kept busy until they no longer felt like engaging in schooling. The resident teachers did not deal with the contradiction. Most of them hated to have to teach the EMR— hence, those of us with the least seniority were assigned to teach in them.

Disagreeing with this whole situation, I decided to make changes at all costs. When asked, the students told me that they would not mind studying bicycles and how they worked. Assuming sole responsibility for taking *these* students to the lab, I had my students work on an old bicycle. Over the following weeks, they took it apart and reassembled it. They studied the gears, how gearshifts worked, and how different combinations of front and rear gears led to different rates of revolution of the wheel. At the end of the unit, the students told me that it had been fun—they had learned something that made sense and that they could really use. A few weeks after the unit, three of my students began part-time jobs assembling bicycles for a department store, receiving $2.50 per bicycle, a considerable amount of money in a town where there were so many young people unemployed.

Even more important than teaching about bicycles, however, was the time that I spent with these students to understand their understanding of the world. I learned that some came hungry to school, eating dry bread and drinking tea for days while their family awaited the arrival of the next welfare check. I came to understand the social relations among these youths and in their families; I found out that "tokers" were less likely to be caught than beer drinkers; and I found out that they came to school because their families were eligible for government child support. By listening, I came to understand the kinds of activity these students would be willing to do and could do.

As a teacher I learned that, for students to be successful, I needed to listen to their needs, enter *their* reality, and come to understand where they are. I also came to know that I could not preplan all the different questions and problems that they might have, but that I could trust myself in coming to understand problems then and there. Once I found out where the students were, I could facilitate further learning. In this book, I develop the notion of *relationality* (Chapter 5) to articulate the ways in which experienced and caring teachers are in tune with students and their current learning needs.

TOWARD AN EPISTEMOLOGY OF PRACTICE

In 1989, after having completed my Ph.D. degree, I returned to teaching. I took a job as the sole physics teacher in a private, all-boys school where I also served as the science department head. Over the three years of my tenure, my understanding of teaching and learning and the relationship between theory and practice changed radically. The first of these radical changes pertained to my understanding of the relationship between traditional psychological research about learning and learning in everyday contexts. My Ph.D. research was concerned with correlates between measures of short-term memory, on the one hand, and measures of learning, development, and achievement, on the other (Roth 1990, 1991; Roth and Milkent 1991). However, when I returned to the classroom, the predictions that I could make based on theory turned out to be of minute relevance to everyday learning. What I had treated as error variance during my doctoral work now became the most important piece of information. To understand Johnny's learning difficulties, it mattered less to know how much short-term memory he had and more to know that his aunt had just died. I began to realize that to be a good teacher, I had to build an understanding of each student in relation to the complexities of his or her "lifeworld." This ultimately led me to radicalize teaching as the praxis of solidarity involving students and teachers alike (Roth 2000).

These years at the private school were crucial in my development, for while I taught, I continued to be interested in theoretical aspects of teaching and learning. I realized that to understand teaching, I needed to be firmly grounded in practice, while continuously attempting to construct a conceptual framework for further developing my existing understandings. In my quest to understand teaching and learning, I came across *Cognition in Practice* (Lave 1988) and *Laboratory Life* (Latour and Woolgar 1979). Both books brought about profound change in my understanding of teaching and learning as everyday activities. Jean Lave, not only through *Cognition in Practice*, but through her work more broadly (Lave 1990, 1991, 1993, 1996, 1997, Lave and Wenger 1991), introduced me to the notion of practice, situated cognition, and knowledgeability. It was also her writing that encouraged me to read the practice-related work of the

French sociologist Pierre Bourdieu (e.g., 1980, 1997) and the work of the German critical (Marxist) psychologist Klaus Holzkamp (e.g., 1983, 1991a, 1991b), who was centrally concerned with establishing a historically grounded, subject-centered way of understanding human activity. By reading Jean Lave, I first encountered activity theory (Engeström 1987; Leont'ev 1978), which in turn led me to dialectical reasoning (Il'enkov 1977). Jean Lave and the authors that I have come to know through her writing have had a considerable impact on my understanding of teaching developed in this book.

First Experiences in "Being With"

At the private school, I had my first experiences teaching alongside other teachers. Being with another teacher was not really planned but rather emerged from the attempts to find better and more equitable ways of evaluating teachers. At the school, department heads were asked each year to evaluate their teachers. Feeling uneasy with fly-on-the-wall–type observations myself, I developed, together with my science department colleagues, a four-level approach that would integrate teacher evaluation and development. These levels included teacher self-evaluation, peer observation, collaborative teaching, and department head observation. All four activities were debriefed, written up, and entered into a portfolio.

The most important aspect of these activities became the collaborative teaching. We noted that we learned a lot just by participating with another teacher, being surprised by some of the other person's tactics and strategies, and by debriefing particular lessons that we had experienced alongside one another. Although I did not know at that time, *being with* another teacher was to become an important practice and a theoretical tool in my work (Chapter 2).

At that time I learned about teaching as reflective practice (Russell and Munby 1992; Schön 1987) and formulated my understanding of teaching in these terms despite the fact that while I was teaching, this framework did not apply to me. Curiously, I experienced myself as unreflective; I was completely absorbed in teaching and unconscious of the passing of time, becoming aware of the context only with the ringing of the bell. I was similarly absorbed when I was joined in my classroom by other teachers, most of them from my own school, others from different schools—the representative of the Ministry of Education, who had observed me several times, recommended teachers from other private schools to come to my classroom. We investigated, together with the students, the problems that they had designed. From one another, we learned to ask questions that led to further inquiry and learning. We learned a lot without being consciously reflective at all.

Breakthrough

After the fact, the key events that led me to a breakthrough in my own thinking about teaching, particularly about the nature of theory and its relationship to practice and praxis, came after I left the high school for a university job (Roth 1998c, 2001). It was not that I left teaching—far from it. I continued to teach, mostly in seventh-grade classrooms, which are administratively placed, here in British Columbia, either in elementary or middle schools. But I did not teach alone. I always taught alongside a resident teacher, a mode of teaching that I have come to call *coteaching* (see Chapters 6–9), to make it distinct from team teaching. But I am getting ahead of myself and past the fortunate circumstances that had led to the emergence of coteaching as praxis and as praxeological concept (as described in Chapters 6–9).

Shortly after beginning my new job at Simon Fraser University, I received two national grants to look at the teaching and learning of science in classrooms, conceptualized as "communities of practice." A colleague introduced me to a school, where the teachers had made the improvement of science teaching their top priority for the upcoming three-year period (Roth 1998a). A survey of their fourth- to seventh-grade students made salient a general dissatisfaction with science at the school, particularly the lack of hands-on activities. The teachers wanted to change but felt that they did not understand the science content or pedagogy well enough. My arrival at the school appeared to be an answer to their prayers—but I declined to do the dog-and-pony shows they wanted me to do. I did not want to design and give workshops or teach their classes while they watched. In my view, they had to have ownership of their own learning environment and their own learning. I agreed, however, that my graduate students or I would teach alongside them, bringing together the expertise in content and the local knowledge about school culture and students, in exchange for the opportunity to document what we were doing. The means of a research team allowed us to record all coteaching and debriefing. I now refer to this activity (in its current form) as *cogenerative dialoguing* (see Chapter 8).

We found that by teaching alongside each other, we learned tremendously—not only because we started to talk about teaching but also, and especially, because we had experienced the events from the perspective of teachers. At the end of the first coteaching experience, we noted that there were changes in our teaching, which were apparent from the comparison of videotapes shot at the beginning and toward the end of the unit. That is, we had changed, for example, the way in which we scaffolded whole-class conversations through productive questioning, even though many aspects of questioning had not been the focus of our cogenerative-dialoguing sessions. For example, a close analysis showed that one teacher had a tremendously powerful way of asking questions, which engaged children in talking about science and engineering (Roth 1996). The other teacher had tremendous knowledge of the children and knew how far questioning could be pursued without discouraging a particular child. Over time, each of the two teachers became more like each other, yet without making many aspects of their teaching explicit and therefore matters of reflection (Roth 1998b). It was at that point that I came to realize the power of learning to teach through coteaching as an everyday activity (Roth 1998c).

Since then, I have cotaught science in elementary or middle schools for up to six months in a single year. One of the most powerful and moving experiences was that of coteaching with an intern, whom I call Nadine in this book, at a local middle school (Roth and Boyd 1998; Roth, Bowen, Boyd, and Boutonné 1998). It was while teaching alongside Nadine that I came to revisit my own biography as a teacher, particularly the role of room to maneuver, or *Spielraum* (Roth, Masciotra, and Boyd 1999; Roth, Lawless, and Masciotra 2001); the gap between the description of teaching skills and skilled teaching (Roth, Lawless, and Tobin 2000); and the phenomenological structure of time in teaching (Roth and Lawless 2001). It was by teaching alongside Nadine that I began to understand and critically analyze my own shortcomings and strengths.

Another lucky, and very important, event allowed me to further develop my understanding of teaching, particularly the practice of coteaching and cogenerative dialoguing. As director of teacher education at the University of Pennsylvania, Ken Tobin had recently changed science teacher preparation, partly in response to particular circumstances, to the coteaching/cogenerative-dialoguing model articulated in Chapters 7 and 8. Ken coteaches almost daily with Penn students, who are assigned in pairs to resident teachers. In their respect, Ken is coteacher, "supervisor," and "methods teacher." When I was in Philadelphia, I cotaught with Ken, his students, and resident teachers, which allowed us to rethink the new roles all of us take in coteaching and cogenerative-dialoguing situations (Roth and Tobin 2001a, 2001b, 2002; Roth, Tobin, and Zimmermann in press; Tobin, Roth, and Zimmermann 2001). It was in this context that I was able to expand my experiences of coteaching and cogenerative dialoguing into urban schools and to understand "implementation" issues in a context in which coteaching and cogenerative dialoguing became the paradigm for science teacher education.

CONTINUED AND CONTINUING GROWTH

Reflecting on the previous sections, readers will note that I experienced, and now view, "becoming a teacher" as a trajectory of continued growth. "Becoming a teacher" was not completed when I received my teaching certificate but rather has been an ongoing process rooted in my being *in* the classroom, especially when I have had opportunities of *being with* another teacher. Being in the classroom and being with another teacher provides opportunities to learn, through both implicit (coteaching) and explicit means (cogenerative dialoguing). The two forms of knowing associated with coteaching and cogenerative dialoguing are not the same and, indeed, are often contradictory. That is, praxis and discourse *about* praxis (i.e., *praxeology*, from the Greek words *praxis* and *logos*, meaning talk) form a dialectical unit. Dialectical units, such as the praxis/praxeology unit, consist of mutually contradicting items, here praxis and praxeology. The tension arising from the contradictions inherent in the unit is a site of growth. In Chapter 9, I argue that rather than engaging in the (futile) attempt to overcome the praxis-theory divide, a brief history of which I provide in the chapter, we ought to embrace the dialectical tension as an opportunity to engage in continuing growth. In my view, "becoming a teacher" ought to be a process that engages teachers, even while they are still at the university and "in training," in the dialectical tension of praxis and praxeology. Coteaching is an ideal vehicle for learning to teach, because it has embedded safeguards that come with collective activity. In this approach, then, we become teachers by being teachers. In other words, by *being* (teachers) in the classroom, we *become* (teachers) in the classroom. To me, there is no reason why this journey of being and becoming cannot start as soon as a person feels the calling or decides on teaching as a career. Once we come to understand new teachers currently in training as a (currently unused) resource in our efforts of assisting K–12 students to learn we can begin redesigning teacher education in terms of trajectories of legitimate peripheral practice. Practical mastery and symbolic mastery would thus no longer be acquired in physically different locations but rather would emerge from the concurrent practice of coteaching and cogenerative dialoguing.

I do not consider my own growth as complete—being in the classroom is a continuous becoming. The most important aspect of my growth and change is that they come out of my experience as a practitioner rather than being imposed from the outside. My conceptualizations are grounded in my praxis, which allows me to submit for immediate testing any new understandings and new action possibilities, especially as they arise from cogenerative dialoguing with coteachers and students.

OVERVIEW

In this book, then, I develop a discourse about teaching that is deeply grounded in praxis, both my own and that of fellow coteachers. In Part I, "Being in the Classroom," I develop the experience-based praxeological concepts introduced in this preface. One chapter is devoted to each concept, including "temporality of teaching," "being in and being with," "habitus," "Spielraum," and "relationality". In Part II of this book, "Becoming in the Classroom," I present coteaching and cogenerative dialoguing as a viable practice for teaching and learning to teach grounded in the phenomenological concepts introduced earlier. Chapter 6 sets the stage for a more in-depth presentation of "coteaching" in Chapter 7 and "cogenerative dialoguing" in Chapter 8. Coteaching/cogenerative dialoguing allow teachers to develop both implicit knowledge of, and explicit knowledge about teaching, factors that stand in a dialectical relation. The contradictions embedded in this dialectical relation and the opportunities for growth such that contradictions present are the topic of the final chapter.

PART I

BEING IN THE CLASSROOM

1

Temporality of Teaching

> This actual participating from a concretely unique point in Being engenders the real heaviness of time. (Bakhtin 1993: 57–58)

Teaching, as all practical activity, unfolds in time, irreversibly, without deliberating each single act, in a continuous series of acts (in the sense of deeds) that constitutes the life of a teacher. As teachers, we engage in the heat of the moment and thereby commit ourselves to consequences, which, depending on the extent of our experience, we can anticipate only to some (varying) degree. Paraphrasing Mikhail Bakhtin's opening quote, we might say that participating in praxis from the concretely unique point of a teacher engenders the heaviness of time. In this chapter, I focus on temporal aspects of teaching—the modes of phenomenological and chronological time, irreversibility, lack of time for deliberation, and the dialectic of experience and anticipation. This inquiry will yield significant implications for the understanding and practice of teaching and teacher education and development.

To introduce the thematic and phenomena in a non-technical way, consider the following classroom situation (recorded during one of our studies). At the time, Nadine was a teaching intern who had engaged in a coteaching arrangement with myself, an experienced teacher, to gain experience in the use of whole-class conversations to develop students' conceptual understanding. Nadine had asked one student, Stephen, to explain to his peers the concept of the "web of life," which he had introduced to the conversation at an earlier point. (For transcription conventions, see the Appendix.)

[MAR 26]
10:06:22   Stephen: It is hard to explain, but, if there is one kind of animal, like,
10:06:26   there is plants, right, there is plants, and then there i s

10:06:30		herbi[vores that-]
10:06:31	Nadine:	[TOM! (1.8)] ENOUGH! (1.3)
10:06:34		OK? (.) I (.) *don't* (.) *have* (.) the (.) *pat*ience today.
10:06:37		Do you under*stand*?
10:06:38		(3.3)
10:06:41		[*She turns head to look at Stephen and nods.*]
10:06:42	Stephen:	-and then there is herbivores eating the plants. And then
10:06:45		there is carnivores that eat the herbivores, and it goes on and
10:06:49		on. But if one of them is taken away, then they all die.
10:06:52		

In this short excerpt we see that Nadine shouts Tom's name in order to stop him from behaving in a certain manner. At the same time, however, she also interrupts Stephen's response to her request to explain what he meant by "the big circle of life." Nadine's interjection is marked by a series of long and short pauses and concludes with an encouraging nod to Stephen to complete his explanation. In a debriefing session at the end of the school day, and while reviewing sections of the videotaped lesson, Nadine reflected on her experience:

Tom appeared to be inattentive, talking to his neighbor. I wasn't really thinking what I was about to say or what I would do. I just went. It was almost as if it wasn't me who was talking- I mean for me, as far as classroom control, it has just all been trial and error; that is, I was learning as I went along, finding what works or what doesn't work. I mean, this class is the way this class is because of the individuals that are in there.

This event, recorded on videotape, is reproduced here in a way that other observers can share. The beginning of the event is datable (March 26, 10:06) and the duration of Nadine's intervention measurable (10.2 seconds). The beginning of each line of transcript, and in fact each word, can be associated with a specific moment in chronological time—that is, each moment can be characterized by its datability, lapse of time, and publicness (Ricœur 1984, 1985, 1988). These characteristics make it easy to come to some agreement about the event in the sense that it is public, and therefore shared. Nevertheless, this temporal framework is limited in that it does not allow us to understand the temporal nature of Nadine's experience then and there, as the teacher in *this* classroom at *this* time. That is, if we want to understand what and how Nadine learned from this event, we need to know how she experienced it herself and how the events affected her. To do this, we must consider the phenomenological nature of both time and action.

Nadine, I suggest, did not experience these events in terms of chronological time or deliberate them in terms of time. Rather, she was absorbed in the situation, which is better characterized by action and its consequences. Nadine did not experience herself as (objectified) subject, a rational actor, who consulted prior knowledge in order to deliberate on a plan to deal with Tom (e.g., "I just went"). She experienced the events as a temporal continuum, a flow, which itself was not measurable in terms of chronological time. Each (verbal) action was directed (forward in time) to Tom but, once uttered, immediately receded into the past, in its completion becoming an act (deed) that nothing could recover from the past. She did not think about talking but talked (shouted), and she did not deliberate a threat, but enacted what was heard as a threat.

At the same time, having been there next to Nadine, we felt the threat, which, after the fact, we attribute in our analysis to the effect of the long intervals and short pauses in Nadine's response. Her interjection "TOM! (1.8) ENOUGH! (1.3)" and the subsequent use of a suggestive pause gave a sense of gravity to her words. The overall significance of the sequence of actions portended potential actions should Tom continue. However, whether Nadine's (verbal) acts would actually put an end to Tom's actions is almost impossible to assess unless we are in the shoes of the teacher then and there. The answers depend, in part, on Tom's (and his peers') subsequent actions, which follow Nadine's implied request to stop whatever he was doing and how the mutual actions were read by other individuals in the classroom. It also depends on the historical timing of the intervention—whether this was the first warning or one of a series of warnings leading to intensification. Time, as experienced in and by the participants, plays an important role in the constitution of meaning of the event.

In each act, Nadine irreversibly committed herself. Unlike the case study scenarios used in her university classes, where she had time to deliberate on several options before committing to an answer, Nadine committed herself irreversibly, both in shouting Tom's name and in waiting. (Pausing also constitutes a form of action and contributed to constituting the meaning of the event for each participant.) For example, by uttering the implied threat that she did not have the patience that day to deal with behavior such as his, she committed herself to take some action in response to his action—some form of punishment. The utterance with its implied threat is one of a series of acts that make up a teacher's life, which amounts to an uninterrupted performing of acts. The social nature of each act implies that Nadine can account for it, and provide a set of rules or reasons, and that she takes responsibility for the effect on Tom. (Of course, Tom, too, is accountable, for his act brought about Nadine's intervention. Here, it is a simple threat that on this day, Nadine does not have the patience for a particular behavior.) Yet Nadine's actions have other ramifications. Not only did she shout at Tom, she also interrupted Stephen. Interrupting another person is normally considered inappropriate, and there is an obligation for the speaker to make such an intervention appear reasonable (unless, of course, it is done in relations where unequal status are produced and reproduced through inequitable distribution of the "right" to interrupt others as with the "speaker" or chair in some assembly, parents interrupting their swearing children, and so on). Therefore, Nadine is accountable and responsible as well as to everyone else witnessing the event.

Praxis, because it is entirely immersed in the current of time, is inseparable from temporality. It unfolds in time, is non-linear, and remains irreversible. Its temporal structure—rhythm, tempo, directionality, and irreversibility—is not only constitutive of its meaning but also the central element that distinguishes praxis as a lived experience from praxis as re-presented (made present again) in theory. In other words, praxis as lived experience takes place at a level of immediacy that does not allow stepping back and taking time out to either reflect or construct a theoretical understanding of the situation before making a rational decision.

In this chapter, I am interested in the phenomenological structure of praxis, particularly its temporal nature. I begin by introducing my theoretical framework, which I subsequently illustrate with a short vignette taken from a series of studies on teaching and learning to teach. Although I describe a situation that some may construct as a pedagogically weak moment, I am not interested in characterizing teachers such as Nadine in terms of the adjectives *good, bad, expert, novice,* or *incompetent.* Such judgments can only be selected based on particular acts interpreted after the fact and in relation to some subsequent outcome, whereas here I attempt to articulate a non-teleological framework that deals with experience as it unfolds in real time.

TEMPORALITY, ACTION, AND RESPONSIBILITY

Conceptual Framework

The temporal nature of human experience has been the subject of reflections and meditations throughout the history of Western thought. As a result, philosophers distinguish phenomenological time (as explicated by Augustine, Henri Bergson, Edmund Husserl, Martin Heidegger, and Maurice Merleau-Ponty) from chronological time (as explicated by Aristotle and Immanuel Kant). Lived experience, including teaching qua praxis, is characterized by oscillations between the two forms of experiencing time. Although chronological time has become the paradigm of science and modern life more generally, I will resist the temptation to use it as the starting point of our inquiry. Rather, I articulate a more general framework, discussed in terms of Figure 1.1, from which I derive the different modalities in which humans experience time. (Because of space limitations, I deal in detail only with some of the salient dimensions in the figure.)

Figure 1.1 depicts a set of conceptual relations (rather than spatio-temporal relations expressed in the two dimensions of a diagram). For reasons elaborated below, past, present, and future each have to be considered from the inside of time, that is, in terms of past, present, and future (Müller 1973). This gives rise to a matrix of nine elements with the structure X[Y], where X and Y each take the values of past (Pa), present (Pr), and future (Fu). Each element X[Y] should be read in the form of "Y as appearing in X." Thus, Pa[Pa] is "the past as it appeared in the past," Pr[Pa] is "the past as it appears in the present," and Fu[Pa]

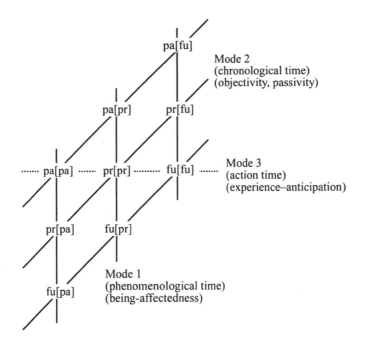

Figure 1.1. Considering time itself under the aspect of time yields a matrix of elements in which time appears twice. The axes linking triplets of elements turn out to be particular modes of times accessible to experience and reflection.

is "the past as it will appear in the future." An example of "the past as it appeared in the past," Pa[Pa], is Nadine's lived experience as the events unfolded. An example of "the past as it appears in the present," Pr[Pa], is constituted by Nadine's account of the experience during our debriefing session. Finally, an example of "the past as it appears in the future," Fu[Pa], is the event as it will appear to the reader (we cannot predict the interpretations some readers will construct). The two modes of experiencing time, chronological and phenomenological, which are at the heart of this discussion, are but aspects of this more general framework (Figure 1.1).

Chronological and Phenomenological Time

Chronological time is an outcome of reflection and, as such, thought from the present (Figure 1.1, Mode 2): Pr[Pa] ("the past as it appears in the present"), Pr[Pr] ("the present as it appears in the present"), and Pr[Fu] ("the future as it appears in the present"). Chronological time is associated with objective experience, arising with the human capacity for reflection and the ability to simultaneously (re-)present objects and events that normally do not simultaneously occur to us. In chronological time, the present is but an infinitesimal instant between the future and the past, an infinite series of "now" points without beginning and end. As a construct in physics, chronological time can be represented as a point on a line, a variable that can be manipulated. As such, it is an expression of time that is external to us, that we experience passively ("time flies") and to which we are delivered. It is a time that is used for reckoning (appearing in lesson plans), marking instances (bell ringing to mark beginning and end of lesson), dating (teachers' plan books), and measuring (amount of time spent on an activity).

As an ensemble, this structure of time simultaneously re-presents events that really occur at different moments of time. In this way, it allows for the construction of logical connections between aspects of the past, present, and future that are simultaneously given in the present. In this sense, this mode makes possible the nature of theory as we know it, which fundamentally requires the simultaneous presence of objects and events that in practice never occur simultaneously: "The process of empirical science has access only to those first-order interactions of temporal modes that contain the present as their first partner, that is, that are of the type Pr[X]" (Müller 1973: 341, my translation). This is because logical connections, as these appear in scientific theories, can only be made when "the presence becomes threefold: the present of the future, present of the past, present of the present" (Ricœur 1991: 210). As is apparent from this exposition, because empirical science is wedded to one mode of time, it captures from the totality of human experience only those aspects that can be made to appear in the present simultaneously, those aspects that can be re-presented. The experience of being affected, because it is inaccessible to "reason," will forever lie outside the realm of formalistic inquiry.

In contrast, phenomenological time is related to the experience of the moment, which philosophers often refer to as the experience of being affected. The sensation characteristic of phenomenological time is characterized as the "duration" of the moment embedded in a continuous irreversible flow. The sensation of duration of the moment arises from a sense of the immediate future and immediate past in the present; it arises from an intentionality that reaches beyond the present, therefore giving the now an extension that the now points in chronological time do not have. When we listen to a familiar song, we do not hear at a particular time just one note; rather, we hear the note as part of a context that includes both the imminent future and the receding past. Nadine has such a sense of the impending future when she begins to admonish Tom, even though she has yet to utter a word. The temporal structure of this experience is therefore Fu[Pr] (Figure 1.1, Mode 1), "the future present" or "the present as it will appear in the (immediate) future." At the same time, with each word she advances, other parts of her sentence irrevocably fade into the recent past. This imminence gives time a certain "thickness" that stands in contrast to the present as an infinitesimal line separating future and past. The temporal structure of this experience is therefore Pa[Pr], "the present as it appears in the (recent) past." "Imminence, the recent . . . constitute intentional relations, internal to the present, not by any means transitive intentional relations, turned toward objects sighted outside, as it were, but longitudinal relations constituting time as a continuous flux" (Ricœur 1991: 210). At the same time, this duration and directionality are experienced as a current against which we cannot swim. Even when we are completely absorbed in a classroom activity and are unaware of the chronological time, we still have a sense of the impending future and of events that sweep us away.

In daily experience, phenomenological and chronological time are complementary; they cannot be lived or thought simultaneously—much like complementary quantities in quantum mechanics that cannot be thought or measured simultaneously with ultimate precision. In other words, the two forms stand in a dialectical relation that constitutes our daily experience. For example, there are moments when we are completely absorbed in an activity and suddenly, with the ring of the end-of-lesson bell, realize that forty-five minutes have passed without our noticing. For these moments, we have lived solely in phenomenological time. The expression that "time flies" arises out of the contrast that, on the one hand, we did not experience chronological time at all and, on the other hand, we recognize that a considerable amount of chronological time has passed. In such instances our Being, as it "engenders the real heaviness of time" orients itself towards something else (the abstract idea of chronological time) and we objectify ourselves as experiencing the real heaviness of our own existence (our Being). In such cases, the dialectic of experience and anticipation of experience become apparent. (In Chapter 9, I devote some space to the nature of dialectical reasoning and the positive value it attributes to contradictions as growth points and starting points for change.) As such, chronological time does not really exist in the concrete (unlike phenomenological time, which exists as embodied), but rather is an abstraction, understood through our own embodied experience.

In the classroom, all of us have experienced lessons in which time did not seem to progress, days that seemed unending in their slowness. We also have experienced moments in which time appeared to race. At the same time, we are also able to constitute time in the way we serialize our actions such as when we pause after making a serious threat to increase the gravity of a situation. Even waiting and doing nothing, or as here, continuing with the whole-class conversation, constitutes an action. Praxis is therefore characterized by two dialectically related moments of time. On the one hand, praxis is shaped by time as it impinges from the outside and leads to a sense of urgency, a practical investment that brooks no delay. On the other hand, in acting, we can also manipulate our experience of time instead of being subject to it by playing strategically with time and, particularly, with its tempo.

Act and Responsibility

The difference between "action" and "act" is related to differences between phenomenological and chronological time. An "act," as with a "deed" (something completed), belongs to chronological time in the sense that it is something (event or thought) that can be made present again (re-presented), deliberated, and therefore objectified. More important, it is no longer a part of the chronological present. In being complete, it has a beginning and end that lie outside the bracketing of the recent past and immanent future. At the same time, from a phenomenological perspective, the act (as a complete event or thought) becomes part of that into which we are always and already thrust. It is relational in that as past, it remains a part of the present because our experience of the moment and of the act located therein is constantly colored by the residue of the past. We cannot speak of an "act" (a complete deed) in phenomenological time but only of "action" (ongoing, continuous, progressive etc.). As act tumbles into act we no longer see each as a separate event but rather now see them as a continuum of acts—that is, as action. Herein lies the crossroad between the chronological and phenomenological concepts of time—actions turning into acts.

Praxis is the locus where the two (complementary) modes of time interact. The series of acts that define a life therefore take place in a third mode of temporality, which has the accumulation of past experience as one pole and anticipation directed toward the open future as the other. Experience, acquired first-hand or vicariously, "is always a matter of overcoming something foreign, of something acquired becoming a habitus. . . . Experience has a layered structure, composed of clusters and stratifications, which allows the past, built up in this way, to escape simple chronology" (Ricœur 1991: 218). In terms of our diagram, experience therefore has the structure of Pa[Pa], "the past as it appeared in the past"; that is, implicit (embodied) and explicit patterns that we have extracted from multiple experiences and that are accumulated in embodied form as dispositions, which I present in Chapter 3 as *habitus*. These dispositions structure future experiences—the way in which we perceive the world, act, and anticipate future events. This anticipation is not in the form of prediction, which in my diagram has the structure of Pr[Fu], "the future as it appears in the present." Predictions are explicit images from the past projected into the future. Anticipation reaches beyond the impending future (Fu[Pr]) and the (statistically) predictable future (Pr[Fu]). It is a sense for the broad range of possibilities that the things to come may constitute. Anticipation therefore has the structure of Fu[Fu], "the future of the future" or "the future as it will appear in the future." Consequently, anticipation can never be fully derived from experience; at the same time, there are no surprises for someone with little experience.

Each (social) act is not simply motivated to do something but is directed toward the other, the recipient. Both aspects are implied by the notion of "Care" (or concern) that is central to Martin Heidegger's (1977) treatment of human action. Acting is always linked to suffering and witnessing. Each act therefore implies a double responsibility. First, once committed a (practical) act cannot be undone; it is the outcome of a once-occurring event. In other words, the notion of the act that cannot be undone and the irreversibility of time are mutually constitutive. An act is not only directed toward another but is also irreversible. As such, each act has, in a strong sense, an irreversible effect, in a reciprocal manner, on the individual agent him or herself. The agent therefore bears a moral responsibility for being the source of the suffering that follows from the act. Second, in each act we are also responsible for its intelligibility. That is, a social act also implies the responsibility to account for one's actions. In acting "each individual not only takes into account others' reactions but motivates his or her action through symbols and values that no longer express simply private features of desirability made public but rules that are in themselves public" (Ricœur 1991: 194). In this public nature, acts are objects of interpretation and are therefore inherently polysemous (multiple meanings). Thus, Nadine not only shouted at Tom—telling him to stop ("ENOUGH!") and warning him that she would not put up with his behavior—but also interrupted the whole-class conversation.

In summary, there are three major issues that arise from our consideration of temporality. First, each (practical) act arises from the dialectical tension between the space of experience (past) and anticipation (future) that is oriented toward the other (present). This simultaneous triple orientation of the act, toward the future, past, and present, is the fundamental principle of being. Second, each act entails moral responsibility and intelligibility. Finally, two modes of temporal experience—chronological and phenomenological time—characterize each act and the associated phenomena of the directionality (flow) and irreversibility of time, rhythm, and tempo. To demonstrate how these aspects of a temporal consideration are expressed in praxis, I offer the following illustration in which an intern teacher wrestles with classroom discipline and management.

CLASSROOM MANAGEMENT

In this section, I illustrate how unfolding conversations reveal and develop the realities of the participants. Whereas a master teacher acts in an appropriate manner at the right moment, the new teacher in my illustration does not yet anticipate the possible ramifications of her actions. She lacks the experience, the dialectical counter-pole of anticipation, necessary for a sense of how "the future will appear in the future." Here, I am not interested in a deficit account, elaborating on what the participating teacher, Nadine, cannot do in this seventh-grade classroom. Rather, I elaborate on the praxis of teaching and the (necessary) experiences along a trajectory of a never-ending process of "becoming a teacher."

My insights into the experience of teaching intern are grounded in a particular approach to doing research: coteaching and cogenerative dialoguing. Coteaching is based on the idea that teaching, as any praxis, can be understood only from the perspective of the practitioner. Coteaching, engaging with another in the activity of teaching students, gives the "me" the unique perspective of praxis as it appears to the practitioner. Cogenerative dialoguing is the setting in which the coteachers articulate their experiences, not only for the purpose of critically analyzing their experience, but also for articulating workable changes to their practices in order to enhance students' learning opportunities. Having been a teacher in this classroom at the same time as Nadine provided me with an insider experience of the temporal nature of teaching that cannot be gained from an observer (outside) perspective.

Nadine was not an average new teacher. Teachers in the school where she did her internship recognized her current abilities and her potential to be a "great teacher." Her principal and university professors highly recommended her when she sought her first employment. As a consequence, she was able to garner full-time employment in a context in which less than twenty percent of newly certified teachers do so. There should therefore be no question that Nadine was an exceptional new teacher; and yet, there were many moments when Nadine struggled. I therefore think of these difficulties that she experienced as endemic to the process of becoming a teacher, a process that we attempt to understand in a positive way, as a necessary part of a process of development rather than as a deficit (of a "novice" with respect to an "expert").

In the course of a four-month study of Nadine's teaching, there were repeated instances when students questioned her request that they leave the classroom. Asking "Why do I have to leave, I haven't done anything?" they refused to leave the classroom so that Nadine could deal with them privately, away from other students. Although such requests sometimes worked with other students, it generally did not work with Tom, the student she had most trouble with during her internship. Nadine felt she was stumbling through the first few months of her student teaching without being able to address important aspects of teaching (discipline problems, productive questioning) in a satisfactory way. In the following excerpt, I twice represent one such event in which Nadine conducts a classroom discussion. The first representation is a transcription as given by the videotape and as it occurred in chronological (objective) time. The second is a narrative account provided by Nadine during a debriefing session some time after the event.

A Moment in Classroom Life

On the previous day, we had taken the class to Henderson Creek, where the students conducted research in order to inform their community about the health of the stream. Nadine had asked me to let her practice questioning techniques while conducting a whole-class conversation. As usual in such situations, I had stepped a little to the side and back, which allowed me to experience the lesson from a teacher perspective and to reenter the conversation at appropriate times. Nadine asked different student groups to describe their research sites in and along the creek. The transcript picks up sometime during this part of the lesson.

[MAR 12]

10:33:55	Nadine:	Blake, what about you, you were sitting at that site?
10:33:58	Blake:	Ahm. We also [found
10:33:59	Nadine:	[Thomas (0.6) Please! Stop talking!

10:34:01		(3.2)
10:34:04		(*Turns to Blake*) Sorry Blake, go ahead.
10:34:05	Blake:	We also sort of found a little bit, a type of gas on the surface of the water.
10:34:11	Nadine:	*Tom!* (2.0) OUT!
10:34:15		So Bryan, you guys also found gas or something like that on the surface?
10:34:19	Tom:	(*Remains in his seat, mumbles*) I didn't do nothing!
10:34:21	Nadine:	(*Stares at Tom*) GO!
		(4.5)
10:34:25		(*Turns to Blake*) What else?
10:34:26	Blake:	I don't know.
10:34:28	Nadine:	Alicia, maybe, third group? What about you guys?
10:34:31	Alicia:	We were at this place there [was almost a small river.
10:34:36	Tom:	[I didn't do nothing!
		(*Tom stays put. Nadine walks up to him, whispers something. Alicia, as everyone else, is watching her walk up to Tom but continues talking. Tom gets up. Nadine begins walking toward the front.*)
10:34:42	Nadine:	Sorry, I am sorry.
10:34:44	Alicia:	There was a little small river . . .
10:34:46		

Subsequent to this, as to most lessons, we reflected on our teaching experience. Talking about this and similar events relating to classroom management and discipline, Nadine noted:

It is difficult to think back about situations such as this one and describing how I felt and what I noticed. I am not so much aware of myself as I am of unfolding events. I was attempting to facilitate the discussion and Tom somehow seemed to interfere with what I wanted to happen. I really had no time to think about what was going on. I shouted at Tom but hadn't really planned to do so. What I said seemed to come from somewhere, but I was not aware of it. I was really focusing on the conversation that I wanted to facilitate. So although I wanted to do what I learned in classroom management, to be in control of the classroom, everything really seemed to happen at its own rate. I never really seem to know what is going to happen until it happened.

The most difficult part for me in going from the university classroom into the internship experience is doing the right thing at the right time. Like, when I look at you [Michael] teaching next to me, I notice that you always seem to have the right thing to say at the tip of your tongue and you always seem to do what is right at the moment. But it is different for me. I remember, at the university you hear all these ways and methods and these idealistic ways. When you actually get out here, everything is different, when you put it into actions. I think I am following all the steps that I have been taught to follow, and I am going in ways that I am supposed to be going. But things aren't changing.

Well, I learned that I have to act in the here and now, right then and there. It's easy to think of, "Well somebody does this to me then I follow this and this and this." But every situation is so different and every student is so different and I am sort of stumbling through these situations. I am constantly battling with things and learning and trying to find new ways or new things right then and there. I don't think I found, I don't feel like I figured it all out because what I see happening is those people, like Tom, that shouldn't be getting disciplined are getting disciplined.

Chronological Time and Phenomenological Time

This episode can be analyzed in terms of chronological (objective) time. The date indicates that the lesson occurred mid-way during the third month of Nadine's four-month internship, on a Thursday, and therefore toward the end of the week. The time of day tells that it was the third lesson of the day. On a more micro-level, we notice that Nadine addresses Tom in ten- to fifteen-second intervals (10:33:59, 10:34:11, 10:34:21, and 10:34:36). Also notice that there were repeated, marked pauses as Nadine was talking to Tom. Each pausing increased the significance of her earlier utterance, which was clearly to be understood as a threat. Tom continued to speak and did not leave the classroom, which everyone else could read as a challenge to Nadine's requests. There is therefore a particular temporal unfolding of the interactions; the event had its own specific tempo. Moments in which the debriefing of the students' field experience continued were interrupted by requests for Tom to stop talking and subsequently to leave the classroom. In conversational terms, Nadine's pauses were long, lending a particularly threatening flavor to the previous command.

Each unanswered challenge seemed to aggravate the situation. There were nearly twelve seconds between the moment Nadine asked Tom to stop talking and the moment she asked him to leave. Another six seconds went by between her first and second requests for him to leave. Analyzing the situation with hindsight, escalation seemed to be inscribed in it from the beginning. Each pause or action irreversibly advanced the events, in this situation leading to escalation. Even if Nadine had had time to consider alternatives, once she committed to a particular action, she could not revert but instead had to deal with the consequences, with the new situation as it unfolded, and with a new constellation. Meanwhile, Tom continued to talk, thereby increasing the seriousness of the challenge to her authority. Nadine's act of pausing for a combined total of nearly ten seconds led to an unbearable tension.

There are certainly merits to analyzing the episode as it lies there before us, in the form of the transcript and, perhaps, by drawing on the videotape to get a better sense of its tempo. Such analyses, however, do not get at the event through the eyes of the beginning teacher. They do not give us a sense of what it means to experience such events in phenomenological time, "first time through," and without knowledge of the result. Comments made with the benefits of hindsight do not help us in understanding Nadine's experience of the moment proper. Yet if we want to know how a teacher learns, in praxis, and thereby gains experience that will ultimately make him or her a master teacher, we require an understanding of his or her lived experience as it unfolded in real time, and without the "revisionist" interpretations that are produced when all the consequences of actions and acts are known to the analyst.

Nadine did not experience the events in chronological time. She had asked to take the lead in the whole-class session and use the opportunity to develop her questioning practice and concentrate on getting students to elaborate on their contributions, justify claims, and explain what they mean. As she focused on the developing conversation, she had the sense that Tom was talking to his neighbor and that this was interfering with what she was attempting to do. As the events unfolded, she did not articulate this sense—there was no time to do so. Asking Tom to stop talking and shouting the request to leave happened without extended reflection. Nadine experienced herself as caught in emergent situations that she had participated in producing but the effect of which she could not anticipate. She felt torn between the demands of facilitating the conversation, enacting the intended lesson, and repairing the breach caused by Tom's actions to an anticipated unfolding panorama of acceptable practices. Having learned early on during her internship that attempting to implement classroom management procedures did not seem to help ("at the university you are hearing all these ways and methods and these idealistic ways. When you actually get out here, everything is different"), she was relying on her sense for acting in the then-and-there of the moment. But at each moment, Nadine had to face the consequences of her acts, as if she were running into them—acts that had taken on a life of their own. That is, Nadine experienced teaching as being complicated by the unintended consequences of action. Here, more experienced teachers have developed a practical sense that gives them more room to maneuver when unexpected situations arise so that they can act more seamlessly with breaches to what is expected.

In the end, Nadine came out of this lesson feeling as though she had somehow failed. As in other circumstances, she had come to send Tom out of the classroom, in order to deal with him separately from the class and outside the constraints of an ongoing lesson that demanded all her attention. In this way, Tom had been punished again, though she noted that he was getting disciplined without deserving it. The transcript and description of the event in chronological time do not convey Nadine's experience. They do not convey her sense of the lack of a time-out for understanding the situation and deliberate actions; of events that irreversibly unfolded in time and outside of her control; of the sense of urgency to do something; or of the limited room to maneuver. She noted that, given these characteristics of teaching, it is difficult to act appropriately in a situation—each one being different from every other one.

Yet it is out of this sense of urgency and lack of a time-out that Nadine acted, that is, requested Tom to stop talking and subsequently to leave the classroom. It is the event colored by her sense of urgency that constituted her lived experience, and therefore the bit of practical experience she gained, the learning in praxis that had occurred. To me, this is a key aspect that distinguishes the lived experience of teaching from abstract descriptions thereof. It is easy to arrive at outside descriptions: "It suffices to step outside of the game, where there are is nothing at stake, to sweep away the urgency, the appeals, the threats, the steps to be taken, which make up the real, really lived-in world" (Bourdieu 1980: 138, my translation). During her internship, Nadine increasingly realized that the one thing she learned in the praxis of teaching, something that she could not have learned by taking classes, was to act appropriately in the "here and now" and "then and there" of each situation. Nadine found out that teaching was not a matter of applying what she had learned at the university but of building and trusting her sense for the moment, to anticipate without having to deliberate what might occur in the near future. However, learning to act appropriately in each situation takes experience.

Classroom Discipline in Theory and in Praxis

Talking about discipline problems removed from classroom praxis, Nadine cited a number of techniques that she had heard about in her classroom management course at the university. These included (a) take the student outside the classroom and talk to him or her without an audience present; (b) write the name of the "misbehaving" student on the chalkboard along with an action to be taken after class; (c) talk quietly to the student and attempt to resolve the issue; or (d) continue the discussion in the forum selected by the student. Which of these (or any other option) would solve the present situation? Nadine found out that knowing these techniques away from classroom praxis, literally in the abstract, did not help her to act appropriately. In the heat of the moment and without time to extensively deliberate on what was going on at any given moment, these options were either not salient or, when she actually evoked one of them, the predicted outcomes were far from what actually happened. Time and again, situations escalated so that she not only sent one student outside to be dealt with later but also asked the entire class to remain during recess or after school. Even if her interactions with Tom seemed to continuously lead to similar problems, Nadine found it difficult to act in such a way that the situation did not escalate. ("Well I think, I think that it's just the here and now. . . . I mean it's easy to think of. . . . Well somebody says *this* to me then I follow *this* and *this* and *this*. But every situation is so different and every student is so different.") That is, explicit knowledge of the patterns of actions derived from explicit descriptions of past events did not assist her; she realized that she had not done the right thing at the right time. ("When I look at you teaching next to me, I notice that you always seem to have the right thing to say at the tip of your tongue and you always seem to do what is right at the moment.") Here, Nadine attempted to take an explicit pattern (which, being derived from the description of past vicarious events, have the structure of "the past as it appears in the present," Pr[Pa]) to achieve a particular outcome (which has the structure of "the future as it appears in the present," Pr[Fu]; see Figure 1.1).

Nadine recognized the essential indexical quality of practical action: "Every situation is so different and every student is so different." Indeed, the appropriateness of an act lies in the here and now of the situation, in the relation between the present action and the possible meaning of the completed act. A particular action that might have helped her to deal with Tom in one situation was not always appropriate in another situation. The temporal unfolding of events is a crucial ingredient in defining the "situation" and therefore in making an action appropriate. Nadine felt that there was no time for deliberation. The situations unfolded and appeared to have their own logic, outside her control. Here, Nadine faced the same openness of the future faced by all practitioners. We cannot know the outcomes of our actions until after these outcomes have materialized. However, experienced teachers seem to be able to *anticipate* possible events that might arise from the present circumstances in a better way, which allows them to position themselves such that negative consequences do not arise. In contrast to new teachers, experienced practitioners appear to be better prepared to improvise their lives and interactions with each other in the here and now. Although newcomers and old-timers experience events as part of a continuous, irreversible stream, they experience the events differently because of the differences in the biographically shaped horizons of practical action (i.e., traces of past experience with the temporal structure Pa[Pa]).

Nadine's ("trial and error") learning is characterized by a developing sense for the relation between actions and acts, on the one hand, and their results and consequences, on the other. Rather than applying routines, she developed a sense for the implications resulting from her actions and the commitment she made—and therefore the answerability that such a commitment necessitates—in each and every act. She explained how she found out, through trial and error, "what works" in her interactions with Tom:

With Tom, what I found worked was when I wasn't always down pounding him, being on his back, and asking to speak to him in the hallway, at lunch time, or after school. I finally took a step back. I found that when I did that with Tom, it really worked and he just sort of did his thing. When he needs help he asks for help. He did not feel like he was being singled out as the one that was in the wrong all the time.

Here, easing off and "taking a step back" are descriptions of a *disposition* with which Nadine began to approach teaching. These descriptions did not tell her what to do in a particular moment, but they framed the character of the particular acts to which she committed herself. Whereas shouting and threatening often led to the same, drastic endpoint of a student being sent out of the classroom (which students interpreted as a sign that she could not handle the class), "stepping back" provided her with additional room to maneuver and the potential to achieve different trajectories of events. We can also say that Nadine had learned to anticipate—not all the time, but increasingly often—the outcomes of particular discipline-related actions. That is, she began to bring about a unity between the performance of an act (i.e., action), characterized by a threefold appearance of the present (Pa[Pr], Pr[Pr], and Fu[Pr]), and its result, which has the temporal structure of "the future of the future." That is, in these successful moments, Nadine acted like the experienced practitioner, who intuits the possible moral implications resulting from his or her act. In their every act, experienced practitioners are aware of the possible consequences and implications, the result of the action. This unity between performance (action) and outcome (act, deed) is relational thinking or *relationality*, an idea that I introduce in Chapter 5. It is associated with forms of temporality that are characteristic of praxis (practical mastery) rather than with the simultaneous presence of the past, present, and future characteristics of abstract, theoretical thinking.

Relational thinking conjoins the performance of the act and its outcomes in such a way that the experienced practitioner almost never ends in a dead-end situation from which there is no way out. Each act provides the experienced practitioner with sufficient room to maneuver. The beginner, on the other hand, acts without a sense for the implications of this act or of how he or she has committed him- or herself. Thus, in my examples, Nadine acts without being able to foresee the implications. It is only when she enters the classroom with the disposition or mood to "take a step back," that is, not to control, that classroom events unfold in such a way that Nadine can be said to have actually been in control.

Irreversibility and Uniqueness

"No man steps into the same river twice"; many scholars since Aristotle have elaborated on this aphorism and asserted its truth, including the temporal characteristics of praxis: irreversibility (directionality) and the uniqueness of each moment. Irreversibility implies that practitioners commit themselves in each act without explicit knowledge about its future meanings (i.e., its content, and outcome). Uniqueness implies that existing knowledge never exactly conforms to (predicts) the open future (i.e., having the structure Fu[Fu]) that practitioners confront each moment. I address, in turn, both issues.

As soon as Nadine said "Please! Stop talking!" she had irreversibly committed herself. At this point, however, she could not yet "know" what her act, the admonishment, entailed. Her acts were not yet characterized by the relational thinking of the experienced practitioner. She could not anticipate that if Tom continued talking, she would have to deal with that possibility. When Tom actually continued to talk (which was noticeable by everyone in the classroom), Nadine found herself in another critical situation. After the fact, we can say that more important than the initial offence was the fact that Tom disregarded the request to stop talking and subsequently to leave the classroom. Raising her voice, Nadine called him by his name. An ominous, conversationally and experientially long pause followed before she raised her voice one more notch and shouted "OUT!" We do not know what Nadine perceived between the two utterances—Tom might have continued to talk or she might have considered possible options for acting.

Calling Tom's name did not yet commit Nadine differently than the way in which she was already committed. Simply calling him by name could have been heard as a reiteration of her previous request to stop talking. However, as soon as she shouted "OUT!" she was committed to deal with his response, which might include leaving, staying put, continuing to talk, or remaining silent. (These options may or may not have been apparent to Nadine in that situation.) If Tom had left, the situation would have been settled for Nadine. She could have dealt with Tom later, once the other students began to work in small groups. In this situation, however, Tom continued to mutter under his breath, "I didn't do nothing!" Again, I do not know whether Nadine heard what he said, merely heard him talking, or simply reacted to his refusal to follow her earlier request. In the context of understanding the interactional nature of teaching, it is not really relevant what she might have thought. More important is what she did and how the situation was therefore made available to all participants. After shouting "GO!" she continued to stare at Tom and wait, further increasing the sense of the severity of the situation.

Despite all this, Tom did not leave. The elapsed (passed) time did not play in Nadine's favor, and the situation came near its pinnacle. The passage of time favored Tom as he ignored Nadine's request. If Nadine had waited less, ignoring the request might have been a less serious offense. Her request could have been heard as an aside comment, making the offense itself less serious. Her long pause, however, defined the act as a serious offence. Now that Tom had ignored it, there was no further way in which Nadine could enforce her threats in public without raising the stakes even higher—for example, she might have asked him to "go to the office" to see the principal, followed by a suspension from school activities.

Teachers, as all practitioners, face not only the irreversibility of their every act but also the uniqueness of every situation. Teachers continuously produce irreversible acts facing singular situations without the luxury of stepping back to articulate the situation and deliberate alternatives. That is, the rhythm and tempo of praxis does not allow teachers to engage in the mode of time characteristic of the theoretician. They cannot stop to simultaneously make present and deliberate the past, present, and future (Mode 2, Figure 1.1). How, then, is "appropriate" action possible under such conditions? Here, experience, as available in the form of dispositions that are the result of past experiences, plays a major role. Experience has the temporal structure of Pa[Pa] because it is based on patterns (tacitly or explicitly) extracted sometime in the past from multiple, recurring experiences that the practitioner has had even further in the past. Experience is associated with a practical sense that practitioners develop in the course of their working lives. Practical sense allows practitioners to immerse themselves in the particularities of a case without drowning in it and allows them to make moral choices: "The man of wise judgment determines at the same time the rule and the case, by grasping the situation in its singularity" (Ricœur 1990: 206). Thinking of the particular case *as* a particular case is but another aspect of "relational thinking" which itself is characterized by a singularizing function. The practical sense makes it possible to appreciate the meaning of the situation, at a glance, in the heat of the action, and to produce an opportune response. It invents behavior suited to the singular nature of each case. The practical sense therefore implies a teacher's capacity to invent conduct (on the spot and without reflection) that will best satisfy the exception required by solicitude. Hereby, the practical sense betrays existing rules to the smallest extent possible.

Responsibility

Completing an act in the real lived-in world of experience means a commitment. We commit ourselves and, in this, become answerable for what we have done—although the exact nature of what we have done cannot be established until some future point. Simultaneously, the irreversibility of time and the uniqueness of the situation make each act special and irrevocable. Each act also has a recipient. The agent therefore has a moral responsibility—is morally answerable—to the recipient for the act performed. Mikhail Bakhtin (1993) expressed this in terms of the notion of "non-alibi": a human being has no right to an alibi, the evasion of responsibility for the act performed. In contrast, when we manipulate rules in order to respond to questions about a case study, we do not commit ourselves in the way we do when acting in the classroom. The consequences are not nearly as serious to the constitution of who we are as teachers. Manipulating rules is not only possible outside the classroom but also permits deliberation that has no consequence to the events under consideration. In manipulating rules (theories), we can make moves, withdraw them, and then start applying a different set of rules.

There are moments in the event that show how Nadine was, after the fact, conscious of her responsibility with respect to the actions she took. For example, she apologized twice to the previous speakers, Blake and Alicia (10:34:04 and 10:34:02, respectively). Both students took the apology as a signal to complete their contributions to the whole-class conversation. In both cases, Nadine had interrupted the current speaker to attend to different matters than the conversation—the behavior of Tom, which, in her experience, was not consistent with her expectations regarding whole-class conversations. But even when she does not mark an act in terms of her responsibility, she is answerable in the sense that she has to live with the consequences, both in terms of her relationship with Tom as well as in terms of the content and structure of the event as experienced by other participants.

BEING AND BECOMING IN THE CLASSROOM

Teaching as Being in the Classroom

My research is concerned with developing better descriptions and a greater appreciation of praxis as it is lived and enacted in subjective experience, without knowledge of the future. As a long-time teacher interested in understanding the work and experience of teaching, I have come to realize the limits of rational choice models and teaching as a rational activity. As have others before me, I have come face to face with theories of teaching that did not describe my experience of teaching. I believe that the ultimate test of theories is their capacity to explain subjective human experience. I therefore endeavor to elaborate with our teaching peers a framework that is consistent with teaching as practitioners experience it. This is not to say that other theories, such as reflective practice or the tripart classification of teacher knowledge into pedagogical knowledge, content knowledge, and pedagogical content knowledge, are inappropriate. I agree that there are certainly moments when they are suitable lenses for classifying data in educational research. Rather, I am concerned with aspects of teaching that neither framework captures, yet that appear to me as crucial elements in understanding teaching, and therefore in developing experiences to induct new teachers. I am particularly interested in the phenomenological structure of praxis, of teaching as lived experience. Reflecting on my own experience, I noted that in becoming a teacher, there was a development in my capacity to do the right thing at the right moment. I am interested in the immediacy of teaching, which is always experienced in *this* classroom at *this* time and with *these* students. And I am interested in understanding the "event-ness" of teaching, for "being presents itself to a living consciousness as an ongoing event, and a living consciousness actively orients itself and lives in it as in an ongoing event" (Bakhtin 1993: xviii).

Praxis proceeds through irreversible acts produced (not necessarily consciously) under pressure and sometimes involving heavy stakes. For teachers, the very notion of Self is at stake. It is difficult to predict how the situation described in this chapter might have unfolded if Nadine had acted differently at any point in her interaction with Tom. She might have asked him early on, for example, whether he wanted to contribute to the whole-class conversation. She might have also brought up the notion of respect for others, which could have been shown here by listening to what they had to say. We can never know what might have happened if she had taken a different road, the one not taken, as Robert Frost deliberates in his famous poem *The Road Not Taken* ("Two roads diverged in a yellow wood,/ And sorry I could not travel both/"). What is important in the present situation is that in her actions, she committed herself in particular ways. As a result, she came out of the situation as a teacher "who can be pushed," "whose requests do not have to be followed immediately," "who is weak and afraid of taking serious actions more rapidly," and as a teacher "who does not know (yet) how to handle difficult students."

I pointed out that "relational thinking," that is, anticipating possible outcomes of one's actions, was a characteristic of experienced teachers. In this context, I find salience in, and similarities with, the notion of "(pedagogical) tact" as a form of knowledge associated with our discussion of temporality, because tact connotes both temporal and social appropriateness of an action. Tact is commonly understood as a particular sensitivity to situations and what to do. Pedagogical tact refers to the "improvisational pedagogical-didactical skill of instantly knowing, from moment to moment, how to deal with students in interactive teaching-learning situations" (van Manen 1995: 41). In the same manner, practical wisdom realizes itself in the act of teaching and thereby resists articulation and reduction to a set of techniques. The right moment and right action to be taken in a situation—for example, of Tom speaking to his neighbor—lies in the appreciation of the situation.

Becoming in the Classroom: Issues of Teacher Development

The nature of time as I have explicated it here has considerable implications for teacher education. Lived experience and representations of such experience are fundamentally different from each other: there is no overlap between the content of an act and the biographical experience of performing it. Did Nadine show practical wisdom and act in the way an experienced teacher would have? Given the information already provided, this is a rhetorical question. Anyone familiar with teaching and teacher education would recognize the beginning teacher in Nadine, based on "objective evidence." It is easy to blame Nadine after the fact, knowing that, once again, she had sent a student from the classroom. After the fact it is easy to say that she should have done this or that. Nadine knew that looking *at* the events, from the outside, so to speak, gives a different sense: "It's easy to think of, 'Well somebody does this to me then I follow this and this and this.'" That is, looking at events and deliberating what to do when "somebody does this" is just what Nadine had done in her university classroom management classes. Deliberating is the easy part. Doing the right thing at the right time in the here and now, when there is no time out for deliberation, is an entirely different process.

Two other teachers in this class appeared to curb any restlessness through the physical placement of particular students or student group in the classroom. These teachers, who were seasoned individuals with long experiences of teaching at the middle school level, interacted with individual students, groups, and the entire class in ways that prevented the kind of problems Nadine experienced from even arising. As experienced practitioners, they did not let such moments develop to the point where they had to completely discontinue the activities and require all students to sit still in their desks, waiting until everything had calmed down. As experienced practitioners, these teachers appeared to be in the right place at the right time. Potential conflicts were avoided before they become apparent to everyone in the classroom so that they had to be resolved in public—and preferably in a way that allows participants to retain their self-respect. But how does a teacher develop from having Nadine-like experiences to the point of experiencing the classroom as a seasoned individual? Furthermore, how does this development occur out of the experiences Nadine had from moment to moment? In my own work, coteaching associated with cogenerative dialoguing has become an alternative to the preparation of new teachers. The model has been implemented with a colleague at the level of the teacher preparation program for middle- and high-school teachers at the University of Pennsylvania (Roth and Tobin 2002). In coteaching, new teachers do the job "at the elbows of" one or more teachers, which provides them with many occasions to experience practical action as it unfolds in the heat of the moment. Cogenerative dialoguing, that is, constructing understanding and (local) theory together with other teachers subsequently provides for an avenue in which teaching can be articulated.

In this approach, the real question in teacher development is one of a continuous becoming in the classroom. For new teachers, the critical issue does not appear to lie in an inappropriateness of theory in practical situations. Given sufficient amounts of time, they might be able to analyze complex classroom situations in the way they previously analyzed case materials during their university courses. (However, our own experience of doing research and attempting to interpret videotapes shows that the analysis and framing of events within a particular theory are not quite self-evident.) Rather, the critical issue appears to be the capacity to do the right thing at the right moment in time. Here, the right thing cannot be theorized independently of the right time, for they depend, in part, on each other. The teacher must act constantly and on the spot, without the luxury of removing him- or herself from the flow of activity to reflect on current events and consider alternatives.

In this context, I also need to question the role of theory in teacher education and its relation to praxis. Nadine abandoned what she had learned in her classroom management course because in her praxis, the relationships between antecedent, action, and result were not as simple as her course seemed to suggest. Why might this be? Theory juxtaposes, in the *simultaneity* of a single space, actions and practices that are never required in this synoptic totality by the necessities of praxis. By stepping outside praxis (where there is nothing at stake), the observer no longer has access to its temporal nature. Importantly, it is impossible to reconstruct biographical experience from any of its representations. By taking university courses before actually finding themselves in the position of a teacher with real children, new teachers first and foremost develop a symbolic mastery. As part of their university training, new teachers (learn to) manipulate synoptically, given atemporal accounts of teaching, where actions can be arranged and rearranged without consequence. However, if biographical experience cannot be reconstructed from theory, then all attempts to force one's way into the lived experience of teaching from a theoretical world that is disconnected from praxis is hopeless. If scholars such as Bakhtin and Müller are right in arguing that there is no overlap between the theoretical and practical world, that is, between formal theories and teaching as lived experience, then beginning teachers will find themselves in a new, unknown world once they enter the classroom. What they have learned at the university appears to be inapplicable to the world in which they find themselves and where they have to cope. Whereas working theoretically and analyzing case materials allowed them considerable time for deliberation, the new teachers have to learn to cope in a world that is characterized by its own temporality. They have to learn to act when there is no time to deliberate yet remain answerable for each irreversibly committed act. This fact ought to have consequences for how we prepare future teachers.

2

Being in and Being with

It has already become quite evident that there is a gap between theory and practice. Both novice and experienced teachers point out, time and again, that what they know, they acquired in the practice, and what they learned in the academy is often inapplicable to the "reality of the classroom." Teachers, particularly when they have the opportunity to work side-by-side in the same classroom, begin to note that what they learn in just a few weeks is more than what they could have learned by taking numerous university courses. In this chapter, I continue to articulate a framework for understanding teaching that has arisen from my own lived teaching experience. I am committed to making my own experience, articulated through rigorous hermeneutic phenomenological inquiry, the ultimate test case for theoretical, or rather, in the present case, "praxeological" frameworks. If theories treat differences, and therefore human subjectivity, as error variance, they will always fail to describe and explain the actions of an individual in everyday situations. This is particularly the case for professions, such as teaching, in which individuals deal with other individuals rather than inanimate objects. I am interested in developing a framework that is consistent with our daily experience of teaching as well as other activities that I, and other teachers, engage in without thinking too much about why we do what we do in the first place. Thus, I eat a meal without reflecting on Newtonian physics, including explanations about why a plate stays on the table rather than falling to the ground. In other words, I want to provide a description of how it is possible that we teachers do what we do without having to be conscious of it.

In this chapter, I continue my discussion of what it means to teach from the perspective of the person who teaches. In the previous chapter, I made passing reference to the philosopher Martin Heidegger's central characteristic of Being. Thus, Being involves the experience of being ahead of itself, finding itself always already in the world, and always and already finding itself being together with others. I introduce the notions of "being in" and "being with," which express the fundamental conditions of human existence from the perspective of phenomenology and critical psychology. Stated briefly, we are always and already in a world and with others so that it makes little sense to think that we could exist without our physical bodies and our relations to others. Being in the classroom and being with others are the core foundation for coteaching, our solution to the problems in teacher development and teacher education, which I describe in Chapters 6 through 8.

BEING IN: FROM THE CLASSROOM

Although being in and being with cannot be separated—as human beings we are always social beings—I present one concept at a time for the purposes of representation and manageability from a reader's perspective. To introduce the concept, I use a short example from one of my research projects on teacher development. In this project, I cotaught with Nadine, the intern described in Chapter 1. She was, as I had said, completing her two-year program with a four-month assignment teaching seventh-grade science and mathematics. Initially, Nadine's cooperating teacher thought to leave her to teach the class by herself. However, when I offered to coteach with her, Nadine gladly accepted because she felt that her science background was not very strong and that she could learn from working alongside an experienced science teacher. I suggested that I could also do some demonstration lessons with equipment from the university and engage the students in whole-class conversations designed to develop a discourse of science within the classroom. For years, I have been pursuing the idea to all students to "talk science" rather than teaching them concepts. This had a considerable consequence on my teaching over the years, as I planned an increasing number of activities that allowed students to talk science with others, including peers and teacher. By necessity, the activities were organized as group activities, sometimes in the form of small-group inquiries (making a concept map, doing an experiment, or using computer models), and, at other times, as whole-class conversations.

Teaching Episode: An Observer Perspective

Prior to this particular episode, Nadine had started a unit on water by telling students that water was composed of hydrogen and oxygen. She had written the formula for water (H_2O) on the blackboard, along with a "Mickey Mouse" figure containing an "O" in the face and an "H" in each of the two ears. Afterwards, I proposed to begin the next lesson with a demonstration that shows two gases coming off an electrode when an electric current is passed through water. (The water also contains some sulfuric acid to increase its conductivity. Students are not told this so that the issues appear less complex than they otherwise would.)

Figure 2.1. In the middle of a demonstration lesson in which students experience the dissociation of water into oxygen and hydrogen, and the subsequent recombination of hydrogen and oxygen into steam (water). (About line 19 in the transcript.)

I prepared the equipment (a water dissociation apparatus, a power supply, and the acid), wrote the water formula H_2O on an index card, and mounted the card behind the apparatus (see Figure 2.1). Next, I connected the leads to the power supply in such a way that hydrogen (which is produced at twice the rate as oxygen) would be collected in the left tube. That is, the hydrogen would be collected on the same side as the *H* in the water formula, as written on the index card. I had also planned that at some point in the demonstration, I would fill a test tube with the hydrogen and ignite it to produce a characteristic explosive noise. Furthermore, I planned to take a glowing splinter and insert it into another test tube, where I would collect the oxygen and make the splinter burst into flames.

My general approach to lessons such as this is to engage students in conversation as much as possible. There was just one mediating circumstance to such an approach. The students in this class were not used to contributing in whole sentences or providing reasons for their guesses. One-word answers were the norm, and it would take some time until students became accustomed to my continuous requests for elaborations.

At this point in the lesson, I had captured some hydrogen from the apparatus and ignited it with a burning splinter. (Figure 2.1 shows the arrangement, corresponding to about line 19 in the following transcript. Students have pulled up their chairs and are sitting closely around a table in front of the blackboard.

Some students sit on top of their desks.) I hold up the test tube and ask if the students can see something in the test tube.

01	Teacher:	Do you see it, do you see something in the test tube?
02	Stephen:	[*Water molecules!*
03	Lisa:	[*Steam!* [
04	Tom:	[*Fog!*
05	Teacher:	What is fog made up of?
06	Karen:	[*Water molecules!*
07	Jay:	[*Hydrogen!*
08	Stephen:	You have been filling it up with something.
09		(*I draw a test tube and write H_2, as shown in Figure 2.1*
10	Brandon:	[It seems like it is water or something.
11	Karen:	[I think it is water molecules.
12	Teacher:	What happens to hydrogen when we light it?
13	Stephen:	[Whooop! Whooop!]
14	Brandon:	[There is no air in] there, so fire can't breath. Like it goes out.
15	Teacher:	But something happened to it! Someone talked about it earlier
16		on. (3.1) What did you see in there afterwards?
17		(*I draw wiggly line along walls inside test tube, writes H_2O next*
18		*to it.*)
19	Tom:	Fog.
20	Lisa:	Steam.
21	Teacher:	But steam is the same as?
22	Tom:	Fog.
23	Karen:	Water.
24	Teacher:	So as the hydrogen burns, it explodes . . . ?
25	Brandon:	It burns out, and the air makes it into steam.
26	Teacher:	It turns back into water.
27		(*I gesture from H_2 to H_2O*)

In response to my question, "Do you see something in the test tube?" several students shout simultaneously one-word answers including "fog." Without hesitation, I follow up on the word "fog" and ask students what fog is made up of (line 5). There are five student responses before I make another discursive move; meanwhile, I re-present the focal situation by drawing an inverted test tube with H_2 written inside. This was not planned.

Important for leading students to an understanding of the demonstration is the production of hydrogen from water and the subsequent (chemical) change from hydrogen to water as the former combines with oxygen during the small explosion (burning). From a discursive perspective, my question "What happened to hydrogen . . . ?" (line 12) indicates that somehow the students' earlier responses are not adequate. Accordingly, it is not surprising that Stephen and Brandon generate new answers. Again, my language at once indicated that the previous responses were inappropriate and encouraged students to generate new responses. In this case, Tom and Lisa reiterate earlier answers ("steam" and "fog"). My utterance shows that the questioning consists of discursive moves to get students to make the connection to water (the substance with which the demonstration had started). Thus, rather than having students make salient the transition of water → hydrogen → steam, my questioning leads students to the transition of water → hydrogen → water. The general direction in which I lead the conversation is that students articulate the change from a test tube filled first with a gas and then with steam (after the explosion).

Being Absorbed: Praxis and Lived Experience

In the first chapter, I pointed out that it is always possible to articulate events in an objective space and in terms of chronological time. Such descriptions, however, capture little of the experience of teaching as it unfolded. While it is true that teachers' own after-the-fact accounts are fallible and may have little relation with their own experience at the moment it unfolded, a critical phenomenological approach allows me to capture some of the experience. The critical approach does not attempt to rationalize the events but rather gives a sense of what it meant to be there at that time. In the following, I attempt such an account, which can be seen as an additional piece of data for making sense of what it means to teach. I wrote it soon after having taught the lesson.

While I am in this classroom, enacting the curriculum with the children, I am not aware of my Self as a distinct entity that stands in opposition to the class or as distinct from the material entities in the room. I am absorbed, focused on the unfolding events in which I take part, but which I do not control on my own. In this seventh-grade class, while teaching one of my first lessons, I am attuned to students' responses, while at the same moment being aware of the terrain I want to cover with them. Although I am prepared and have a general sense of what needs to be done so that the lesson can be described a posteriori as "successful," I do not know beforehand when I will ask particular questions. I do not even know whether I will have to ask particular questions, for the students may articulate many of the issues that are salient from a scientific perspective. So I go into these whole-class conversations with a sense of a general readiness, trusting my sense of what is right at any moment. This cannot be planned in advance. In fact, if I were to attempt to stick to a certain plan, I would be lost from the beginning, for like classical computer programs, I would not be able to adapt to the needs of the students and situations. It is perhaps for this reason that teachers often lecture and use initiation-response-evaluation sequences, because they retain the control in this way.

Lucy Suchman (1987) uses the analogy of the canoeist planning to go down a wild water channel. Despite all his or her planning, the canoeist cannot know exactly what will happen. He or she simply begins to get in a certain mood, which will allow him or her to be in tune with the situations that unfold. The canoeist is therefore ready to act, whatever the situation will be. I see myself in the same way. I am planning some demonstration—really I am preparing a set of resources. But then, in the classroom, I abandon myself to become part of the "wild waters," all the while intending to get down as quickly and safely as possible, I am working with the flow, going where the stream of the unfolding conversation takes us. I am attempting to take advantage of what I recognize in the heat of the moment as "teachable moments." I am willing to pursue a line of questioning to follow up some student idea, to probe and find out about students' current understanding (language), and finding out about the discursive resources that they bring to the curriculum (as disciplinary structure).

When I reflect back on situations such as this episode, I particularly note that I was not reflecting during the sequence or on the questioning process itself, nor on the way in which I interacted with the students. Much like during my years of rowing at an international level, if we began to "think" about what we were doing, we were certain to lose the very competitive edge that had brought us to this level in the first place. I attempt to get in tune with the situation and then rely on my embodied knowledge—which allows me a considerable flexibility with surprises that arise—to enact questioning. Later, with the help of videotapes and other people, I reflect on what has happened and on what might be improved.

Some colleagues might be tempted to critique me for "abandoning" myself to the situation and refusing to enact a more reflective (i.e., controlled) approach. But in a conversation with other people, professional or private, we do not plan ahead of time what we say, irrespective of the other person. If we were to do so, we would be regarded as being very insensitive to other people. Responsive teaching is very much like responsive conversation. We enact it without taking unilateral control, relying instead on our sense that we will say and do the right thing at the right time.

In the previously described episode, I brought particular resources, including the equipment and the little card with the formula of water. I paid attention as I set up the apparatus to connect the leads so that the hydrogen would be produced on the same side as the H_2 in the water formula. I thought that this orientation might be something like an affordance for a "discovery," a linking between the number 2 and the relative amount of the two gases. But all I was doing is setting up a range of resources that we could use in the conversation. In the same way that the wild water canoeist or a skier walk the stretch that he or she subsequently will descend, I got myself ready and into the proper frame of mind. But no planning would determine the unfolding of the events, unless I was failing to relinquish the control of what was being said to the children, unless I was failing to allow a conversation to unfold, merely interested in taking the students from guidepost to guidepost, without any concern for listening to their voices to learn whether they were actually with me.

When I am teaching, I can rely on spontaneously enacting my knowledge of chemistry and physics, without having to stop and think what science might say about the current situation. One analogy is that of driving a car or riding my bike somewhere where I have not been before. I do not have to think about my car or bicycle, or about changing gears. Rather, and more so than in a familiar situation, I am focused on the unfolding geography of the unfamiliar context. This is not to say that I know everything there is to know about the physics or chemistry of water—far from it. But when I talk with students about various aspects of water, I feel I am treading familiar terrain, where I do not have to constantly consult a map and my feet seem to take me to the right places.

Most important, when I teach—in the same way as when I write research articles or analyze data—I am not thinking about my Self. I do not reflect on the process of writing while writing these lines. In fact, if I were to do so, I would probably never be able to write these lines, instead always remaining caught in reflection and in infinite regress. Rather, when I write and teach, I do not seem to exist as a person; instead, I become so absorbed in the activity that nothing else seems to exist. There is a sense of flow, but there is no longer an "I" standing against the world out there. There is no more a distinction between myself as a living being and a social or material world that contains me but is distinct from me. In teaching, questions seem to form themselves, the events unfold, with myself an integral part, but there is no "me" that could say the things in this way. When I teach, the lessons go so fast that I lose track of time.

When teachers teach, they are generally unreflective about their own praxis in the same way that we remain unreflective about most everyday situations. In fact, it is the strength of our background understanding that we can do most of the things we do everyday without having to consciously think about them. We drive to work, shop for groceries, eat our daily meals, or walk to school without having to think about these activities. Even when we have conversations, we engage in the unfolding dialogue with little reflection on either the process or the unfolding content. We simply participate and are absorbed in the conversation.

In teaching, we are there in the classroom as if the situation presented itself to those of us who are present. We are there, dynamically enacting the teaching, and no longer "me" as separate from the classroom. This is not to reject the fact that when there is time, we reflect on our teaching. For example, I often have students conduct investigations in small groups; while they work, I usually move from one group to another to interact with them. On my way to each group, we usually have time to think about what has happened, how we asked questions, and how the students responded. That is, we have time to reflect on an exchange that has already passed. However, my interest is in those moments in which, for example, I am engaged in an exchange and do not have the time to reflect on the exchange or on the topic. I simply become involved in the situation, which unfolds and seems to have its own dynamic. In this part of teaching, in the heat of the moment, I do not have the resources to re-present what has happened in order to reflect upon it. Nevertheless, I still seem successful in these exchanges. How is such an immediate involvement possible without my conscious control?

BEING IN: THEORETICAL REFLECTIONS

Everyday understanding, acting in familiar situations, and using common sense have been the topic of phenomenological research for nearly a century. Phenomenological approaches to knowing and learning are non-reductionist. Rather than taking a being apart and separating it into individual organism and environment, phenomenologists theorize our fundamental condition as *being in the world* and everyday knowing as arising from the irreducible unit thereof. To understand a particular being, that is, a particular student or teacher, in his or her environment, we need to know more about how that person experiences the world.

When we look at teaching situations from the outside, we are often tempted to describe the unfolding events in terms of intentionality. Accordingly, some individual (mind) decides to engage in an action (or series of actions) and then implements these actions following the intended plan. However, while such a move is always possible, research in the field of artificial intelligence suggests that we can also impute intention to action even if there are no intentions at all. For example, in one kind of artificial intelligence experiments, robots were not preprogrammed but were still able—given simple action options such as stopping in front of a hurdle, turning left or right, and moving again straight ahead—to learn to navigate through their world. Human observers unfamiliar about the way in which robots had come to their knowledge ascribed intentional (perhaps programmed) behavior to the robots, including for activities such as seeking out soft drink cans hidden in holes. Other robotics researchers were able to build languages synthetically using a bottom-up approach. They first let robots construct a world and then, by providing rudiments of interactional behavior (e.g., looking at the speaker, turning in the direction of the object talked about), allowed these robots to evolve a simple language. The difficulty in this was that different robots had different experiences and often constructed different worlds. Furthermore, these robots needed to somehow agree upon a common language. Once all of this was achieved, the group of robots had a much greater chance of survival than any individual robot or group of non-interacting individual.

What we see in these examples is an empirical confirmation of some fundamental ideas about human cognition and development put forward in particular by the French philosopher Maurice Merleau-Ponty (1945) in his *Phénoménologie de la perception* and further developed by the French sociologist Pierre Bourdieu (1997). Merleau-Ponty inquired into the fundamental conditions of knowing and learning. He suggested that the human body is central to our understanding of the world. For example, we come to understand objects as objects, not because we find them out there somewhere, but because we learn to coordinate multiple perceptions of an object that we come to know as such only after we know that the perceptions to pertain to the same object. Similarly, our senses of space and time are built up from the experience of moving about in a world and correlating it with changes in sensory experiences. Like fish that are born into the water and whose mode experience is shaped by being in the water, human beings are thrown into a physical and social world that shapes how they interact with both the physical and social aspects of their situation.

In a similar manner, we need to question whether actions and action sequences such as those in which I engaged are intentional in the way we traditionally think about it. Thus, my action may be assembled on the spur of the moment, in a haphazard fashion. But how would we begin to conceive of such a new way of looking at teaching that appears planned and intentional but is not causally driven by plans—as we know from my account of my teaching experience.

As a first step toward a non-reductionist way of understanding teaching, let us consider the metaphor of knowledge as an environment. In familiar environments such as the neighborhood in which we have lived for many years or the city in which we have spent several decades, we are familiar with the available resources and know how to access and use them. We shop without having to plan where and how we go, how far we will drive the car, where we will leave it, and so forth. Thus, we can decide to shop for groceries without making a plan about the details of our shopping trip, even though we might visit several stores. We simply rely on our background knowledge and understanding of how the world works.

In the same way, we might think of teaching in a domain that is very familiar to us. If I, a trained physicist (physical chemist, statistician), teach some topic such as the chemical dissociation of water, I am in familiar terrain. In the world of the classroom, I am familiar with the chalkboard, desks, windows, ceiling, and many other objects that make and frame it. I do not make these things thematic while I teach, I take them for granted—at least after I have become somewhat familiar with the place. I do things in these classrooms without reflecting on what to do next—I pick up the chalk to write on the board without having to think "Now I move, lower my arm, pick up the chalk . . ." and so on. Rather, I just do it in the way we always do it.

Teachers begin to think and reflect only when there is some sort of *breakdown*. We find ourselves in such breakdown situations when the chalk we had placed next to the board is no longer there or the board has already been filled with text and labeled "Do not erase" etc. In the case of the experienced science teacher, scientific objects, events, and pedagogies are present in the same way as the classroom and the chalk in our example. In the experienced science teacher's case, these things include atoms and molecules of substances such as hydrogen, oxygen, and water; different models for visualizing the relationships of atoms within a molecule and between molecules; and an understanding of how to teach the subject matter. We enact scientific conversations without having to consciously reflect on whether something we say is true or appropriate at the moment. We know it is true by the mere fact that we are saying it. In teaching, however, it does not suffice to be in familiar terrain with respect to the subject matter content. Rather, being familiar with the range of perceptions and languages that students bring to science lessons is also an important aspect of successfully navigating a whole-class conversation. Let us pursue the idea of "breakdown" for a while. The notion of a breakdown points to reflection, another mode of being, which has dominated educational theorizing and research for some time. As I pointed out, being in can be described as a mode of transparent coping in the world. Much of what we do and the things we use are not noticed, or noticeable. For example, as I am writing these lines, the keyboard is completely transparent to the activity of writing. The primary activity is one of communicating ideas to the readers. As part of this activity, the keyboard is transparent, and does not seem to exist; instead, what is salient to includes the words, sentences, and ideas. It is not unlike driving to the grocery store: the car and the related practices of shifting gears, activating the turn signals, or depressing the gas pedal are transparent while we engage in a conversation with the person next to us. However, when something does not work in the usual way—when there is a "breakdown" in our normal mode of being—we begin to attend to particular things. Things that did not exist as such up to now become objects of our inquiry; consequently, we begin to re-present them and attempt to figure out what is not working. For example, when what shows up on the computer screen no longer conforms to our expectations (letters are missing or a seeming stream of the same letter appears), we think "keyboard." Our access to the keyboard is no longer immediate but rather mediated by our thoughts and formal (and formalizable) knowledge about keyboards.

In my experience, teaching is exactly the same. Normally, we teachers just do what we do, without having to think about what we are doing. When "things go their way," we cope with the unfolding lesson in an absorbed fashion. Without attending to it, our moving around in the classroom has an effect on what students currently do, although we are not consciously aware and therefore know what it is. We do not attend to proximity, yet it has considerable influence on what students say, how they contribute, and how they interact with each other. Some restlessness, unrest, or talk in one corner of the classroom makes us move without ever attending to what is happening, we continue our questioning sequence. But although we move into the direction of the disturbance, it is something that is not salient; it seems to occur in the background and almost in spite of all the other things that are occurring. The disturbance disappears, and we continue to move. It is only if it does not disappear that we begin to consciously think about that situation. At such times, we might stop the lesson, explicitly ask students in the corner about what is going on, and then deal with the situation. Alternately, we might even think about a next move or perhaps even reflect on alternatives.

Relation of Planning and Enacting

In recent years, curriculum has been conceptualized in a variety of ways, including as content structure, as a planned set of activities to teach the content structure (planned curriculum), or as an unfolding of events when teachers and students engage in a set of activities (enacted curriculum). I begin this discussion by noting that educational researchers and theorists have not sufficiently attended to the difference between planned curriculum and enacted curriculum, between plans and situated action.

In a curriculum that is to go exactly as planned, there really is no place for students. It is a world completely controlled by the teacher and interactions have to be minimized—because each time another person is allowed to act we introduce the possibility of changing the situation in a manner that had not been foreseen. If we move away from such a rigid view of curriculum and allow it to evolve in and through the interaction of students with each other and the teacher, the enacted curriculum will only proximally resemble what has been planned. For example, I could not know that Tom would shout the answer "fog" (line 04) and therefore could not plan to have an appropriate response or follow-up question. In the flow of regular conversations, there is also little time to reflect on what to say next. Rather, we teachers know that we are ready to give an appropriate response *to this particular situation*. In other words, since we know that we are in relatively familiar terrain, it suffices to mark particular points that we want to reach and then interact flexibly with students to reach or approximate these marks.

My notion of being in as absorbed coping, which implies a being in tune with the situation no longer requires "control" in the traditional sense. By being in tune, a teacher can rely on competence to enact a curriculum that is appropriate to the situation. We need to follow what we have planned only in the sense of the wild water canoeist who plans the descent. Planning prepares us, puts us in a state of readiness to cope with the unexpected, which, by definition, we cannot know in advance. In fact, we are ready to enact alternatives that only become apparent to us in response to the particular situation. (I come to this idea again in the next chapter, on *habitus*.)

BEING WITH

Humans are social beings through and through. The ways in which we know, learn, think, and act are deeply social. In this section, I articulate the essential dialectic of the Self and the Other, subjective and intersubjective experience, which arise (in ontogeny, as the infant matures) and have arisen (in phylogeny, over the evolution of the species) together in human development. Other and Self stand in a dialectic relation, not just as counterparts of each other but as necessarily involved in the constitution of their meanings.

Phenomenological Perspective

Being in the world makes salient that we exist not only as material bodies, but also as social bodies among other social bodies. Martin Heidegger (1977) alerted us to the fact that each human being is a being with others. It does not make sense to think of our Being and knowledge as independent of a world that we always and already share with others, a social and material world that shaped us before we were even capable of thinking of ourselves as Beings. Thrown into a world shot through with meaning, our (social and material) bodies are formed by the (social and material) world that envelops them.

In the phenomenological view developed by Pierre Bourdieu (1997) and Paul Ricœur (1990), our bodies are open to the world. In this openness, they are susceptible to be conditioned by the world, formed by the material and cultural conditions of existence in which we are placed at birth. Through our bodily inclusion in the world (e.g., classroom and school), we are therefore subjected to a process of socialization in which individuation, the formation of our sense of "Self" (e.g., as teacher or student), is itself a product. That is, our bodies (as "flesh") mediate between the intimacy of the self and externality of the world and enable the joint emergence of intersubjectivity and subjectivity.

We grasp the social as lived experience, through day-to-day praxis, and the singularity of "me" (as a teacher) is worked out as we enact, and emerge from, each social relationship. A teacher's identity and competence therefore presuppose a condition of being with. Our bodies—gestures, attitudes, and facial expressions—are used to provide the contextuality and indexicality that are the fundamental conditions and stabilizing features of everyday interaction (communication). It is because the world comprises us, because it includes us as entities among other entities, that we can comprehend it. We acquire an understanding and a practical mastery of the "us"—including space—by means of this material inclusion (which rationalist theories do not allow us to perceive and which is therefore repressed in them). We also acquire an understanding by means of the social structures embodied in the dispositional structures that we develop from this material inclusion.

Origins of Sociality

The simultaneous emergence of individuality (Self) and sociality (being an other to Another) has been theorized in an attempt to provide a historical grounding to psychology through a categorical reconstruction of the human subject (Holzkamp 1983). We best understand a thing if we understand how it became what it is. According to critical psychology, the human psyche developed in two major steps. The first step involves tool use. Some animals also use tools. For example, chimpanzees use twigs that they rid of leaves and stick into entrances in termite mounds to pull out the insects and eat them. (Gestalt psychologists had shown how chimps convert things into tools to get at food.) However, these animals use tools in response to the immediate situation. That is, they make the tools when they need them. What is particularly human about tool use is that we make tools to be used by others or in other situations at different times and locations. This is a profound shift from means to ends in the character of the tool. The object that initially served as a means to mediate our relation with the world now has become an end in itself. This shift, which critical psychologists call means-end inversion, encourages abstract thinking in the sense that it is thinking about other than the present situations.

A second major shift occurs when the toolmaker and tool user are no longer the same. Although there are social divisions in primate groupings, they take on completely new dimensions with the division of labor between maker and user. This involves a new, deliberate social arrangement. Survival is no longer solely linked to biologically determined features but now depends as well on the characteristics of the particular society. With the accomplishment of this second step, the specifically human form of existence is achieved. That is, whereas earlier forms in hominid evolution relied on a direct relationship between the animal and the world, early hominids began to have mediated access to the world. This mediation works in two different ways. Let us look at simple tools such as a hammer or a knife. These tools mediate our relationship to the world: and we no longer interact with the world in an immediate ("im-" or "non-mediate") way, but with and through the hammer and knife. More important, others make the hammer and knife; others therefore always mediate our use of a tool. If this double mediation of our relationship to the world is true for such simple tools, it is even more so for complex tools such as pedagogies or theories of teacher knowing and learning.

These mediations, and in particular the division of labor made possible in societies, have an important consequence. We no longer need to pursue immediate individual needs but contribute, as individuals, to the needs of society as a whole. Our individual actions are an integral part of the options available at a societal level. In fact, individual actions are concrete realizations of action possibilities in the society as a whole, where they are available as generalized action possibilities.

These mediations that we appropriate as we learn to get around the world are also responsible for our constitution of Self—who we are as teachers, parents, lovers, and so forth. That is, the recognition of our personal Self comes with the recognition of the Other as a Self to whom we are an Other. I not only perceive the other from my standpoint, but the other also perceives me in a similar way, also knowing that I perceive him or her in the way he or she perceives me. Our perspectives cross over into each other. Our intersubjectivity and our subjectivities emerge together.

Learning to Teach by Being in and Being with

We are born into a world that is always and already entirely social. As such, much of our learning develops by participating in a world that the presence of others always and already mediates. This realization is embodied in apprenticeship. Apprenticeship situations have always taken advantage of, and adopted, a shared praxis as the principal mode of learning. In traditional societies apprenticeship constituted the main context in which newcomers were inducted into a specialized area of practice, such as becoming a tailor, blacksmith, or midwife. Additionally, in many modern-day professions, we come to know a lot by working along with others, that is, by participating with others in getting the day's job done. For example, the social organization on the bridge of navy vessels is such that it allows newcomers to participate and learn increasingly complex skills as they progress to take on new tasks and positions on the bridge. Pilots, too, learn much of what they know by participating as copilots before they actually become pilots. In all these cases, learning and becoming knowledgeable are intimately tied to being in praxis and participating in ongoing work. In particular, being with another practitioner allows newcomers to experience praxis from the position of practitioner rather than as an observer. Here, the participant view is quite different from the observer perspective, much like playing a soccer game versus watching it.

My research shows that beginning teachers who work alongside one or more (experienced) teachers, learn tremendously. They are not just in the classroom, "with others" in a loose way. They are in a mode of being like a co-pilot with a pilot on a plane. They develop a teacher identity by being part of a learning community that allows them to share the lived experience of teaching without the fear of failing. These beginning teachers grasp the social as lived experience, through day-to-day praxis. They develop competent practice and teacher identities as they participate with other teachers in the everyday world of teaching.

In teaching, things usually are a bit different. The traditional approach is that, first, we learn theories and techniques at the university and then we transfer them into the classroom during brief student teaching assignments and later as beginning teachers. For the most part, however, the apprenticeship of observation is extended from the high school to the university setting, where students witnesses their own, student-oriented perspectives. Few teachers have been in the position of learning to teach by teaching in a participatory manner side-by-side with another teacher. Being with another teacher in the same classroom, doing what has to be done—teaching—is not the norm. Yet, if the research in other domains is valid, there should be tremendous possibilities in learning to teach by being with another teacher and sharing the experience of being in this particular classroom.

Learning to Ask Productive Questions: A Case Study

In this case study, we want to show how learning occurs among teachers being in the same classroom and being with each other. In this example, I focus on Chris, an experienced classroom teacher, as she cotaught a unit on the engineering of physical structures developed by another teacher, Birgit.

Chris was the regular (part-time) classroom teacher and had twelve years of experience teaching at this grade level. She was also recognized at her school as a good teacher and was regarded as an exemplary science teacher by her peers.

She was kind and very student centered, being concerned for students' well-being and learning. Birgit was a curriculum developer and graduate student with four years of teaching experience; she had developed this engineering unit and also given teacher workshops about it.

During my initial observations in this classroom—which began three months prior to the unit and during which I began to participate in all classroom activities—Chris asked questions that were close-ended (factual) and utilized a tripart, initiation-response-evaluation structure. This form of questioning was consistent with her frequent use of worksheets. The questions asked by students during the presentation and discussion of student-produced artifacts also were of factual nature. When Birgit joined Chris in the classroom to teach with her, the content and structure of the questions began to change. Starting from the close-ended questions that had been characteristic of Chris's practice prior to the study, she gradually changed to using the content-oriented and open-ended ones characteristic of Birgit's practice. This led to questions that are more productive that extended children's thinking and led to much higher cognitive achievements in this unit than Chris had observed in a previous class. Over time, Chris and Birgit's questioning became increasingly similar, though they often were not conscious about the changes. Even the students began to ask more open-ended and reflective questions (e.g., "What would you have done if . . . ?" "What did you do when you were struggling . . . ?" or "What were your problems . . . and how did you resolve them?"). Gradually, the questioning practices in this classroom community (teachers and students) began to change.

After about four weeks of teaching alongside Birgit, I noted some major changes in the way Chris asked questions. There was one lesson in particular where the videotapes showed a considerable (and, as I later noted, lasting) change. At the beginning of the lesson, Chris still asked questions that demanded very specific answers, such as, "Can you enlarge [the tower] in this (vertical) direction?" "Can you stabilize this with triangles?" "Can you put something on the bottom?" "Can you make this [piece] the top part?" and "Are you going to work on this [part]?" Other questions (implicitly) suggested what she wanted students to do, such as enlarge the tower by adding a base or a top or stabilize it by adding triangular braces. The boys answered with "yes," "no," or "We can do that. It's very easy."

About sixteen minutes later, Birgit joined the same group of three boys, thus providing them with an opportunity to talk about their engineering project in a formal way. Meanwhile, as she had done frequently throughout their coteaching, Chris stood nearby to hear Birgit ask questions involving these particular children at this stage in their project and this stage in their learning. Intending to engage students in talking science and engineering, Birgit asked questions such as, "Do you think there is anything you want to change to improve [the tower]?" "I am a fellow engineer who wants to buy this tower, how can you sell it to me?" and "What are the features that would make me want to buy this [tower] rather than someone else's?"

We notice that Birgit asked students to identify weaknesses, strengths, or salient features of their design and construction or to explain characteristic ("leaning") aspects of the current tower. It was evident that the students answered Birgit's questions in more elaborate ways than they answered questions asked by Chris. Birgit had engaged in an interaction that was productive and had encouraged the students to reflect on what they had done or wanted to do. In contrast, as Chris later admitted, her interaction failed to help the students reflect on their collaborative work or practical and theoretical engineering issues related to their construction. However, changes in Chris's practice of capitalizing on or creating such opportunities became apparent later in the lesson when she questioned another group of students. It was quite apparent that this particular event became a turning point in her teaching. At some later point, while sitting around a table with others who had shared in the experience, Chris suggested:

This is one of my first days when I started realizing, "What kind of questions am I asking?" and "What can I do to extent the kids' thinking?" I did not ask why it was a big challenge, but what it was- I asked the question, "Where is the tower going to break?" and Birgit asked the question, "Why is it going to break?"

By stepping aside and listening to Brigit interact with the three boys, Chris became aware of the difference between her own questions and those that her teaching partner asked. It was in this moment, when she was not directly involved in questioning, that she was able to reflect on questioning, while the lesson was still going on. Overall, she considered Birgit's interaction as much more productive. Commenting on the instance with the three boys, she emphasized the positive outcomes of Birgit's questioning and contrasted them with her own questions, which to her sounded very negative.

Near the end of the same lesson, my cameras captured Chris again, this time interacting with two boys. The tape shows that Chris initially asked the same type of questions that she had always asked: "What kind of shape was more stable?" "Where is the engine?" and "What kind of engine is it?" Then, suddenly, her questions changed. She began to ask questions such as, "If you had to do it again, how would you change it?" and "If I was an engineer and I wanted to buy this [tower], what would be [its] selling feature of the tower?" In these later question we can hear that Chris has appropriated some of Birgit's ways of asking questions.

From this day on, my videotapes show a tremendous increase in the frequency of open-ended questions. Within a three-hour period, Chris included several productive questions within each interaction, and throughout the remainder of the unit, she continued to improve this aspect of her teaching.

In this (perhaps fortunate) instance, I saw how one teacher's questioning changed quite dramatically. What my observations did not reveal, however, was how this change of practice was brought about, that is, *how* Chris had learned it. While watching the videotapes of this lesson, Chris indicated that she had noted the difference between her own and Birgit's questions. She recognized that her own questions were not productive and that she "was going nowhere." At the same time, she was impressed with the questions posed by Birgit. This suggests a conscious change process. On the other hand, she indicated at the same time that she would not have used the questions (such as, "If I were to buy your tower . . .?") had she read them in the teachers' manual. However, experiencing the question in context "put it into her being" and "made it become part of her." Chris commented upon the fact that her questioning had begun to resemble Birgit's in the following way:

I probably copied all the questions like the kids copied somebody else's triangle shape in order to improve their own. . . . I was trying to use her words, because I needed to put it into my being. I needed to practice exactly what I had seen and heard before it was part of me. Now it has become much more part of me, and I can extend those question. . . . I am such a visual learner. I have to do it, touch it, feel it, or see it. Because I am with Birgit, I actually hear a question. It goes in, and then I can use it. While if someone gave me a list of questions, I could not use them.

Here again, Chris reconstructs her learning in terms of explicit and tacit aspects. On the one hand, Chris consciously tried to use Birgit's questions and practiced exactly what she had seen and heard. On the other hand, she emphasized that watching her partner helped her to make the questions part of herself, something she would not have been able to had she read the same questions in a resource book. Actually hearing a question helped Chris to appropriate a way of questioning, that is, a way of being with and relating to the children. Here, Chris addressed a critical aspect of learning by being in and being with another teacher. She also pointed out the difference between this type of learning and trying to implement a question from the teachers' manual. Chris could not verbalize that aspect of her learning in which we were most interested, that is, the difference between the experience of hearing Birgit ask a question and reading the same question in a book. Chris merely explained: "I am such a visual learner. I have to do it, touch it, feel it, or see it." Initially, productive questioning was not something that was salient to Chris or in her questions. Being with Birgit, Chris and the children changed the ways in which they questioned each other. Chris also noted that what the children built and learned seemed to be different from what the children in another class had learned during a similar unit on bridge building that she had taught during a previous year. Again, she attributed much of the children's learning to the difference in questions, which helped children obtain a cognitive benefit from their experiences. Through productive questioning, she was able to see content knowledge being made salient concurrently with the processes of knowledge construction. We all felt that the productive questions ultimately led to the success of the unit in her class.

In this example, I focused on Chris, specifically on how her questioning changed as she worked side-by-side with Birgit. Birgit's own questioning also changed in the course of being in this classroom and being with Chris. For example, in the course of this research, we all realized that the questions Birgit asked became increasingly appropriate for each particular child. Birgit expressed this learning in terms of the "appropriateness and timing" of questions. She attributed her learning to the fact that she was working next to Chris. Birgit, too, described what was happening to her during the work at the elbows of Chris as knowledge in action "that goes in," is "soaked up," or is "made part of her." Here, for Birgit and Chris—as for other teachers who participated in my coteaching research—being with another teacher leads to learning, some of which goes on without being aware of it. This is not to say that we learn *only* while in the mode of being with, but we do learn essential parts of teaching as situated practice by working with others. I will return to the role of reflection in the context of cogenerative dialoguing involving coteachers and students (Chapter 8).

Independent of the contingencies of the moment, expertise is characterized by (a) appropriateness of questioning, (b) availability of multiple questions, and (c) absence of deliberation. Given this description, we might therefore ask, "How is it possible that teachers enact appropriate questions without reflecting in the moment of asking?" "How can it be that experienced teachers always seem to have the right question on the tip of their tongue?" and "Why is it that experienced teachers do not waver to produce the next question?" To help answer these questions, in Chapter 3 I introduce the notion of *habitus*. Habitus is a set of dispositions that the practitioner develops in and through his or her experience that allow him or her to see and hear the present situation in particular ways.

3

Habitus

In the previous chapter, I articulated being in the world as a non-thematic, unreflective, but concerned absorption in everyday activity. Moreover, it involves a world characterized by physical and social regularity and immediately endowed with meaning because we have been exposed to these regularities since birth. However, this alone does not explain why we get around and participate in interactions without conscious control and reflection. There must be something else that shapes our perception and lets us do what we do without having to deliberate. To explore this question further, I begin with the idea that physical and social regularities affect our sense of what it is like to be then and there.

STRUCTURED STRUCTURING DISPOSITIONS

To become attuned to the phenomenon of interest in this chapter, let me return to the lesson presented at the beginning of the last chapter. I had asked a question about the contents of the test tube in which I had previously ignited the hydrogen captured from the water dissociation apparatus.

```
01    Michael:   Do you see it, do you see something in the test tube?
02    Tom:       [Water mo[lecules!
03    Lisa:      [Steam!  [
04    Stephen:               [Fog!
05    Michael:   What is fog made up of?
```

Although I had conducted this demonstration many times during my years as a junior high school teacher, I had never heard the description "fog." Furthermore, in this particular instance, the conversation unfolded in such a manner that there was no time to reflect on this answer and instead I responded by asking what this substance is made of. In looking at the transcript, we can begin to understand how this seemingly simple question has the potential to lead students to the more usual "steam" or "water" description as to the results of the burning of hydrogen. My question embodies an understanding of the relationship between fog and water and sets ups an appropriate avenue for students to make a connection between the two. From this simple illustration, a series of important questions about interactions arise, including, why do teachers respond to the contributions of others without having to reflect? Why was the relationship between fog and water immediately available to me without an extensive search for the connection? In other words, why do competent teachers have many different options for continuing a conversation, even without reflecting about the content and pedagogical content knowledge involved in teaching? In answering these questions, I turn to the work of Pierre Bourdieu (1980) and, in particular, his notion of *habitus*.

According to Bourdieu, habitus consists of systems of dispositions that generate activities, including perceptions, expectations, and (outward) actions. These systems of dispositions are patterned and obtain particular structures. We may also say they are pigeonholes that frame our perceptions, expectations, and actions. For the most part, we see or use cups as cups, hammers as hammers, and pliers as pliers and in this respect, the world is pre-constructed in many ways. Cups are used for drinking, hammers to drive nails, pliers to bend some metal or pull a nail. That is, we see and use objects *as* objects (tools) that afford us engagement in particular activities. Additionally, these objects typically do not even enter our consciousness. It is only when we need something that is currently not available (situations of "breakdown") or through the imaginative play of a child that we come to see and use familiar objects in new ways, such that two cups may be used to hold up a baking sheet or a pair of pliers becomes a toy that can be used in place of a person. In most instances, however, we see and use objects and tools in particular, structured, or patterned ways. We do not have to reflect to see a cup as a cup, a hammer as a hammer, or a pair of pliers as a pair of pliers. In the same way, we talk in patterned, grammatically correct sentences before we ever know what grammar is, and most people are not even aware of the fact that there are culturally patterned ways in which people take turns in conversation.

Habitus generates patterned actions and is therefore a structuring disposition. However, these dispositions are themselves formed through inhabiting the world. That is, these dispositions are themselves structured by the structures of the world. There is therefore a reflexive and mutually constitutive relationship between habitus and the world. For example, habitus is responsible for perceiving the world as a structured environment (full of physical and social entities), while at the same time, this structured environment (as perceived by the individual) is responsible for bringing about habitus. Habitus, our systems of structured structuring dispositions, results from a (long) process of formation.

Let me now return to the example in which I interact with the students. My discussion of knowing as environment and habitus shows that we do not need to think in terms of intentional behavior and plans to understand that a long-time teacher (like myself) enacts questioning in patterned ways. Being familiar with physics and physical chemistry, entities such as "water," "hydrogen," "oxygen," "chemical reactions," burning, "2 H_2 + O_2 → 2 H_2O," "steam," "states of matter," "phase transitions," and so forth are familiar (structured) resources that I employ in my (discursive) practices. There is no need for me to reflect in order to talk about water, combustion, or the production of water from the burning of hydrogen. I talk about water, combustion, and the production of water in the way I walk rather than (consciously) placing one word, or foot, in front of the other.

Habitus generates the patterned ways in which we interact with the world, including those practices that embody actions, perceptions, and expectations. There exists a mutually constitutive, and therefore reflexive, relationship between the structures of the world and the structures of habitus. Being exposed to and formed by the world, habitus is structured by the world. But because habitus generates our actions, perceptions, and expectations, the world is structured by it. Habitus therefore constitutes a system of structured dispositions in which the past is constituted in the present: our dispositions are always historical and biographical products. Because habitus was formed by the regularities of the world, it is enabled, as I showed in Chapter 1, to anticipate these regularities in its conduct. This assures me a *practical* comprehension of the world that is entirely different from the intentional and conscious decoding acts normally attributed to the idea of comprehension. Habitus therefore temporizes itself in praxis through a practical mobilization of the past in the very moment it anticipates the future.

Habitus cannot be described in the abstract. Central to the notion of habitus is that it only reveals itself in reference to the particular, that is, in definite situations. Thus, what has to be done cannot be prespecified in the abstract, but rather emerges from the contingencies and temporalities of each situation. For example, even though it is highly desirable for teachers to plan thoroughly in order to enact a curriculum, it must be remembered that the most appropriate course of actions cannot be prespecified if the actions are to be reflexively accountable to the unfolding present. The teacher's relationship to the enacted curriculum is similar to that of the canoeist about to descent on approaching rapids. It is not possible to know whether a particular move is appropriate unless one is there. Similarly, it is not possible to sit on the side watching a teacher and class and specify a correct course of action to adopt. Thus, habitus produces given discursive and material (perceptual, classification) practices only in relation to the specifics of a setting. The easiest way to acquire habitus is by coparticipating in situations with others who already have acquired habitus. The formation of any habitus therefore requires being in situations and being with others. It is this being in/with that is central to apprenticeship and enculturation theories as well as studies of the cultural reproduction of practices. Relative to teaching, being in/with is the central underpinning of the "co" in coteaching.

Habitus is not static and closed but an open system of disposition undergoing a continuous experience-dependent transformation embodying its own history and experiential trajectory. These experiences either reinforce or modify existing structures of habitus such that it will sustain more viable practices. Importantly, habitus is not merely formed by being exposed to the social and material world. Rather, as Bourdieu points out, it "can also be transformed via socio-analysis, i.e., via an awakening of consciousness and a form of 'self-work' that enables the individual to get a handle on his or her dispositions" (Bourdieu and Wacquant 1992: 133). Thus, reflection on action is an additional, though not principal mode, by which habitus is formed and transformed.

Habitus generates our patterned actions in and with the world because it takes (and can take) the world for granted. However, this does not mean that strategic choice and conscious deliberation are ruled out as modalities of action. First, the sequences of actions generated by habitus may be accompanied by interests, strategic calculation of costs and benefits, and by other concerns prevalent in the situation. Second, in times of serious breakdown, when the normal forms of interacting with the world are disrupted, rational choice indeed takes over—at least in those agents who are in the position to be rational.

Becoming a teacher therefore means forming the habitus that, according to Pierre Bourdieu, can only be formed by the experience; if we coparticipate, rather than individually constructing, we participate in patterned activities and practices, which in themselves make sense: we "are the ways we do things." We understand ourselves in the way we objectify our experiences of being with. These experiences constitute the ground that reflexively elaborates (objectified) discourse about teaching. As teachers, we never simply do things in a stable world but interact with students who are also agents themselves. Thus, students and teachers construct their Self-Other continuously and in an emergent way, always in situation. "Teacher" and "student" arise out of the dynamic of each situation, and personality can only be attributed to individual bodies in a retroactive manner. To be a teacher requires more than simply exposing a stable self in the classroom. It requires that we engage in a continuous construction of "teacher" arising from the interactions in and with the (social, material) classroom.

HABITUS OF AN INEXPERIENCED TEACHER

In the case of teaching, expertise involves the development of interaction in such a way that allows students to learn. This includes a large range of possible discourse options that allow for room to maneuver in an appropriate manner. The habitus of an expert, therefore, enables the generation of different options for doing what comes next, even without reflecting about it. In such situations, what comes next resides in the current state and the ways in which salient elements can be transformed to bring about the next state. Expertise can be characterized in terms of this room to maneuver. The more room to maneuver a practitioner has, the more options to act are available and the more options for still subsequent actions are created. We come back to this concept of *Spielraum* in the next chapter.

In contrast, when novice teachers first begin teaching, they often act in ways consistent with past experiences and thereby re/produce the structures that they themselves had been subject to. Although they have not yet (or little) participated in teacher-student interaction from the teacher's point of view, their habitus (system of structured structuring dispositions) structures the way they question, itself having been structured by the questioning sequences they experienced with their own teachers.

Let me take the following episode from a lesson by Nadine, an intern teacher near the end of her two-year program, which she completed with a four-month internship. She is teaching in the same school and in the same class where she had taught already during a previous six-week practicum (student teaching). She therefore knows the students and acts in accordance, not only with her own experience as a student, but with the norms that underpin questioning in this school. Her students already expect to engage in teacher-student interaction in a certain way, which is, in many ways, similar to what we had seen happening in the split fourth- and fifth-grade classroom taught by Chris (Chapter 2). They, too, have developed a habitus for participating in teacher-student interactions. Together, Nadine and her students both produce and reproduce a particular culture.

The episode comes from a lesson in which Nadine wants students to learn about some of the characteristic differences between the solid, liquid, and gas phases of a substance. As water is one of the most available substances that can be illustrated at room temperature, she has filled different beakers with water and ice. Her goal is to arrive at a statement about the quality of liquids that fill containers. She holds up a glass of water (Figure 3.1) and asks:

01	Nadine:	What do you notice about the liquid here? (3.5 s) Are there
02		spaces?
03	Stephen:	No.
04	Nadine:	No. When a liquid is poured into something, it fills all the
05		spaces.

In this episode, we have the traditional triadic dialogue: teacher initiates with a question (lines 1–2), a student provides a one-word response (line 3), and the teacher provides an evaluation (line 4), which here comes in the form of a confirming repetition of the students' answer. It is an instance of the IRE sequence typical of classrooms. Thus, although Nadine was just beginning to teach, she was already enacting a way of asking questions that is typical for traditional schooling. She participated in producing and reproducing the IRE sequence.

Figure 3.1. Nadine questions students about the liquid state of water. Her interaction follows the triadic model that constituted the world in which she grew up and was formed.

Given that Nadine's own learning experiences occurred in classrooms where such questioning was enacted, it is not surprising that she herself enacted a similar style. Being exposed to the questions both in content and format (triadic), her habitus was being formed. Not surprisingly, her mode of interacting with the children in her care reflected exactly the same questioning strategies that had provided her with a context, and therefore reflected the forces that shaped her. Now, when Nadine observed me asking "productive" questions and began to realize that there are different ways of interacting with students in addition to her triadic method, she decided to change. However, change, as much as we desire it to happen, does not come about easily. (In the past, researchers assumed that they just had to tell teachers what and how to change and to expect such change to happen.) Consider, for example, attempts to stop smoking and how it involves more than simply not lighting up anymore.

During the brief period while I smoked, cigarettes always were a part of coffee breaks. Whenever I had a coffee, I also smoked. I began to notice that I had hardly smelled the coffee or taken a sip before my hand was searching for the pack of cigarettes. Thus, quitting smoking meant having to break the link between coffee and cigarettes or between end of meals and cigarettes. This relation between smoking and coffee or end of meals is an example of a habit rather than a habitus. However, habitus is even more difficult to change than habits, for it goes deep into the mechanisms that generate the structured ways in which we perceive and act toward the world. At first we have to understand that there is something problematic about IRE sequences; to understand, we need to be able to see IRE sequences for what they are.

Nadine did not know about IRE pattern and asked questions in the way she knew teachers asked questions. There was no reason for her to do otherwise—habitus that is not interrogated is like ideology. However, when Nadine began to teach alongside me, she started noticing the differences between her questioning and my own. She felt that I had questions "right at the tip of [my] tongue." Furthermore, she felt that she let students get away with one-word answers, whereas I asked them to elaborate on their responses. Above all, I asked why questions, which forced the children to provide rationales for their claims.

After Nadine brought up the issue of questioning as a topic for learning, I talked to her about the IRE-type questioning and how it has come under serious criticism. Because it leaves control of the talk entirely to the teacher, students are relegated to filling in individual words. As a result, students do not learn to articulate descriptions and explanations. Nor do they learn to articulate elaborate responses to open-ended questions. Rather, such questioning supports the development of a fact-oriented discourse. Nadine decided that she wanted to make a conscious effort to change her questioning. However, she found that this was not as easy as she thought. Although she wanted to change her questioning and make it more like mine, making this change meant that she had to deal with the deep-seated dispositional structures that led her to enact the triadic IRE dialogue forms. Thus, change came slowly, but it was, in tremendous ways, facilitated by the fact that she experienced questioning in action, while she taught lessons together with me.

In the following section, I take another look at Birgit and Chris, who wrestled with changing their questioning practice. In the previous chapter, I described how Chris came to ask more generative questions and mentioned that Birgit learned to make her questions more appropriate to the needs of particular students. In the following, I show how habitus accounts for the difficulties associated with changing the patterns of asking students to respond to questions.

HABITUS: IMPEDIMENT TO CHANGE

Relation of Rules and Actions

Why might it be so difficult to change practice? If competent practice means that we follow rules, then a change in practice means that we simply have to change the rules that we are said to enact at the moment of practice. But a lot of research shows that change in practice does not come easily. Even if, as shown next, teachers know what they want to do differently and can describe the new practice in the form of rules, they still experience difficulties and impediments. Why do (can) traditional theories of teaching not articulate these difficulties? There is some (little-heeded) suggestion that much of the cognitive research on the relationship between rules and actions has simply put the cart before the horse.

Ethnomethodological research on plans (rules) and situated action suggests that our understanding of this relationship has traditionally moved in the wrong direction. Whereas most theories postulate rules that drive the actions they describe, ethnomethodologists suggest that it is the other way around: actions are only subsequently described in terms of their (non-)conformance to particular rules. Thus, this research suggests that rules are part of an accounting mechanism rather than at the bottom of an action-determining mechanism. Harold Garfinkel (1967) suggested that people are not cultural dopes who follow sociocultural rules in a blind way. Rather, actions are thought to be the result of a highly artful, contingent composition. Rules are discursive resources to account for the actions in particular contexts.

It may be more fruitful to think about teaching in this same way. Teaching is an activity that consists of highly spontaneous and contingent actions. There also exist various forms of accounting discourse, in the form of rules and precepts, which are used to describe and explain teaching after the fact. But we need to keep in mind that actions precede the accounting process; whether a particular action conforms to a rule is only established after the fact (though any actions can often be predicted with a certain probability). Once we abandon the relationship in which rules drive actions, we need a different way of explaining practices and why they are so resistant to change. Habitus provides us with such a concept.

Habitus and Change

Habitus is formed with time and through experience. This formation contains both a historical and a dialectic component. Because habitus shapes the way we perceive and act in the world, what we teachers respond to and what makes us learn is already patterned by our habitus; it structures our learning and therefore its own future shape. Consequently, habitus is a historical construct and therefore must be studied through historical methods. At the same time, habitus makes change possible, despite its own nature as a conserving force: habitus embodies a contradiction of both resisting and enabling change. As such, it is a dialectical construct, embodying a contradiction that itself is a driving force of change (Il'enkov 1977).

Because of the conservative tendency of habitus, it takes considerable time and effort to bring about changes in practices—change in practice requires a change in habitus. But change in habitus does not come easily, as habitus is formed and transformed in and through practical experience. However, habitus can also be changed through considerable socio-analysis, that is, through an awakening of certain forms of self-consciousness and self-work that enables practitioners to get a handle on their dispositions. One way of enacting such self-work is through reflection on practice. This has to be accompanied by a form of radical doubt to break with accustomed ways of looking at situations—lest we be caught in (commonsense) prejudice (here viewed in its positive form as prejudgment that arises when habitus generates practices of perceiving and talking about experience). The pre-constructed is everywhere: What we perceive as the self-evident character of the world (of teaching) arises from the fit between the structures of this world and the structures of habitus, which stand in a mutually constitutive relationship.

This self-work is made difficult by the fact that habitus is not revealed directly but only through the practices it generates. As a corollary, habitus reveals itself only in reference to the particulars of a definite situation, that is, in praxis. It is only *in the relation to* the specific structures of practical situations in the classroom that habitus produces the discursive (and other) practices characteristic of teaching. Thus, teachers often face difficulties when they want to change their practice if the main venue for change is restricted to talk about action. At the level of accounting for (talking about) practice, we may therefore observe conflicts in the rules teachers use to account for what they do. They want to use new (sets of) rules, which may be in conflict to other sets of rules. But if, as I described, rules do not cause actions but only serve as accounting devices, teachers' struggles become understandable. Change cannot occur if the work is limited to a level of accounting for practice. What really needs to undergo change is habitus. In the following case study, I present the struggles experienced by two teachers (Birgit and Chris) as they attempt to make their classroom more gender equitable in terms of participation in whole-class conversations. Their effort to enhance girls' experience of science became for me an opportunity to study practitioners who consciously tried to change their practice, and in doing so, disrupted the spontaneity of their actions. These difficulties may be characteristic for many teachers as they attempt to change their practice as a result of outside input (traditional supervision models) or self-initiated individual or collaborative reflection on action.

Impediments: Case Study

Birgit and Chris were very keen on changing the traditional ways in which boys and girls are enculturated to science. Birgit was particularly attuned to the need for bringing about change early on in the children's experiences. In her work as a curriculum developer, she had developed a workshop for teachers designed to make them aware of the structure of past practices that favored boys over girls and to provide teachers with instructions for enacting curriculum in alternative, gender-balanced ways.

When Birgit first came to the classroom, she noted an imbalance in the way boys and girls contributed to whole-class conversations. Without attempting to be malicious, boys appeared to monopolize the discourse while girls remained quiet. (Of course, this is an interesting phenomenon given recent reports that boys lag behind girls in school achievement.) Birgit talked to Chris about this imbalance, and they decided to work on providing opportunities for more equitable participation in the science class that they cotaught.

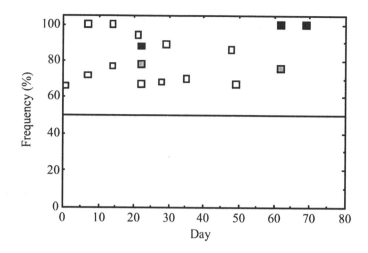

Figure 3.2. Frequencies with which teachers (open), boys (black), and girls (shaded) called on boys to respond to a question.

Nobody knew at the outset how difficult that was going to be—at the time, we did not know about habitus and its conservative force. Although Birgit and Chris wanted to provide equal opportunities for boys and girls, we were all struck by the pair's interactions with the whole class. At the beginning of the unit, Birgit and Chris called on boys about four times as frequently as girls to answer questions in a whole-class situation. On the basis of the videotapes we made, Birgit and Chris then began to consciously attend to gender issues. They attempted to make boys and girls respond in equal numbers to teacher questions and to structure classroom activities in such a way that would allow girls to be more active in conversations and question-and-answer sessions. They asked me to monitor the frequency with which boys and girls were called upon and to provide them with feedback.

Figure 3.2 shows that throughout the unit, in a whole-class setting, boys were asked more frequently than girls to respond to a question. Even under the best circumstances, boys were asked twice as many times as girls to provide an answer. At worst, there were two whole-class interactions during which boys were asked seventeen and twelve times but girls were asked once and not at all, respectively. The figure also shows that children also contributed to this phenomenon; boys and girls reproduced the patterns. That is, the figure suggests a culture in which girls do not get to participate in exchanges in the same way as boys. Despite the conscious effort mounted by Birgit and Chris, their attempt to bring about change was largely a failure. Regardless of feedback, Birgit and Chris did not manage to change interaction patterns in any significant way for either whole-class discussions, student-centered presentations, or question-comment sessions. In fact, when several outside observers (elementary teachers from another school) of a particular lesson pointed out the gender imbalance, Chris and Birgit were astonished. They had experienced this particular lesson as one where they had actually managed to ask an equal number of girls and boys. However, when we later counted the frequencies from a videotape of the lesson, we discovered that the ratio was actually thirty-six boys to eighteen girls.

Here, I do not attempt to blame the teacher; I am not certain that I could have done any better. Rather, I attempt to understand the phenomenon, and in particular, the resistance to bringing about the change that Birgit and Chris had articulated as desirable. I simply want to show that talk about and reflection on practice, in and of themselves, do not bring about change. Even when reflection occurs during an ongoing lesson, it does not assist in bringing about the desired change—in fact, it may interfere with the ongoing lesson. Because habitus continues to make them perceive and act in particular ways in particular situations, the teachers continue enacting old practices although their discourse suggests that they want to change them. Nevertheless, intention does not necessarily lead to action. During debriefing, Birgit and Chris constructed various discursive resources to account for what they were doing in class. But the rules that these resources embodied were partially in conflict, resulting in a system of rules that accounts for their practice but also has considerable exceptions.

Much of the two teachers' struggle to provide equal opportunities for boys and girls in their classroom had to do with their habitus, which they did not change just by reflecting on action and making a conscious decision to select an equal number of girls and boys to respond. In the situation, Birgit and Chris acted spontaneously, asking their questions and calling on students as a matter of course. However, when they accounted for their actions afterwards, they used "rules of action" to describe what had happened. These rules included, "Never ask the person who puts the hand up first" "Ask as many girls as boys" and "Ask boys and girls the same kind of questions." But interestingly enough, they experienced trouble when they wanted to act in accordance with a new rule.

At the heart of their effort to bring about change was the rule, "Ask as many girls as boys." Change meant that they would act in such a manner that retrospectively, the rule accurately described what they had been doing. But when events turned out otherwise, the teachers produced a range of other rules in order to explain why what they had done did not conform to the rule that they really wanted to enact. Much of their struggle can therefore be understood as an attempt to reestablish the practical adequacy of each precept in the light of a (desired) new practice. The present analyses provide a view of this work. In the following excerpt, Chris and Birgit raised several crucial issues related to their effort to ask more girls to respond to questions.

Chris: I never ask the person who puts the hand up first, unless. You know sometimes I do, but I really try not to. That is something I don't do.
Birgit: And I had to consciously do that as well. So this is the question I have. I have felt uncomfortable in a whole class setting—when there are five boys with their hands up—consciously to ask girls. You know that I do that,

right, "Carla, what do you think about that?" But you know my struggle is that there is something going on within me about relating to that girl. I feel uncomfortable. I have a real hard time with my wait time. I have to consciously count to five. But I guess my question is, "Is it right to put girls on the spot in front of the class like that or are there other ways to draw them out that they are more comfortable being drawn out?"

When the two talked *about* their questioning practices during whole class interactions, they framed them as a rule, "Never ask the person who puts the hand up first"—even after a five-second lapse. However, this rule was not universally applicable ("You know, sometimes I do. But I really try not to. That is something I don't do"). The videotapes of their questioning confirmed this assessment; there were times when this rule could not be used to account for the teacher's actions. Depending on the situation at hand, they waited sometimes but not at other times. Just when they waited or did not wait was something they were not able to articulate. We can understand that in terms of their practical sense, their habitus allowed them to act, in situation, without being able to articulate (even after the fact) just why they had acted in that particular way.

In many situations it did not appear to disturb either teacher that they had asked up to ten or twelve boys without directing a question to a girl. At other times, this imbalance appeared to be noted, and after five or six boys were asked, a series of questions was directed to girls. Birgit talked about these situations; the awareness of a girl/boy imbalance during questioning led her to construct several exceptions during a whole-class conversation. Her rules in this respect were "Ask as many boys as girls" and "Ask boys and girls the same kind of questions." She questioned, however, "is it right to consciously ask girls when there are five boys with their hands up and they are real keeners?" or "Is it right to put girls on the spot in front of the class?" In this context, she constructed a second conflict involving her rule "Always wait five seconds before accepting an answer."

With some of the eager children—particularly the boys—Birgit and Chris acted in a way that reified their rules. But they felt uncomfortable waiting in the case of some girls where they could "see their discomfort, sort of squirming." In one instance, for example, Renata was called upon. Renata uttered her first words in that answer, haltingly and with big sighs. Chris immediately asked another student to continue. She later noted that she had not waited to allow Renata to respond ("I got her off the hook really fast"). While reflecting on the event, Chris considered two conflicting rules to account for her actions, "Let a child respond fully" and "Keep a class going." Acting according to the first rule helps children in their conceptual development, but its implementation may take time and interrupt the flow of the class, thus conflicting with acting according to other rules, such as the second.

In the context of gender equity, Birgit had further opportunities to consider the adequacy of her rule, "Do not ask close-ended questions." She had to establish the adequacy of this rule as a descriptor in the context of two other rules,

"Do something for every learning style" and "Do not ask risky [too difficult] questions." In order to accommodate different learning styles, especially those of individuals who seek definite answers and clearly defined situations (among which she counted most girls), she used tasks and questions that have only one correct solution. That is, her accounting rule about close-ended questions was modified in the context of gender-related learning styles. For example, one activity required students to induce the rule that it takes $n - 3$ straws to stabilize a polygon with n sides. The ultimate failure of the activity in this class encouraged Birgit to construct it as inadequate to implement her learning style rule. Then, and partially overlapping with the previous rule, both teachers asked close-ended questions in order to avoid situations in which students "felt on the spot," "uncomfortable," and "embarrassed." Thus, they modified their rule about asking close-ended questions in the context of gender equality. This then accounted for why they asked questions that were "not risky."

A risky question is not only determined by the content and the person asked but also by the context. Thus, "provide a safe environment" was a rule that Chris used to talk about her practice. While Chris spoke to the students about storing projects, Damian appeared to make reference to the fact that Clare had forgotten to properly stow away a notebook so that it was accidentally destroyed.

Damian: Clare, but what if you forget it? That's [where-   ]
Chris: [Damian!] Can we have positive
          comments or none at all!

As the transcript indicates, Chris interrupted Damian's talk by calling his name while he was still talking. Chris acted here, apparently without reflecting, thereby in effect cutting off any further ironic remarks Damian may have made. She later used the "safe environment" rule to explain and legitimize her (discursive) action.

I think we are trying to make a classroom that just encourages positive comments all the time. I mean, who was it that made some weird comment today, Damian or something? And just instantly that was it, "You shut up kid," and I told him so, in no unclear words, "You don't say those kind of things in our class." So I think that is a kind of positive classroom atmosphere that most teachers try and make that they can feel safe then to respond. That's probably why we see Renata responding more than at the beginning of the year, because she knows that nobody is jumping at her for stupidity.

Chris's account of her practice is interesting in several respects. First, she was uncertain whether telling a child to "shut up" and "You don't say these kinds of things in our class" in fact causes a classroom to be safe ("I think we are trying to make . . ."). However, she assumed that as a consequence of practices that can be described in this way, students like Renata were more likely to respond. Second, acting such that the rule "Provide a save environment" was reified did not lead to unequivocal practices; there was no logical necessity for specific practices to emerge. Deciding whether the rule was able to account for what she had done had to be worked out for each specific situation. Whatever she was doing, after the fact she provided this and any mediating rule for explaining why she had acted in a particular way. In effect, her practical actions differed from student to student, and even for the same student in different circumstances. In the present situation, she used this rule to explain why she told a student to "shut up." In a different situation involving more students, she used the same rule to explain why she stopped all classroom activity, called the students together, and told them, "I am not comfortable going on in this way" and "Let's think about it." Finally, Chris did not recall what Damian had actually said; there was a discrepancy between what the two video cameras recorded and what Chris claimed to have said. Her situation definition was different from ours. It was not clear whether her statement "You shut up kid" and "You don't say those kinds of things in our class" communicated something about her stance; the same uncertainty characterizes what she really said when she admonished Damian: "Can we have positive comments or none at all!"

These data document the struggles both teachers experienced when they tried to provide opportunities for girls equal to those for boys. They experienced these struggles although they had identified the problem themselves and chosen to change their practices. As they tried to change, they found that some of the rules that they used to account for their practice were no longer adequate. Before, they just did what they did, without thinking about it. Now, their sense of the "right thing to do" was lost, meaning that they had to deliberate the practical adequacy of each rule. In this case, their interactions with the class became stilted. At one point, both boys and girls remarked that teachers were attempting to act differently than usual. The boys asked, "Why are you calling on so many girls?" and the girls asked, "Why are you calling on us even if we don't want [to answer]?"

As a set, the rules of actions described by each of the two teachers were only marginally adequate to account for what they were doing. Neither Birgit nor Chris could articulate the specific conditions that made them act in one of two quite different ways. However, it does not seem that this is a problem in and of their practice. Rather, they continued in a fairly consistent way (as shown in Figure 3.2) to ask many more boys than girls to respond to their questions. Instead, the problem is at the level of accounting for what you do, that is, in the notion of rules as the driving force for what people do. Once we abandon this notion and accept that rules serve to account for actions after they have occurred (post hoc), we have made a first step in understanding the difficulties of altering practice. That is, if we view patterned actions as the product of a habitus that is not directly accessible, we understand the complexities involved with bringing about change.

PRAXIS AND (IMPORTED) PRAXEOLOGY

Reform is often unsuccessful because discourse about action changes without corresponding changes in the actions. This is not surprising given that, in the same manner as any literary text, actions are open to interpretation. Thus, the same action or set of actions can be "read" in different ways, or, in other words, can be described using a different observational language. Thus, there is nothing illogical about changing one's descriptive and explanatory language to account for teaching without requiring any change in the praxis of teaching. In an interesting study, Brigitte Jordan (1989) showed how traditional (Mayan) midwives underwent training by the United Nations Educational, Scientific, and Cultural Organization (UNESCO) for the purpose of bringing their practice "up to standards." It turned out that these midwives were very good students and, during the workshops with Western doctors and nurses, learned to talk about what they were doing in Western medical terms. But when Brigitte Jordan followed them around after they had returned to their villages, there was little or no change—the midwives were doing what they had always done. Surprisingly perhaps, in the follow-up workshops, the midwives again spoke about what they were doing in Western medical terminology.

In my own experience, similar phenomena can be observed among teachers. New discourses are continuously imported into school system and schools, and practitioners adopt these new discourses to describe and explain what they are doing. These new discourses, however, frequently do not require any changes to occur in the practices themselves. The teachers do the same lecturing, using the same overhead displays that they have used for the past twenty years, but they now talk about their practice in constructivist terms.

Past reform efforts have focused too much on changes in teachers' discursive practices and spent too little effort in assisting willing teachers in changing their habitus. Given the amount of effort required to create a change in habitus, it is not surprising that few researchers, most are caught in their own set of accounting (publishing practices), were interested in the long-term relationships required in supporting substantial change. Typical for reform efforts in the past were short and sometimes repeated summer workshops. But the problem of these workshops is that habitus is not involved because teachers are not in the environment that sets their habitus in action. All the changes that occur in such workshops are changes in the language used to account for practice rather than in the habitus, which is necessary for a change in practice.

The trajectory from bringing a particular practice into the domain of discourse to bringing about a desired change of practices is not straightforward. Teachers often experience considerable conflict when they attempt to change their practices. We now know that these difficulties have to do with the resistance built into the nature of habitus. If we accept that rules do not drive practice but are descriptions of practice whose adequacy can be established only after the fact, it becomes clear why change is difficult. Teachers enact a lesson and, through subsequent analysis, can evaluate to what extent their practice corresponded to the new description (rule) that they wish to adopt. That is, although they can attune themselves to change, habitus has a tendency to reproduce past practices, which we notice in the discrepancy between what we desire to do and how we actually behave. We can change our attunement, or through reflection become aware of what we are doing, but the next time we have to deal with the same problem we typically abandon ourselves to our habitus. It is out of this contradiction, therefore, that we come to change what we are doing in the classroom.

It is important to note the difference between the learning that was going on between Birgit and Chris as we described it in the last chapter and the kinds of changes that they wanted to bring about in the present situation. Although they had the intention to change what they were doing, change was difficult and, in this particular instance, did not come about. In the first instance, learning and change were seemingly effortless and coincided with participation *in* practice. The changes to be brought about by reflecting on their practices were difficult. Much effort was expended without apparent results. In the first instance, Birgit and Chris initially enacted different practices, and learning was visible in the increasing similarity between the two different forms of questioning. (When people move into new contexts, they often "pick up" new dialects and intonations without being aware of it. They find out that this has happened to them when they see others from their previous contexts, who notice these changes.) In the second instance, the practices (and therefore habitus) of Birgit and Chris were quite similar. As such, there was no internal force to drive the change. In the end, their conscious effort to bring about change remained unsuccessful, and Birgit and Chris still found themselves asking boys much more frequently than they asked girls when they interacted with students in whole-class situations.

4

Spielraum

In Chapter 3, I suggested that one of the defining characteristics of expertise is a habitus that includes a wide range of possible options for action. This Spielraum, or room to maneuver in an appropriate manner, sets up a dialectic that generates new options for subsequent actions. In this chapter I develop the notion of Spielraum and illustrate its use in praxis. I begin by developing a contrast between popular ideas about reflective practice (particularly as it is developed in much of the educational literature) and the actual experience of teaching as understood within the phenomenological framework of time developed in the first chapter.

FROM REFLECTION TO SPIELRAUM

In the past, epistemologies of practice have been elaborated on the assumption that any setting of action is constituted by objective properties at hand that are available to the analyst in the same way they are to the practitioner. But these epistemologies have largely failed to capture the essence of the teaching experience. The failure of such epistemologies lies in the fact that they do neither describe the lived experience of teachers nor the reality in and toward which their actions are directed. In turn, a popular response has been to adopt a reflective stance towards our own pedagogy. Much of this change was inspired by the work of Donald Schön (1983, 1987).

One of the benefits of Schön's work is that it provides us with a new rhetoric with which to discuss the practical activities of teaching. Inevitably, however, each new paradigm evokes the need for clarification and continuing development. In particular, I focus on one concept within Schön's framework of reflective practice, namely, *reflection in action*, which concerns itself with the ability of the immediacy of the relationship between thought and action to redirect a problematic situation. I suggest that given the temporal constraints of teaching in terms of the immediacy of the demands of classroom interactions, the concept of reflection in action is incomplete. In particular, I contend that when expert teachers are "surprised," there is no time for reflection as I understand it. Rather, these teachers use their Spielraum (room to maneuver) to explore and develop students' understanding within the immediacy of the given context.

Reflective Practice

Pedagogical development is grounded in a reflective stance towards one's thoughts and actions. However, descriptions of reflective practice are often confounded by a lack of conceptual clarity about the nature of reflection itself. To circumvent this problem, I offer a general working definition of reflection that allows me to deal with the central issue of the temporal constraints of teaching as well as the problematic of reflection in action. I suggest that reflection is a pragmatic (goal-driven) action that attempts to objectify, conceptualize, or thematize a problematic phenomenal experience. In this, reflective thinking is fundamentally purposeful and involves an initiating perplexity. Given this understanding of reflection, the concept of reflection in action is confounded by the failure to distinguish between reflection as an individual cognitive event and emergent transactional events involving and embedding students and teachers. It is in the latter events that a widely construed concept of reflection in action becomes problematic and begins to break down.

Reflection in Action: A Temporal Problematic

Central to the development of reflective teaching is the concept of reflection in action or the logic of on-the-spot experimentation. Recently, however, the limitations of the concept of reflection in action have been outlined and its usefulness for understanding pedagogical transactions has been questioned (van Manen 1995). Much of this criticism focuses on the temporal constraints of enacting reflective practice within a classroom environment. For example, if reflection in action is to include any element of reflection as we generally understand it, then it must also involve a degree of detachment, because reflection necessitates an object (a representation of the world) to be operated on. Yet representing and reflecting are processes that take time, which does not exist in the experience of ongoing action. Nevertheless, expert teachers are still capable of acting appropriately, even without the luxury of a time-out for reflection.

Given the constraints of the immediacy of classroom transactions, the examples used by Schön are simply not analogous to the lived experience of working in a classroom with twenty or thirty active students. Take, for instance, the example of building a garden gate, which Schön used to illustrate an action context framed in terms of reflection in action. First, he made a drawing. Next, he began to build the structure from pickets, but stopped to think about how to make it square before continuing to nail the pieces to complete the gate. Of particular concern is the temporal characteristic of his actions: namely, his account is full of descriptions of time-out. Schön continuously stopped to think about his next move. Meanwhile, the gate in progress waited patiently, all pieces staying in place until Schön decided what to do next. Yet from our experiences, teaching cannot be likened to the action of building a gate. Students, conversations, and activities do not wait; they continuously act and unfold. In real classrooms, teachers would soon be out of synch if they were to engage continuously in such a process of time-out. Unlike Schön, teachers must act, without extended periods of time for representing (objectifying) students, conversational topics, and the classroom. Teaching is a continuously unfolding event, and teachers must engage in the right action at the right instance, even when the context has changed in unforeseeable ways. In each situation and moment, an action is required, even if it is non-action. More important, I suggest that experts relate to the setting with a non-thematic, non–self-referential awareness. There is no longer a subject that experiences itself in an objectified world—there is only enacting performance that constitutes an event. Experts are so involved in the activity that they do not experience themselves as separate from the activity. Martin Heidegger (1977) called this absorbed oneness *Dasein.*

Teachers' Dasein: Being in the Classroom

Novice teachers often feel that despite their subject matter knowledge, teaching skills, and understanding of educational theories, they remain unprepared for life in the classroom. They experience a gap between theories of teaching (classroom management, learning, and curriculum) and the praxis of teaching: a gap between what is being said about teaching, and what they experience as actually happening in the classroom. If theorizing of teaching is based on *Dasein,* I am able to describe practice in ways that teachers can relate to their own experience.

Heidegger postulated *Dasein* (literally, "being there") as the fundamental mode of human existence. According to Heidegger, we always and already find (and therefore understand) ourselves as being at some place and at some point in time. As Dreyfus points out, "In understanding, a particular Dasein takes a stand on itself in a local situation by appropriating a for-the-sake-of-which and some in-order-tos from the world" (Dreyfus 1991: 192). *Dasein* combines Self and world into a single irreducible entity: being in the world. As *Dasein,* we are always somewhere, for some purpose, at some time, and absorbed in some activity. As teachers, our experience is one of being in *this* classroom to teach *this* subject matter to *these* children. The classroom is not some removed entity that can be given in terms of its objective (shared) properties but an experienced world in and toward which we act by investing ourselves and introducing possibilities. Thus, it is because being in the world and participatory belonging precede any subject-object relation that we find ourselves *first of all* in a world to which we belong, physically and socially, and in which we cannot but participate (Ricœur 1990). Only *subsequently* are we able to set up objects (including the signs on which reflection is based) in opposition to ourselves, objects that we reclaim as objectively knowable. That is, only subsequently do we explain and theorize our teaching, or, in the case of Birgit and Chris in the previous chapter, construct rules that explain our actions.

Teacher development, that is, the evolution of being in the world involves a concomitant transformation of being, world, and the relation signified by "in." The world is comprehensible and immediately imbued with sense (always and already shot through with meaning) because Self has the capacity to be present outside itself (that is, as an Other to Another) and in the world, and to be modified by the world as it is exposed to its regularities (Bourdieu 1980). Having acquired a system of dispositions appropriate to these regularities, the *body* (mind and senses) is apt in practically anticipating these regularities leading to an em*bodied* knowing, a practical comprehension of the world that is completely different from the conscious reading that one ordinarily takes as understanding. *Dasein* is primarily constituted by possibility—a developing *Dasein* increases its possibilities for acting in its constructed world, its reality. These possibilities do not arise from a particular skill, but rather from the readiness for action correlative to the current situation, and without cogitating one's next moves in a detached way. Readiness for appropriate action, whatever the unfolding events, means that the agent has Spielraum, the room to maneuver appropriately in the current situation. As Dreyfus explains, this Spielraum "is a version of originary transcendence" (Dreyfus 1991: 191). The trajectory of increasing mastery is therefore characterized by an enlarged system of (virtual) possibilities of integrated and simultaneously available action and an increased readiness for enacting these possibilities.

Spielraum

Dreyfus articulates what we consider the difference between Schön's (1983, 1987) reflection in action and what I conceive of as possibilities in the Spielraum of the agent. The individual agent has Spielraum, room to maneuver in the current situation in terms of the range of possibilities that he or she identifies *without* reflection. Schön did not operate in this Spielraum when he built his garden gate but rather stopped and reflected. Such contemporaneous reflection in situations, however, allows for a stop-and-think kind of action that may differ markedly from the more immediate action required in classroom interactions.

Classrooms, as complex settings, can be described and structured in many different ways. Changing one's positioning within (and the particularities of) the setting will change what is salient. Master teachers, therefore, position themselves to increase their possibilities for acting without having to frame the setting in conceptual terms. Familiarity expands the reality, and with it, the Spielraum and therefore the possibilities for acting. "The range of possibilities that Dasein 'knows' without reflection, sets up *the room for maneuver* in the current situation" (Dreyfus 1991: 190, emphasis in the original). Thus, the possibilities open in any *particular* situation can be thought of as a subset of the *general* possibilities making up what is significant to the agent. These possibilities reveal what constitutes appropriate action in a specific situation. Spielraum, therefore, contributes to classroom interactions in two distinct ways. First, the teacher's readiness for action allows an unfolding of a realm of appropriate possibilities within the immediacy of the student-teacher transaction. Second, this realm of possibilities, in turn, allows the teacher a point of entry from which to elucidate the reality of the students' understanding.

Theories of teaching need to account for the ongoing evolution of events in order to explicate the actual experience of teaching. To understand the Spielraum of a teacher, we need to understand his or her common-sense, taken-for-granted world; in situations of breakdown, we need to understand this world's salient elements. To demonstrate how the concept of Spielraum operates in a classroom situation I present two illustrations in which a master teacher uses his Spielraum to develop and reveal the students' conceptual understanding.

UNFOLDING CONVERSATIONS, UNFOLDING REALITIES

To be a master teacher means to be able to act at the right moment and in an appropriate manner. This requires considerable Spielraum in the face of all the contingencies that real-time interactions pose to the participants involved. The following episodes are taken from an ongoing study in a local middle school where I coteach with teachers and interns. I cotaught with several teachers in the same school; consequently, there were many opportunities to reflect on commonly experienced teaching events with colleagues at different levels of professional development. All collaborations between the teachers and myself were constructed under the auspices of professional development using a participatory action research design.

Episode One: Challenging Mickey Mouse Models

Teachers who use demonstrations as opportunities to explore ways of describing and explaining scientific phenomena find that whole-class discussions can be full of surprises. Teacher-student conversations represent "good" teaching when they respect students' cognitive and emotive needs, follow an internal dynamic that unfolds in an intelligible manner for all participants, and reach specified curricular goals. Good teaching also demands that the teacher maintains a presence and enacts a poise and effectiveness that enables him or her to achieve a close relationship with the students. With this presence comes a readiness for action, which, because there is no time-out, precludes reflection. Master teaching is characterized by this readiness for action, which is a highly developed improvisation and the bipolar opposite of "winging it." Such readiness for action is exhibited in the following episode.

The following scene took place in a seventh-grade classroom where students were engaged in a four-month unit designed to explore the physical and chemical properties of water. During a previous lesson, I had elicited students' hypotheses about the nature of the bubbles that are visible when water is boiled; these hypotheses included the four substances of vapor, oxygen, hydrogen, and air. To construct a context that might allow students to eliminate two of these hypotheses (oxygen, hydrogen), I set up an apparatus (see the figure in the following transcript) that produced oxygen and hydrogen. The purpose was to demonstrate characteristic reactions when glowing and burning splinters are brought into contact with each substance (oxygen makes the glowing splinters burst into flames; hydrogen, when lit, results in a small explosion). I prepared the experiment in such a way that, from the students' perspective, hydrogen would be produced in the left-hand column, corresponding to the position in the chemical formula (H_2O). An additional environmental clue to the nature of the gases could have been the fact that there was twice as much of the gas in the left column as in the right column. The figure in the transcript shows an electrolysis apparatus as presented in the class. The chemical formula was written on the chalkboard so that the environmental cue (H_2, on the left-hand side of the formula) would be consistent with the nature of the gas to the left, hydrogen (H_2). The current from the battery splits the water molecules, resulting in hydrogen and oxygen, which are seen as bubbles rising in the two columns; that is, in chemical terms, two molecules of H_2O change into two molecules of H_2 and one molecule of O_2. The chemical equation describing this reaction is $2\ H_2O \rightarrow 2\ H_2 + O_2$.

Before starting the tests of the two gases (the episode that was featured in Chapter 2), I decided to ascertain that students clearly understood the nature of the gases. (For transcription conventions, see Appendix.)

01	Teacher:	These (*Points to columns.*) contain different gases. Which one do you think is hydrogen, and which one is oxygen, given that you already know that this (*Points to H₂O.*) is the chemical formula of water?
02	Tony:	Hydrogen is right, oxygen is left.
03	Teacher:	Why would you say that this (*Points to right column.*) is hydrogen?
04	Tony:	'Cause there's less hydrogen and more [oxygen in a water molecule
05	Teacher:	[(*Points to "2" in H₂O.*)
06		Does everyone agree with that?
07	Stan:	Yeah.
08	Jon:	Yeah.

To me, Tony's answer (line 2) was unexpected since, in my fifteen years of teaching science, I had never heard students make the claim that the smaller amount of gas should be hydrogen. I had set up the electrolysis apparatus and written the chemical formula for water in such a way that, from the students' location in the room, the hydrogen and oxygen columns and the order of these atoms in the formula were both the same. For the students, however, the physical arrangement (that brought the larger amount of gas and the H_2 in the formula into respective proximity) did not necessarily constitute an environmental cue. For me, this was a novel situation, an unexpected twist. Before I could proceed with demonstrating how hydrogen and oxygen reacted in the presence of glowing and burning splinters, I needed to be sure that students identified the gases correctly. Rather than switching to a telling science mode, the situation became an opportunity for exploration. Above all, I needed to understand the students' understanding. That is, I needed to know what they understood, how they understood, and the nature of the reality in which they operated; as much as possible, I needed to know the world through the students' eyes. The most appropriate teaching move, therefore, would be to elicit what salient perceptual elements led students to such a claim. At the same time, in my experience of the moment, I did not reflect. Questioning simply unfolded as a matter of course and without objectifying distance. Despite the unexpected nature of Tony's response, his next question (line 3) elicited an explanation for the earlier response. Whereas the "2" in the chemical formula H_2O could have meant that there was more hydrogen, Tony's response suggested that he thought the opposite. My immediate action was to ask whether other students agreed with this answer which seemed so inconsistent with my own understanding. Nevertheless, other students agreed with Tony (lines 7–8).

09	Teacher:	Where did you get the information from that there is more oxygen than hydrogen in the water?
10	Tony:	There is two little ones and one [big one, and one big oxygen.
11	Teacher:	[(*Points to "H₂" in H₂O.*)
12	Stan:	The little Mickey.
13	Jon:	With the ears.
14	Stan:	The little Mickey Mouse.
15		(5.3)
16	Tony:	(*Walks to blackboard, draws Mickey model.*)
17		These two (*Points to the small circles.*) are the hydrogen and this (*Points to the large circle.*) is the oxygen.

My subsequent move (line 9) effectively invited students to further elaborate on their response. Tony, Stan, and Jon then collectively disclosed the source on which their argument was based. As they had seen drawn by Nadine (the intern teacher), Tony drew a Mickey Mouse–like figure (see lines 15–16 in the transcript) and identified the big circle as oxygen and the two smaller circles as hydrogen. Here, students reasonably inferred that if there are size differences in the atoms, there should be differences in the volume that these gases take up. However, from the scientific worldview that constituted my reality, this inference was inappropriate since gases, in their molecular form, take up the same amount of space, irrespective of the size of individual molecules (and atoms). Furthermore, as the Mickey Mouse model of water had not been a part of my own reality before, I did not expect this image to be used as an argumentative resource. At this point, I was in a delicate situation from which I had to get out, *then* and *there*, without the time-out required to reflect (deliberate) on possible actions or evaluate the relative benefits of each one. At the same time, I had to continue to explore, then and there, the children's reality—their understanding, the conceptual structure of their reasoning, and the concomitant elements of the world as they saw it. All the while I remained committed to the development of the conversation. The research with Nadine showed that the most difficult aspect of becoming a teacher lay exactly in acting appropriately in the "here and now," to do the right thing at the right moment without having time-out for reflection. Dealing with the unique character of the here and now is one of the distinguishing characteristics that separates the analysis of teaching (i.e., as a preservice teacher sitting in a methods class analyzing some case study) from actual teaching. The implications of this difference are explored more fully in Chapter 7.

When I questioned whether students generally agreed (line 6) with Tony's proposition, several "yes" answers made it necessary to find out more about the nature of the students' understanding. If there had been a "no" answer, the students could have been asked to elaborate on the opposite positions. However, since this was not the case, a unique situation emerged as a result of the conflict between the students' conceptions and the teacher's. Nobody had expected this situation, even though everybody contributed to its emergence; however, only I could elicit its pedagogical properties. My next action (line 9) positioned me so that I was able to elicit students' descriptions in order to develop a better understanding of their reality: The question elicited the nature of the resource on which students' argument were based. The subsequent exchanges brought forth just that. After Tony had drawn the Mickey Mouse model and the three boys had constructed their explanation in the public space of the whole-class conversation, I was able to enter the students' reality yet position myself such as to retain my *Spielraum*. Thus, my subsequent questioning continued the conversation, engaged students in further inferences, elaboration, and explanations, and disclosed further aspects of the students' reality.

My experience of this event can be described as analogous to the improvisation work of a jazz musician working off the play of other musicians while at the same time projecting his or her own presence, all the while moving the musical piece forward. Throughout the sequence, questioning was immediate and excluded time for reflection. Rather, I acted within a large set of possible questions that were available. Emergent questioning was constituted by an appropriate next move, which not only allowed me to understand the students' reality but also to engage them in widening their horizon and therefore enlarging their reality. In the process of enlargement, new aspects of the students' reality came to be known, including unexpected elements, which provided a new playing field on which to enact further questioning. In essence, I created a Spielraum, using the range of possibilities available in my currently salient world. At the same time, I did so without consciously reflecting prior to each move.

Episode Two: Building Models

The following episode describes an interaction between three students and myself while exploring the role of molecular models in explaining the states of matter (solid, liquid, and gas). For me, the central point of the unit was the nature of models as explanatory resources. Prior to this episode, Nadine had displayed an overhead transparency with drawings of the particulate models of solids, liquids, and gases, along with a definition of each. In the post-lesson debriefing, I suggested that students probably copied the drawings into their notebooks without actually understanding the role of models in explaining the three states of water. (To students, the drawings may had been simply drawings rather than models that have, in the work of scientists, a reality of their own, including their own properties and behaviors.) I then proposed a small-group activity: Students would first build models in separate groups, followed by a whole-class discussion in which they could explain why they built the models in the way they did, as well as describe how the models account for the observable physical properties of matter. This lesson would then lead into another one that allowed students to develop understanding of solid-liquid and liquid-gas phase transitions (melting ↔ freezing; and boiling ↔ condensing) by constructing explanations based on their previously constructed models.

There are different scientific ways to frame the phenomena at hand. The one to be developed with the students here focuses on the strength of the bonds between molecules. If bonds are strong, they are also rigid, leading to a solid at the macroscopic level. If the bonds are weaker, the molecules begin to move with respect to each other but are held together by the tension at the surface of the substance, leading to a liquid. Finally, if the bonds are very weak or absent, the molecules can dissipate, therefore resulting in the gaseous state. Scientifically correct models that explain the different states ice, water, and vapor should therefore have stiff, loose, and no bonds, respectively, between the models of the molecules (here, small and large marshmallows).

On the day of the model building lessons, Nadine and I provided students with a variety of materials from which they could freely choose components for their models. We both moved about the classroom to interact with students in their small groups. As I approached one of these groups, the following conversation ensued.

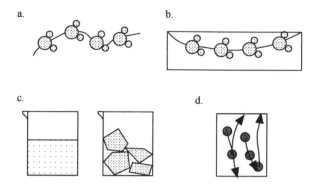

Figure 4.1. a. Sara's string-based model of a liquid. **b.** Tim's string-model mounted into a shoe carton. **c.** Beaker with water and ice used by Michael for engaging students in comparisons between models and physical materials. **d.** Model of liquid state of water in Bill's notebook.

01	Teacher:	So you are building a solid? (0.6)
02	Tim:	No, a liquid.
03	Bill:	Liquid.
04	Teacher:	Why is that? (*Points to string/marshmallow model shown in Figure 4.1.a*).
05	Sara:	I don't know, ask them (*Points to boys.*)
06	Teacher:	You explain it to me. (1.9)
07	Sara:	I don't know, maybe they should go together, see. (*Points to model shown in Figure 4.1.d.*)
08	Bill:	In the book. (*Points to model shown in Figure 4.1.d.*)
09	Tim:	In the book. (1.8)
10	Bill:	It's here in the book.
11	Teacher:	But I want you to explain it to me. (2.2)
12	Sara:	They'd be moving around more, so they'd be a little farther apart.
13		(*Gestures toward the slack between the marshmallows on the string as shown in Figure 4.1.a.*)
14	Tim:	I go by what the book says.
15	Teacher:	(*Gets beaker with water and beaker with ice, as shown in Figure 4.1.c.*)

At the start of the conversation the students had already built their models. However, when asked about various aspects of the structure they were not certain why they actually had built their models in the way they did other than because they corresponded to the drawings provided earlier by Nadine (lines 5, 7–10, 14). To move the conversation forward, I went to get two beakers containing the two substances to be modeled, ice and water (line 15). This served to produce a Spielraum adapted to the children by facilitating their reflection upon the relationship between the models they were building and their referents in the phenomenal world.

1 6	Teacher:	What is the difference between the ice and the water here?
1 7	Bill:	This is closer (*Points to water.*) and this (*Points to ice.*) is farther apart.
1 8	Teacher:	Do you see that?
1 9	Bill:	Yeap.
2 0	Sara:	There's gaps right there. (*Points to ice.*)
2 1	Bill:	Yes! See it is immersed.
2 2	Teacher:	So there are gaps, what does that mean for the water?
2 3	Sara:	It is supposed to be together.

Here, I hold up the two beakers and ask students to identify differences between the two substances. Bill suggested that something is closer in water than in ice (line 17). Since the conversation was initially about the model, one could interpret his suggestion as a statement about the state described by the model in which molecules are closer in water than in ice. But the statement could also refer to the macro-state, in which the ice cubes have gaps between them. Evidently interpreting Bill's suggestion in the first way (line 18), I ask the student if he could see the difference in the distances. The student laconically responded with "Yeap," which was elaborated by Sara, who pointed out the gaps between the ice cubes. (She actually pointed to the beaker in general rather than to a specific gap.) I followed up on the description of the gaps by asking students what could be concluded about water (line 22). Sara suggested that water "is supposed to be together" (line 23). Although this may not have been salient to all the students, or even Sara herself, she provided a starting point for the description of liquids, namely, that they fill a container without leaving spaces.

2 4	Tim:	No, it (*Points to ice.*) is like one lump of salt. That is really all close together. Here (*Grabs beaker with water.*) they are spread apart. See here, in my diagram. (*Points to diagram of solid.*) They are close together. (3.4)
2 5	Bill:	Liquid.
2 6	Teacher:	Can you tell me what the water does that the ice doesn't do?
2 7	Sara:	It moves more.
2 8	Bill:	It moves more, closer together.
2 9	Tim:	The molecules are closer together.
3 0	Sara:	Because the water is more compacted.
3 1	Teacher:	OK, so the water is kind of compact. So, if you said, is one of them taking the shape of the container? (0.9)

We can see here how the students draw on the resources provided elsewhere (and by another teacher) to understand the situation at hand. They associate the spaces between the ice cubes in the beaker with the spaces between molecules in their notebook drawings. While there are spaces in both cases, the cases really are of different logical types and therefore cannot be compared within the standard scientific discourse. The challenge for me is to help students move from where they are and from what they see, to a different way of describing, and therefore perceiving, and explaining the phenomena at hand without doing violence to their current (but scientifically incorrect) perceptions. A good teacher does this in the then-and-there of the unfolding events and without taking time-out for reflecting. The task, therefore, is to enter the students' world, and by interacting with it, develop understanding; that is, he or she has to enable them to construct new avenues of perceiving, describing, and explaining what physics takes as its fundamental objects.

Not wanting to do violence to students' observations and description imposes at least two important constraints on teachers. First, they cannot simply impose their vision, since students often see the same event in incommensurable ways. Second, in order to enter the reality of students, they have to listen empathetically and congruently. Therefore, they are obliged to use their questions as tools to help explore and understand their ontology, the world they experience, and their explanations. But to do this, they have to remain open to their responses and therefore ready for action in situations in which they cannot know the specific descriptions and explanations that students will produce in the next instance.

If Bill's description and explanation (line 17) referred to the particulate model of water, he would be incorrect. However, rather than suggesting that his statement does not conform to standard science, I ask whether Bill could see these distances (line 18). This question, although it had unfolded from the ongoing events rather than from lengthy reflection, comes from the Spielraum available to me, which opens up at least two possibilities. First, the student might refer to the gaps between the ice cubes, so that his description was a phenomenal one; or second, he might describe (in a scientifically incorrect way) the particulate model of water, his perception already informed by theory. My move (line 18) opens the conversation up for clarifying this point, which in turn allows me to enter Bill's reality, including his ways of perceiving the materials and models (drawn and built) before him. The question has practical significance in that it takes the inquiry further, as well as epistemic qualities, in that it changes what and how the teacher knows about the situation.

Bill's laconic answer, "Yeap" (line 20) does not allow for inference about how he perceived the situation, but Sara's comment clearly identified the gaps between the ice cubes; water was more compact than that because it did not have such gaps. This came up again in the interaction following my question about "what water does that the ice did not" (line 26). Sara and Bill suggested that water moves more (again we do not know which aspect they described, but they may have referred to their experiences of water as fluid and ice as solid). Bill subsequently explained that this makes the molecules move closer together (line 28), and Sara added that the water was more compacted (line 30).

In general, such a description of solid and liquid states would be inappropriate because molecular distances are smaller in solids than in liquids. In water, however, the situation is reversed. The molecular arrangements in ice (and the hydrogen bonding mechanism between molecules) actually make the distances larger (leading to a higher volume of a specified mass of the substance, and therefore to a lower density, which causes ice to float on water). A description that students had not yet provided was then introduced by me (line 31), namely, that the water takes the shape of the container. The scientific theory indicates that the bonds between water molecules are weaker and, therefore, allow for free movement of the molecules relative to each other. Thus, the students' model, if they were to reflect the observation that liquids "fill" a container completely, needed to reflect the weak and flexible bonding between molecules. On the other hand, the observation that solids are inflexible should be reflected at the molecular level by rigid bonds (e.g., skewers, tooth picks) in the students' models.

In fact, the diagrams the students drew in their notebooks reflected models of solids and liquids in general but were inappropriate descriptions for ice and water. This conflict needed to be resolved without simply telling the students how I saw the events commensurable with my disciplinary understanding. If I wanted to be successful at all, I had to simultaneously facilitate the conversation to take certain turns and help the students individuate aspects of the situation that lend themselves to a scientific description and explanation. At the same time, my actions needed to recognize that the students' perceptions were likely to be different from my own. Thus, to be successful, I needed to enter the reality of the students and engage students on their ground, such that they could develop perceptions, descriptions, and appropriate explanations. Although Tim's (line 24) description and explanation appears commensurable with a scientific description, I could not assume that all students, or even Tim, would consistently provide scientific explanations for other aspects of the theorization of ice and water. In fact, Tim provided a scientifically incorrect description because he used notes taken during the previous science lesson as explanatory resources: In his diagram, the particles in the solid were closer together than the particles in the liquid. What my question (line 26) about the properties of ice and water did was to deflect any possible impact of Tim's statement (line 24) and shifted the focal point away from the drawings to the properties. Basing his conclusions on the drawings, Tim had already become theoretically informed. He perceived the water as a substance in which the particles are farther apart than in the solid.

If I had not shifted the direction of the conversation, I would have been in the impossible situation in which students explained water and ice in terms of a scientifically inappropriate model, or I could have confronted them with the fact that the drawings were incorrect, at least for the water. Another option was to defer such a discussion and refocus the present conversation to the nature of the bonding, leaving unanswered the questions about the relative distances between the particles in solids and liquids. At this point, then, I introduced my description of water as a substance that takes the shape of the container (line 31). This was not a move that resulted from reflection, for there was no time-out to objectify the conversation and its topics; therefore, there was no time to reflect upon possible conversational moves that I might have instigated to change the evolution of the conversation. If I had done so, the point of attachment of my speaking turn to a particular previous student turn would have passed. Rather, my comment refocused the conversation upon the properties of water and ice as evidenced in Sara's rejoinder (line 32).

32	Sara:	That one. (*Points to beaker with water.*)
33	Teacher:	Why is that one taking the shape of the container?
34	Sara:	Because.
35	Teacher:	Think about your model here, your water here (*Points to model.*), does it take the shape of a container? (*Forms container with hands.*) See, I have a weird container, can you put it in here?
36	Sara:	(*Places molecules in hands.*)
37	Teacher:	Does your model take the shape of the container?
38	Tim:	Not really.
39	Bill:	They are more compact, they need to be closer together.
40	Sara:	They need to be pushed together.
41	Bill:	To form the shape of the.
42	Sara:	Just push them closer together?

I developed this aspect of the topic by asking for an explanation (line 33). Thus, after the "taking shape of container" was made salient in the case of the water, I refocused again shifting to the students' models. Here, "is one of them taking the shape of the container?" (line 31) is not giving a correct answer to students, because this fact is already part of the students' world. My question, which also sought confirmation for a matter of fact, made this scientific fact salient within the students' reality.

From a scientific (detached) perspective this is an important move, for the models are used to explain the phenomenal properties of the world. To me, the nature of models as explanatory resources was the central point of this part of the unit. Rather than letting the descriptions unfold anew, I shaped the context of Sara's answer by asking her to think in terms of the drawing. I literally formed an odd-shaped container with my hands and asked Sara to place her model into it. I followed through by asking whether the model took the shape of the container. Rather than focusing on the fact that the marshmallow molecules rested wherever they fell in the cupped hands, the students' descriptions made salient the remaining gaps. Tim, Bill, and Sara (lines 38–42) pointed out that the model molecules needed to be closer together if they were to appropriately represent the water.

Again, there was a conflict between the possibilities of models and the phenomenal observations made, interfering in fact with the teaching of the scientific vision and division of the phenomena. The problem here was that the model showed spaces within and between the molecules that were unfilled. The water in the beaker, however, did not have such gaps. Within the students' reality, this was a conflict which could only be resolved by pushing the model molecules together until the same gapless continuity could be observed in the model as was observed in the phenomenon (water) to be explained. My next move again had the potential to further enter students' reality (line 43).

43	Teacher:	But if you were looking very close (*Points to water.*), what do you think you would be seeing?
44	Tim:	Bubbles.
45	Bill:	Movement [water] less (*Points to ice.*) movement. (2.5)
46	Teacher:	(*Looks intently at water and ice.*) Movement of what?
47	Bill:	Molecules.
48	Tim:	Water.
49	Bill:	Because, it takes the shape of the container. (2.1)
50	Tim:	Ours (*Gestures marshmallows on string.*) are moving (*Vibrates string.*), like water in a container.
51	Teacher:	Yours are moving?
52	Tim:	Like water in a can. (*Vibrates model.*) This is vibrating like water in a container. And it goes all around.

Specifically, my question ("what do you think you would be seeing?" line 43) encouraged students to construct in public space possible descriptions of hypothetical close-up observations. Such moves are not designed in a reflective sense, for in my lived experience, there was only instantaneous (but deliberate) action without reflection (qua deliberation). Explanations of expertise in teaching need to account for this experience rather than simply dismiss it because it does not fit into structural descriptions.

Sometimes, I did not use questions to redirect the movement of the conversation, but simply asked students to elaborate and explain previous utterances. For example, students' responses (line 44–45, 47–50) were constituted by laconic, short utterances. I responded with equally laconic questions that repeated student utterances (line 46, 51) resulting in further students' elaborations. Here, Tim and Bill provide the descriptor "movement" of water/molecules at the phenomenal level and movement of their two models (Figures 4.1.b, 4.1.c). When no more answers appeared to be forthcoming from the group, I picked up on the last comment by putting into question the last student comment, "Movement of what?" (line 46). In the subsequent exchange, students then elaborated parallel descriptions at the model and phenomenal levels. For example, Bill suggested that the model takes the shape of the container (lines 47, 49) and Tim explicitly connected this to his own model. In this model, water molecules were stringed and suspended in a shoe box which vibrated like water in a container or can, and which "goes all around" in the box in the way water would be seen to do at the macroscopic level (lines 48, 50, 52). From a scientific perspective, this model had tremendous power, for it showed both the relations between the molecules thought to exist at the microscopic level, and the phenomenal properties of water at the macroscopic level. (This likeness was later further explored and demonstrated when Tim subsequently [line 56] actually pushed the molecules closer together so that they could no longer move with respect to each other.)

In these excerpts, my questions had a double function, one pragmatic the other epistemic. On the one hand, my questions scaffolded the talk of students who were encouraged to express themselves about the ice, water, and the model for a liquid in front of them. On the other hand, by listening to the students' responses I entered the reality of the students, including their ways of perceiving and explaining certain topical elements. That is, the questions made possible the disclosure of students' current understandings. Therefore, while each question contributed to the unfolding shape of the conversation, the unfolding conversation, in turn, shaped students' understandings of the current topic and my understanding of students' relation to this topic.

Some teachers, interested in right answers, might have halted the conversation at this point or told students that they were correct and had achieved the lesson objectives. However, I expanded the conversation so that the water model would be contrasted to solid (and later again, to a gas).

53	Teacher:	How would you make a solid?
54	Tim:	A solid? You'd like, put them all really close together.
55	Teacher:	And why would you do that?
56	Tim:	Because we learned that (2.8). Like these (*Moves marshmallows close together on string.*) have to stick together.
57	Sara:	When they are close together, they don't move. But when they are separate, they are spread apart, and then occasionally, they move closer together.

After Tim had so vividly demonstrated the properties of water and of the model designed to explain them, the students were now facing a new reality with a question that asked them how the model of the solid should be made. This question contrasted with the immediately preceding explanation of the liquid model so that the answers formed a textual contrast to the previous answers. Here, Tim at first suggested moving the molecules in the model closer together (line 54), but I encouraged him to elaborate on his design move by asking for an explanation. In his rejoinder, Tim did not really provide an explanation other than deferring to the authority of his regular teacher ("because we learned that") but insisted that the molecules had to stick together. Sara provided a description of the model that is commensurable with a scientific description: There is more movement when the molecules are "spread apart."

Here, then, we have a transition whereby the question changed the situation, and in doing so, provided students with Spielraum to expand their reality and to perceive and explain the differences that they experienced. Although I did not reflect on the move, its effect was to bring about the students' reflection on situating their model and their task in the context of other models and tasks. A posteriori, one might suggest that my next move could have been to ask students again to explicitly address the relationship between the model and phenomenon. However, I continued to expand the context anew and asked how a model of gas would be different from the models for a solid and liquid they had elaborated thus far.

58	Teacher:	And how is gas different then?
59	Tim:	It goes wheeee.
60	Sara:	It goes apart, spreads out (*Gestures into the air.*), and when it moves, it is all independent.
61	Teacher:	So if you were to model a gas, would you model it with a string? (*Points to the string model.*)
62	Sara:	Gas?
63	Teacher:	Yes. How would you model a gas?
64	Tim:	I don't know, you'd have to.
65	Jon:	Like we have the water molecules, but really far apart.
66	Sara:	Like I know, you would put the marshmallows into a bottle or a box, and you would put the water molecules on the toothpick. When they, maybe, you can have them in there.
67	Teacher:	And how far can they move apart?
68	Tim:	The water vapor would leave the container.
69	Bill:	Very far, until they hit the walls of the container.
70	Teacher:	But if you don't have a closed container?
71	Tim:	They would go into the clouds.
72	Bill:	They would go into the atmosphere, and then come back with the rain.
73	Sara:	But they wouldn't be able to leave the room because of the ceiling.
74		(*Intern stops the activity and has students clean up.*)

In this last segment, my questions encouraged students to design and explore the model of a gas. In response to the question how gas would be different from the other two states, Tim and Sara provided phenomenal descriptions of gas, but neither one addressed the nature of the model. My question (lines 61 and 63) raised this as the issue. Jon brought the notion of distance into the conversation—which has to be large—and Sara suggested that the model molecules had to be detached from each other. The episode concluded with a scientifically appropriate description of what the model for water in its gaseous state would have to look like.

This end has to be considered temporary, for it is only during subsequent lessons that I can find out if students' language remains consistently scientific across a variety of situations. I cannot know whether students were aware at this point of the differences between water and other substances, or what *exactly* they were thinking independent from what they express. Aware of these dilemmas, I engaged students during the following lesson in conversations about the anomaly of water in terms of the relation between inter-atomic distances and state of matter. Nevertheless, my research showed that these students changed their concept of the water molecule and models of water in its three different states. Furthermore, these students clearly demonstrated these developing understandings on quizzes and unit tests. I therefore assume that *these* interactions with me have led to important student learning.

REFLECTING ON SPIELRAUM

In my previous work, which was conceptualized in terms of reflection in action, I missed an important aspect of understanding the immediacy of classroom events. To develop this understanding I have adopted a phenomenological framework that begins with the concept of being in the classroom. To understand the Spielraum of teachers, we need to understand their common-sense, taken-for-granted world. In situations of breakdown we need to understand the salient elements that constitute their world.

In the first episode, when the students suggested that the gas with the greater volume should be oxygen (because the Mickey Mouse head portrays oxygen as a much larger atom), I found myself in an unexpected situation. The new element was a description I had never heard before. Consequently, I positioned myself to uncover the source of the unexpected answer, and thereby create new possibilities and a greater Spielraum for action. Questions that elicited the students' perceptions permitted me to see the world through their eyes as well as allow them to reconstruct these perspectives. Similarly, in the second episode, students' perceptions of ice and water included elements that were not entirely expected, such as the fact that students saw spaces in ice (a posteriori, we know they saw spaces between the ice cubes). Rather than saying that there were no spaces in ice, my moves created Spielraum for developing the conversation with students, which in turn disclosed their perceptions. From there I could then contribute to the conversation and help the students reframe their descriptions of the phenomena and reorient their perception.

In each instance, I felt ready for appropriate action although I could not know in detail what the students would contribute to the conversation. At the same time, my knowing in action was actualized in my being in the classroom. The practitioner knows the world, but only in terms of lived knowledge that is not external to a knowing consciousness. Paraphrasing Pierre Bourdieu (1997), we may say that the practitioner knows his or her world too well, without objectifying distance, precisely because he or she is part of it and inhabits the world as he or she does his or her habit (costume) or habitat. In the reality of teaching, the teacher as practitioner inhabits the classroom. His or her fundamental mode of existence is that of being in a classroom. Here, there is no time-out, no time to reflect on and consider alternative actions. In the reality of teaching, we seldom stop and deliberate our next moves. As experienced practitioners, we enact good questioning and live our subject matter knowledge. This was also true in the present episodes, as evidenced in the comment I made during a recorded debriefing sessions on the teaching episodes presented previously.

In this situation, I was not thinking about wait time, or productive questioning. These are ways of describing teacher knowledge but they do not describe my reality of teaching. In this situation, I was simply ready to seize the moment. When I think about teaching, my declared intentions are to increase the discursive competencies of students. I want to reach this through the engagement in conversations. As the conversation unfolds, I ask questions that appear to be the most appropriate at this moment. My universe is this group, the materials water and ice, the models students had constructed. I am also aware of what I want, approximately, models which have some explanatory pedagogical power.

Thus, the conversations unfolded. I did not have time to reflect, although I had to do my part for the conversation to unfold. At no point during either episode did I remove himself from interacting with the students to go and look up some information (i.e., seek to re-represent the situation in terms of some symbol or sign, then figure out a solution which he could implement in his questioning). Such reflection would have been prohibitive in terms of time and energy as well as lead to a loss of synchronicity within the unfolding conversation. If I was to be successful in my questioning, I had to enact questioning on the spot, without a time-out for reflection. As an experienced practitioner with over twenty years of teaching physical science, I had developed an extended capacity for creating Spielraum, which enabled me to unfold the students' realities.

Unfolding Students' Realities

Phenomenological (and constructivist) presuppositions hold that our realities differ because the experiential horizons that frame our perception and interpretation differ. With extensive experience and training in physics I have my "reality of physics"; but my students' experiences are different and so is their reality. My questions opened up students' reality, but at the same time they expanded the boundaries that determine their current interpretive and perceptual horizons. In this sense, the questions guided or scaffold students because they always tested the outer edge of students' current reality. The questions therefore can neither be completely in my reality of physics, nor completely internal to students' reality, but always along the interface of the two. The students required opportunities to explore their own horizon on the basis of the world that is currently familiar to them. But simultaneously, the conversation had to engage them in a journey that took them beyond what they already know and without the understanding of where this will get them.

For teachers to do an appropriate job, they need to find out what the reality is like, in which reality students are operating, how they situate themselves and the subject matter in it, and where their horizons are positioned. Masterful questions that come from the Spielraum available in the then and there of the unfolding classroom events have the double purpose of unfolding the existing reality of the student as well as expanding the boundaries of the horizon that constitutes this reality. The movement, though instigated by the teacher, has to come from the students. They are the builders of their own reality. The teacher can encourage students, provide scaffolds, or stop someone from taking a blind alley, but only students themselves can enlarge their own reality.

In the present episodes, the students made diverse connections and observations that did not fit into my questioning scheme. For example, they suggested that there was more oxygen than hydrogen in water and proposed that there was more space between the molecules in a solid than in a liquid. In the world depicted in the Mickey Mouse drawing, this was a correct inference. Nevertheless, the students thereby made salient elements that are not relevant, and even run counter, to the conceptual aspects of the subject matter required by the curriculum guidelines. Here, the students perceived that water presented itself in a closed form, whereas there were gaps between the ice cubes. This was an unexpected comment, and, if the situation was to lead to learning for the students (if their descriptions were to change to become commensurable with current scientific standards) I needed to contribute to the discourse in ways that allowed such a change to occur. It would not have helped if I had provided students with a description and explanation in my own physics reality, for it is highly probable that the students would not have been able to perceive or understand what I said. (Some of my own research in an Australian high school had shown that although watching the same teacher demonstration, different students actually made quite different observations.) Here, despite the unexpected nature of particular student responses, I was not unprepared and still had Spielraum available for developing the lesson.

Thus, when we try to understand what a teacher does and how a student learns and constructs his or her new world, we need to understand their reality then and there, at the moment of the interaction between them. It makes little sense to describe the teachers, students, and context in terms of an objective reality. Instead, we need to understand the salient elements that constitute the teachers' and students' contemporaneous worlds, for these are the worlds in which they act and react in an absorbed manner, without objectifying or representing the situation.

Toward a New Vision of Teacher Education

Novice teachers often feel cheated because what they learn in university classrooms does not seem to apply to their practice as teachers. This was the case for Nadine, a novice teacher who cotaught with me the four-month unit on water. Her trouble was not that she was ill prepared. She had been a successful student in her classes and had acquired a stock of discursive resources on which to draw for implementing discipline. That is, she could talk about the necessary forms of teacher knowledge as well as the need to reflect on her teaching in general. In conversations outside the classroom, her pedagogical discourse was quite elaborate, and she had many resources to bring to discussions. Yet however hard she tried, she found it impossible to "implement" the knowledge that she had acquired in her university courses. When it came time to enact a curriculum in the here and now of the classroom, she felt at a loss—and ultimately felt cheated by her university teachers. In the end, after all else had failed, she began to enact, in a trial-and-error fashion, a search for appropriate responses in a here-and-now fashion. That is, Nadine had to find ways in which she found herself acting in *this* classroom with *these* students at *this* time. This kind of knowledge is not always transportable since robust knowledge is always situated and situating. But this too is consistent with the realities of teaching, and many teachers found himself in situations where whatever they have done and tried in the past does not seem to help with this class, at this time, and in this context.

Rather than focusing on the teacher and blaming him or her for not being competent, or focusing on the students and blaming them for being a "bad" class, our focus should be on the relations of this particular teacher in the reality of this particular class. We need to ask, "What do we need to do to develop this relationship in the most appropriate way?" I suggest that there is a need to think about and theorize teaching in a non-rationalist way. Because some aspects of teaching are akin to a craft, practice without theory, it therefore requires a different pedagogy. Teaching requires a pedagogy that goes beyond the need for explicit procedural and propositional knowledge, which only produces teachers who talk well *about* practice yet are unsuccessful when *enacting* practice. Much of what is to be communicated about teaching exists as a modus operandi, a mode of production (and reproduction) that presupposes a mode of perception and set of principles of vision and division. Furthermore, one of the best ways to appropriate it is in practical operation, by coparticipating with a more experienced other. This allows novice teachers to experience how teaching operates in the face of practical choices without necessarily explicating them in the form of formal precepts.

If teaching is so embodied and tied to our experience of being in the world of the classroom, it comes as no surprise that learning to teach requires the personal experience of teaching in classrooms. By coteaching, that is, teaching alongside a more experienced other, novice teachers can observe and begin to emulate the more seasoned peer. They experience how the coteacher walks about the classroom, calls on students, waits, feels confident, and deals with a difficult situation then and there—and they can generally expose themselves to the knowing in action that lies at the heart of Schön's work. It is towards this theme—becoming in the classroom through the experience of coteaching—that I will now focus my attention. In the second part of this book, I will show how coteaching at the elbow of another teacher allows a lot of learning to go on.

5

Relationality

Two fundamental interests ground my approach to understanding and developing enacted pedagogy. First, I have adopted a phenomenological perspective that begins with the idea that we (teachers) are and evolve in a holistic way as "individuals in a setting." That is, we always and already experience ourselves as being in the world. Second, I am frustrated with popular images of reflective practice. While many researchers have embraced the possibilities of this new approach to developing pedagogy, many others remain frustrated by the lack of clarity with the central concepts of reflective practice. For example, as I noted in the previous chapter, the very concept of reflection seems to necessitate removal from immediate action, which in turn requires a span of time that practitioners do not always have. Nevertheless, despite this absence of a "time-out," the masterful teacher is still able to act in an appropriate manner. To understand this phenomenon, I have turned to a wide field of scholarship (i.e., phenomenology, sociology, critical psychology, artificial intelligence) and teased out a number of ideas to help explain how this can occur, including being in and being with (Chapter 2), habitus (Chapter 3), and Spielraum (Chapter 4). The last concept I want to add is that of *relationality*. Briefly, relationality is an attempt to deal with the phenomenological concern of restoring teachers' lived experience of relating adaptively, knowingly, and thoughtfully to events and others. In unfolding this concept further, once again, I use data from a four-month study on coteaching to illustrate characteristics of relationality as enacted by both a novice teacher (Nadine) and an experienced teacher (myself).

REFLECTIVITY VERSUS RELATIONALITY

Much of teaching involves action that is not preceded by or reflection. That is, reflection presupposes a removal from immediate action since it necessitates the conceptualization of an object (representation) separate from the acting subject. Consequently, reflection deals with a re-presentation of the world and action rather than with the world as it presents itself in action. Representations have two disadvantages: they have to be constructed, which takes time, and they provide mediated, rather than direct, access to the world. Reflection therefore takes the practitioner out of action in a double sense: it demands removal from action in both a conceptual and temporal respect. As such, popular images of reflective practice are therefore limited in that they are always removed from action. For a teacher to act in a reflective manner would require mediated access and temporary removal from direct relations with class or student.

While reflection on teaching implies a removal from the immediate class context and unfolding events, in contrast, teaching praxis (dimensions of practical decisions) is typically intuitive as well as what Max van Manen (1995) refers to as tactful. Consequently, Pierre Bourdieu argues, the result is a

saving in time which is no small matter when one remembers that the characteristic of practice is that it operates in a condition of urgency and that the best decision in the world is worthless when it comes after the battle, once an opportunity or ritual has passed by. (Bourdieu 1980: p. 177 note 14, my translation)

Bourdieu goes on to say that analysts often forget to consider the temporal character of practice; that is, they fail to recognize the consequences (i.e., practical penalties of being too late) when an individual agent takes the time to reflect on the ongoing situation. In its exteriorizing, detemporalizing, and totalizing movement, reflection fails to retain hold of the experience of the irreversible and relatively unforeseeable succession of practices enacted by ourselves, as teachers, in our daily praxis of teaching. Therefore, reflection in action is not achievable without disrupting knowing in action.

Relationality, on the other hand, is a matter of knowing in action without reflection. It involves a direct rapport between two beings and can only be displayed "in the situation." Relationality manifests itself by, through, and within the ongoing knowing in action. Indeed, it is well known that many types of activities (e.g., jazz improvisations or hitting a baseball) are incompatible with a stop-and-think attitude, because the practitioner opens him- or herself up to failure through a loss of synchronicity. In respect to education, these events might include dealing with problematic incidents or exploring students' understanding of scientific phenomena. There is a knowing in the action involved, but it does not require reflection. Highly developed knowing in action is endowed with its own capacity for supervision without reflection.

Knowing in action arises from relationality, because it is only in relation to particulars that human beings produce given discourses and practices. The genesis of relationality is associated with the development of teachers' range of actions or room to maneuver (Spielraum). In advanced teachers, this range of actions develops into an integrated network of action possibilities that empowers them to establish an extended relationality, which is coextensive with action that is self-conscious and thoughtful by itself without enacting a stop-and-think mode.

Relationality involves, not only the objectified knowledge about the reality, but also the construction of the reality at hand (e.g., classroom and students). Pierre Bourdieu (1980) distinguishes these two forms of knowing in terms of *sens objectivé* (objectified sense) and *sens pratique* (practical sense), respectively. For example, to establish a harmonious relation with the student, the teacher must enter his or her reality. Entering a student's reality is not possible if one has not constructed it. By construction, I do not mean simply to have knowledge *about,* but to relate to the student feelingly and knowingly, in the here and now. Knowing in action means relating in action: it is a matter of being *in relation to* something or someone. Knowing is therefore more than being situated, context bound, and reactive; knowing in action means actively situating oneself in, participating in, and shaping the setting.

In the course of this chapter, it will become clear that relationality constitutes a more viable indicator than reflectivity for understanding the climate and degree of harmony of the teacher-student-classroom world. Whereas reflection emphasizes logico-mathematical knowledge—associated with detached reflection and objectification—relationality expresses the rapport of the teacher with his or her experienced reality—associated with transparent coping, absorption in praxis, and practical understanding. This rapport displays teaching and learning situations in holistic, rather than reductionist, ways.

RELATIONALITY IN TEACHING

In teaching, the relations between being and situation are characterized by a readiness for acting; or an inextricability of thinking and acting, that is, by relationality. In daily life, teachers are constantly on the spot, with little opportunity for a time-out; decisions have to be made in the here and now of the situation, at the spur of the moment. True reflection seems to be possible only to a limited extent. That is, at the moment of teaching, we are curiously unreflective because we cannot step back and reflect (take time out) to consider various alternatives to actions that are not actually at hand, and their consequences. We always commit ourselves to action, and each move we make is enacted within a Spielraum that intentionally links agent, action, and context. Since our Spielraum is either more or less extended, depending on our construction of being in the class, we teachers are either more situating (active) or more situated (reactive) in the class context.

Many teacher educators have come to realize that there are problems with the "practice as the application of knowledge" model of teacher education programs and that this approach falls short of effective professional preparation (e.g., Cochran-Smith 1994). New teachers often feel that however well they have been prepared and however much they have studied, the knowledge base of their subject matter, subject matter pedagogy, teaching skills, educational theories, and so forth fails to adequately prepare them for life in the classroom. That is, throughout their preparation, there is a failure to appreciation the full effect of what Hugh Munby and Tom Russell (1992) referred to as the authority of experience. As I see it, part of what is missing is an elaborated relationality that can only be constructed in praxis. For example, in one of my studies of coteaching, both teachers, after having taught together for a two-month period, suggested that in this experience they learned more than they would have by taking three university courses. In their coteaching experience, both teachers extended their relationality by being with each other in day-to-day praxis. Without making their learning thematic, each teacher developed they capacity to relate appropriately to students (asking productive questions and timing questions in an opportune manner). As such, there exists a gap between theories pertaining to teaching, classroom management, learning, and curriculum, on the one hand, and what actually happens in the real-life classroom, on the other.

In the following sections I describe and analyze relationality in praxis as it pertains to an actual classroom situation. I draw on an episode from the seventh-grade science class that I cotaught with Nadine. I depict and contrast Nadine's relationality with my own, a more experienced teacher. I want to show that relationality is constructed out of practice and that it furnishes a more viable understanding of certain aspects of teaching in action than does reflectivity.

AN EPISODE FROM SEVENTH-GRADE SCIENCE

My work on coteaching is in response to problems with traditional models of teacher preparation. This work is concerned with the peculiar phenomenological structure of practice and the immediacy that characterizes every minute of the ongoing activity of teaching. This work is also concerned with the induction of new teachers into the field, and with finding appropriate modes of doing so. To illustrate relationality in teaching, I chose a typical episode videotaped during a whole-class activity in which I follow up a student question from the previous lesson regarding conductivity. I prepared the activity by setting up an open electrical circuit including a battery, a light bulb, and wires that connect them. Two leads are open such that when they touch or when a conductive material connects them, the bulb lights up (Figure 5.1). Nadine, who was completing a four-month practicum in the class and who cotaught with me, had momentarily removed herself from the interaction to observe.

After following one student's suggestion to place the open leads into water ("For water is conductive"), I commented:

Teacher: Nothing? OK, so, there is no light coming on. This is amazing because they- Aren't they telling us on TV that water is conductive?
Bill: But we need to add salt!
John: Maybe it's the wire?
Teacher: OK, someone said salt, someone talked about salt. What do you think happens if I [put that in the salt here?

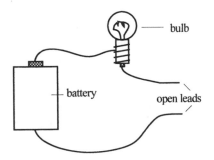

Figure 5.1. Equipment for testing conductivity. If the open leads are held in or to a conductive material, the bulb will light up. A light bulb is therefore an indicator of the conductivity of a material.

	[*Holds the two leads*
Bill:	Well, nothing.
Stan:	You got to add the water also.
Arlene:	Try it.
Teacher:	OK, we'll try it. (*Puts the two leads into the salt.*) Nothing is happening!
Bill:	You need salt in the water for the whole, it'd give you more of a chem. I think it'll
Chris:	We'll have a chemical reaction.
Teacher:	OK, What happens if? What happens if we had some of the salt [in here?
	[(*Points to*
	the beaker with water.)
Bill:	Mix it, mix it around!
Teacher:	We have to, we have to mix it. (*Mixes the salt in the beaker.*) What happens if I put the wires in there *now*?
Tony:	It'll work.
Stan:	Chemical reaction!
Tony:	It'll work.
Teacher:	Why would it? Explain! Who has an explanation?

During a debriefing session after class, Nadine made the follow remarks about this particular episode:

I notice that you are asking them, "What does this mean?," "Can you tell me about X?," "What is it?," "Why is this like this?," and "How do you know that it is like this?" rather than just say, "Yeah, you're right," or "No, you're wrong. This is it."

As an experienced teacher, I did not script my interactive relationality with the students. Having taught science for many years, I did not have to script (plan) this lesson on conductivity any more than people have to script (plan) conversations about the weather. We say the appropriate things about the weather without having to stop and think what we learned *about* weather at school. Therefore, as the events unfold I ask questions that open up an inquiry in which all members of the class contribute. Question stems such as "What do you think will happen if . . .?" encourage students to enact an inquiry. Instead of imposing my universe of knowledge, I enter that of the students by using my questions to prolong their examination of the phenomenon at hand. At the same time, my questioning is deliberately enacted to gradually orient the students' learning process toward larger possibilities. In other words, my knowing in action makes me feel how students, as thinkers acting in the relatively new world of physics, are actually relating to the phenomenal object before them. The goal of my intervention is to give students opportunities to substantiate the object and act on their knowledge of and about it by enlarging their own world of physics. In brief, teaching physics is not a matter of knowledge transmission; it is a matter of developing students' relationality in physics.

Meanwhile, having ceded the lead, Nadine literally stepped back from the event, allowing her time-out from the demands of having to interact. Now, she is in an observer position and, between observations, can engage in short reflections on what is happening as the activity unfolds. From this position, she can now make a question and its response present again, that is, she can re-present it, make it an object of thought, and think about what she can learn from it. A few days later, in a quiet classroom without students, Nadine and I watch the videotape of this lesson to make it present again. We then try to understand what has happened and how my relationality with the students was qualitatively different from hers.

RELATIONALITY AND MASTER TEACHING

In this case, we have three different forms of relating to the classroom event around the conductivity of water, salt, and salt water. As I engaged with the students, I was in an unreflective relationship with the physical and social situation. There was no time out for standing back and turning his experience into a re-presentation that is required for reflecting. That is, I acted promptly but thoughtfully and with an open mind toward the unexpected turns that the whole-class inquiry would take. Rather than following a fixed plan, I harmonized my interventions with students' reactions and made use of opportunities that opened up as the activity unfolded. These opportunities found their existence out there because my Spielraum provided me with many action possibilities—that is, to actively and relationally be engaged, as well as engage others, in the situation. Opportunities emerge out of an expanding and enveloping understanding of the dynamic teaching-learning process of the class, not from a mind withdrawn from the ongoing action.

Consider, for example, the situation in which Bill suggested that salt was needed to make the light come on. Without time for reflection, I strategically asked the question of what would happen if the two open leads were pushed into the salt; the student's suggestion had opened an inquiry into the question of whether salt is conductive. Of course, after the fact I can explain that he knows salt is an ionic substance, and that the conductivity comes from the dissociation (in water) of salt molecule (NaCl) into the two ions (Na^+ and Cl^-). The salt molecule itself is not conductive, and therefore he would not expect the light to come on. However, the fact that I talk about the physics of solutions in this way after the fact does not mean that the content of this talk is present to me in the same way while I interact with students in praxis. Now, students have already seen that water did not conduct electricity (at least not well enough for the light to come on) because only one-tenth of one-millionth of water molecules (H_2O) are dissociated (in ionic form, H^+, OH^-), which makes them conductive. Therefore, there was an opportunity that students would experience a cognitive conflict, which would make them think about the question of why neither salt nor water appear to conduct electricity, although a mixture of the two does.

In the same way, when Bill suggested that water was needed, I did not have to reflect strategically to capitalize on the moment in order to ask, "What would happen if salt were added to the water?" Again, not only was the question appropriate with respect to the scientific knowledge required to understand the phenomena at hand, it was appropriate in terms of the pedagogical content knowledge required to move the students towards an awareness of their own understanding of the phenomena. That is, rather than asking a close ended question, the stem "What would happen if . . .?" opens the inquiry. And again, when students' answers were laconic ("it will work" and "a chemical reaction"), rather than accept these answers, I readily asked them to further elaborate and thereby connect them to other parts of their discursive repertoires. The overall effect is that of altering the students' discursive pattern from simply answering questions toward "talking science." I was not only interacting with the students—that is, simply exchanging at their level of relating to the object of learning—as an experienced teacher I was transcending their answers, and thus reorienting the process in a more developmental direction.

We can say that to me, all of this "information" is embodied. I do not have to think about it—it is part of my lifeworld, of my relationality. When asked, I can talk about all the different components of this physics knowledge. But if I had had to search for this "information" it would have taken considerable amounts of time, in fact so much time that the "teachable moment" would have passed. As Pierre Bourdieu (1980) would say, it was my practical sense (*sens pratique*) that allowed me to appreciate the situation, in the heat of the moment, and produce the appropriate action. Through training and experience, I built up dispositions that allow me to talk physics in the way people talk weather. In contrast, for someone like Nadine, who has little science training, the ability to act in such a fluid manner does not yet exist.

In this situation, the event is unfolding, unforeseeable in its details and with shifting salient elements and continuously shifting interpretive horizons. The event can be rationally accounted for in terms of the knowledge I can provide and my explanations for every move. On the other hand, from the (detemporalizing) perspective of the theorist, who analyzes action after it has happened, the event can also be deconstructed into a series of elements and reconstructed into the same and alternative actions. But this analysis does not capture the lived experience of *that* moment. For at the moment of the event, there was no time for reflection, the event continually unfolded, and my questions, if they were to be effective, had to be asked in a timely fashion.

We also see here that there was, for me, an opening for developing the whole-class interaction that did not exist for Nadine. Asking open-ended questions is not something that I have to stop and think about. It is part of my being in the classroom. I continuously enact open-ended questions, despite being unable to foresee what the next situation will be—though, over the extent of my teaching, I have come to experience many similar situations (now embodied in my habitus) in the same and similar topical areas. Sensing the opportunity for a teachable moment, I made a move. The move constituted thoughtful action that was intentional but not premeditated. In short, I did not reflect, I simply asked the question.

The situation was different for Nadine. Having given up the lead, she was not required to act as teacher and therefore could stand back and disassociate herself from the flow of communication both physically and epistemically. Consequently, while she was observing the events, she was able to follow in a more reflective way. Nadine later described what she had experienced after I had taken over.

I was listening to your questions and how you've formatted that question at that moment. And that helped me then and there, because it triggers something in my head. Like I would go, "Oh yeah I should be thinking about that," or "I should be asking about that," or "That was a good question that really got them going on this tangent or brought them back or got them more focused." Yeah, that was helpful for me to, to listen to your questions and hear your questions *then and there*, as it happened, and then to think about how it related to the demonstration and where you were trying to go with that question.

In this account of her experience during the lesson episode, it is quite clear that Nadine was reflecting, possibly with a slight time lag respective to the action. She thought, "Oh yeah I should be thinking about that," but could only do so if "that" (the question, topic, etc.) was available in its entirety. That is, as she made the already-passed situation present again (i.e., to re-present it as an object of reflection), she distanced herself from the ongoing situation. But while continuing to follow the action, she had time to reflect on events enough to consider questions and their topics as objects.

RELATIONALITY AND CLASSROOM MANAGEMENT

Most new teachers struggle to develop their classroom management skills. Nadine was no exception, particularly in situations where students did not interact in the way she wanted. For example, Tony, who was already a tall young man, often engaged in activities other than those Nadine had indicated. Frequently, she sent him out of the classroom, but Tony did not easily give in and began to argue with her, instead arguing "I haven't done a thing. Why are you kicking me out? Why do you always pick on me?" As Nadine became absorbed in this situation, problems started to emerge in other parts of the classroom. Students began to talk, kick each other, and take pencils away from other students. Tony had hardly left the class when Nadine was compelled to attend to another student, then yet another, until she started shouting desperately and as a last attempt to gain control, began a countdown, "Five, four, three . . .," the signal that something serious was going to happen. Within a minute after Nadine began to deal with Tony, the situation had escalated to the point that she stopped all activity and told the entire class that they had to stay behind at recess.

In this instance, the difference between acting and reflecting became salient as Nadine talked about the difference between knowing classroom management techniques and enacting classroom management. Even though she had reflected, and even consulted other teachers on what to do to maintain control of the class, she had little success. In such instances, her university courses seemed to offer little solace:

I think I remember at the university you're hearing all these ways and methods and these idealistic ways and when you actually get out there it's different putting it into actions. I am following all the steps that I have been taught to follow, and I am going in ways that I am supposed to be going. But things aren't changing. I don't know what anybody else did, but I was sort of stumbling through things myself. I am constantly battling with and learning and trying to find new ways or new things.

One possible source of Nadine's frustration may be that her reflection was not based on an experienced relationality but on knowing about something (i.e., via the detour of detached, objectified representations). In the instance with Tony just described, Nadine's use of explicit knowledge acquired at the university and through discussions with other teachers did not permit her to make instructional choices that were appropriate in this particular situation. As soon as she took time out of the flow of action, she had already lost control of the situation. Her actions came at a time when they were no longer appropriate. Upon realizing this, she began to abandon reflectivity and began, in an active, experiencing fashion, to build a repertoire of moves that she could enact on the spot and that might be appropriate for each individual case at hand. In contrast, working alongside an experienced practitioner allowed her to increase her relationality without having to make thematic all aspects of this learning.

Throughout her practicum Nadine found herself at times in a situation where she felt she had acted inappropriately. During such instances her actions were stilted and out of time with the continually evolving situation and unfolding events. In contrast to such moments, there were times when an interaction turned out to be beneficial in that it did not disrupt the activity of the class as a whole. In these situations, her actions were prompt, timely, and exhibited greater mastery.

RELATIONALITY AND CLASSROOM SETTING

In my teaching, the ingredients needed for an extended relationality were not always present. Indeed, what I found difficult initially, and what interfered with the full range of possible action was that I did not know the students' names. Furthermore, Nadine and her cooperating teacher, in their function as homeroom teachers, often shifted tables and changed seating arrangements; therefore, as I was only coteaching science with Nadine, I often faced new and unexpected classroom configurations. Shifting tables interfered with my feeling for the place and hindered any development of habitual ways of strategically shifting position in this classroom. I know from my own previous experience that a transition from one school to another can have a dramatic effect upon a teacher's pedagogy. In a similar respect, even a simple change with respect to individual students and the entire class can change the nature of the interactions and conversations that emerge within classrooms. In this instance, continual changes in students' places made it difficult for me, the visitor, to become familiar with the students and the place. When I talked about this classroom, I often compared it to those classrooms that where "my own." Even if I was a competent teacher, being in a *new* classroom reduced my relational capacity. A similar situation in the relationality occurred in the teaching of my friend and colleague, Ken Tobin (see Tobin 2000), a thirty-five-year veteran teacher who taught for the first time in an urban school and experienced failure despite his highly evolved relationality in suburban and rural classrooms. What Ken calls his "lack of rapport" and the necessity of "building rapport" with the students is exactly the kind of situation that relationality is intended to cover.

While the physical setting can work against the practitioner, it can also be used to improve practice. Nadine felt that she needed assistance in asking more productive questions, questions that in fact help students to situate their query in an expanded cognitive frame and to produce longer, reasoned answers. We therefore decided to post the words "explain," "justify," and "elaborate" in large letters to the air ducts, visible from the teacher's position at the front of the class. Nadine suggested that this change in the setting acted as a constant reminder to build these stems into her questions without having to think about them. She picked them directly from the environment when she needed them, without having to expend attentional resources for keeping track of these pointers and deploying them. (Granted, there were times when, in the heat of the moment, she literally did not see this postings.) As Nadine suggested, the three stems that ask students for better answers "were just there." They triggered mindful questioning without reflection; they made actions available without planning; and they helped bring thoughtful question stems to the tip of her tongue.

DEVELOPING RELATIONALITY

Over the course of her coteaching experience, Nadine's skill and insights into her own teaching continued to develop. Part of her growth stems from a number of important factors. First, development was facilitated by the opportunity to reflect upon a set of mutual interactions and experiences that she shared with a more seasoned practitioner (myself). Such experiences can also lead to a form of empathy that seems to arise when we find ourselves in the condition of being with another teacher. Second, and just as important to Nadine was the experience of participating in the enactment of the curriculum and a sense of the authority of experience that develops from that experience. Third, coteaching with an experienced practitioner allowed her the opportunity to directly experience proven ways of engaging students in inquiry and control of the class—that is, my presence in the class. At the highest levels of experienced teaching, the word presence refers to the quality of a personality, of a teacher's acting in concert with the whole class without having to be a disciplinarian. Students feel such a presence. They know that the teacher is there—omnipresent, in charge, leading their way to knowledge and to self-development, and so on. All these integrated masteries reflect a highly evolved relationality.

Relationality characterizes the complexity and temporal character of professional practices such as teaching when there is no time out for reflection more appropriately and holistically than does the framework of reflective practice. In contrast to reflectivity, which works outside direct action, relationality expresses situated and situating knowing in action and thinking in action. In other words, relationality refers to practitioners as they develop within the interactive component of their professional world, while reflectivity necessitates the construction of, and action on, representations, which always requires time out and therefore removal from action. Consequently, relationality is part of, and develops in, praxis. Interested and engaged practitioners continuously evolve in their rapport to the Other and the world. This growing rapport involves two correlative poles: the practitioner's self-development and his or her progressive construction of the world of practice. Epistemologically, this means that the knowing subject, the known object, and their intimate existential rapport evolve concomitantly.

Throughout the opening chapters, one of the principal questions I have attempted to address is how experienced teachers are able to act appropriately and knowingly in action. In developing descriptions and possible explanations, I have contrasted my own actions with those of new teachers as these contrasts were framed by teachers themselves, and I have framed my work within what is essentially a phenomenological-sociological perspective. One of the results of this approach is that concepts tend to weave into each other, and so being in and being with, habitus, Spielraum, and relationality become interdependent or layered on top of each other. This points toward an image of teaching as a complex menagerie of interactions between personal and professional experiences and knowledge as well as between Self and Other. In contrast to research that attempts to break teaching down into a set of propositional and procedural knowledge, I believe my approach to be more realistic by virtue of its complexity and the struggles and frustration that emerge from it. In the following chapters, it is precisely these struggles that I use to illustrate this approach to learning to teach.

PART II

BECOMING IN THE CLASSROOM

6

Becoming in the Classroom

> I found that during much of their work, teachers acted "without thinking about it." As their lessons unfolded, the teachers did what was "right" in spite of the irreversibility and continuity of unfolding practice. I showed that by participating in practice, one teacher learned to ask productive questions and the other to get her timing right. (Roth 1998a: 370)

Teaching, like any other craft or practice, involves many complex activities that draw their reasons from the particulars of the situation rather than from some overarching theory that is consistent across contexts. There are many situations where teachers act masterfully without reflection. The introductory quotation highlights the assertion that it is difficult to teach how a teacher comes to do the right thing at the right time. Rationalist models of teaching, including the best-intentioned models focusing on reflection in action and reflection on action characteristic of master teachers, however, do not capture considerable aspects of complex teaching activities. What is it then about teaching that seems so hard to capture in a theoretical framework? Furthermore, if there are important aspects of teaching that are not easily captured, how can we teach these to new generations of teachers? Here, I respond to these two questions. I begin with a discussion of an episode of masterful questioning from a recent four-month study about teaching and learning in a seventh-grade science classroom in which I had cotaught with a teaching intern whom I call Nadine.

MASTERFUL QUESTIONING

Being an experienced teacher of science at the middle- and high-school levels, I had prepared a demonstration to illustrate the difference in the volume of a material when it undergoes a change of state from gas (water vapor) to liquid (water). At this time, Nadine had stepped back a little to observe. I had heated a tiny amount of water in a soda can, inverted it, and brought it in contact with a cold water bath, which caused the can to implode. After the students' excitement had subsided, I asked them to describe and explain what had happened. Following Tony's description that the can had imploded, I requested from the class an explanation while at the same time projecting a transparency with the drawing of the inverted can just before it touched the water. Tony and Stan suggested that "it [the can or the vacuum] is sucking." Without hesitation, I asked the students what was inside the can and then led them to construct a scientific explanation. In my experience of the situation, the questions (which a post hoc analysis revealed as central to students' development of understanding the phenomenon) had come without reflection; it was as if the situation had drawn the questions from me. (In fact, I do not even experience myself as separate from teaching, and "I" or "me" separate from the unfolding event.) That is, in this, as in many other situations, I enacted questioning as a matter of course, without reflecting which question I should ask or why. I could not know beforehand what the students would say, and yet I enacted what others experienced as a fluid performance, without the luxury of previous reflections.

Masterful questioning in science classrooms is a complex activity. However, although I have had a lot of experience and have done research on teaching and learning for many years, my actions were not *driven* by conceptual knowledge about science or teaching. I did not think about the science *before* asking a scientific question, nor did I think about questioning strategies before asking a pedagogically justified question. Actions were not immediately preceded by a reflective thought. Rather, I appeared to act appropriately in the here and now of the unfolding and emerging conversation with the students, without stopping to think about the next question. It is this aspect, acting appropriately without prior reflection, that traditional models of teacher knowledge fail to capture.

This is not meant to say that reflection in action, reflection on action, or pedagogical content knowledge are useless for thinking about teaching. On the contrary, during our debriefing sessions, I frequently talked about the physics involved in demonstrations. I explained the collapsing can in terms of a phase change: when a gas (e.g., steam) is cooled to the condensation point, it will turn into a liquid (e.g., water). Eighteen grams of steam take up 22,400 milliliters, whereas the same amount of liquid water takes up only 18 milliliters. Thus, when the steam in the can condenses while the mouth of the can is temporarily locked by the cold water, the pressure inside the can decreases to virtually nil, with the result that the outside air pressure suffices to compress the can.

When asked about the subject matter pedagogy, I talked about the importance of discrepant events to young students' learning, about the importance of moving back and forth between the model students built and the phenomenon they are to explain, or about students' pre-scientific ideas with respect to gases. Finally, when asked about general pedagogy, I talked about wait time I and II, which *describes* my teaching, the amount of time I wait until the first student responds and the amount of time I allow for *this* question to be resolved. I talked about how I walk up to a disruptive student and, without interrupting the lesson return my attention to another student's contribution; and I talked about how the research on target students fit the episode.

Thus, although I could talk about the descriptions for masterful practice, these descriptions did not actually describe my experience of questioning. As I listened, I was ready to respond to a student's question, elaborate on a student's comment, ask for elaboration of an utterance, wait for a student to complete a comment despite delays in its production, or frame another question that scaffolds the production of a scientifically correct description. My lived experience was characterized by the readiness to participate in the conversation; without reflecting on what to say or ask, I experienced room to maneuver (Spielraum) and created learning opportunities for the students. That is, without having to reflect on what the students said or on the history of the unfolding conversation, I related to the situation and had a presence, a level of relationality that was not unlike that observed among karate masters and canoeists during competition. Furthermore, the situation itself was not that which we might describe in terms of objective properties of the classroom: the students present (e.g., number, gender, race, social class), size and layout of the classroom, or materials available for teaching. Rather, as the teacher, I acted in a reality of my own with a unique rationality, including salient physical properties, ongoing conversations, overriding concerns (e.g., listening), and background activities. This reality was not the same as those of others in the classroom, such that the experienced curriculum is primarily an individual experience before being a shared matter.

Being in the Classroom and Spielraum

New teachers often tell me that they feel cheated. Despite university courses designed to build a knowledge of subject matter, subject matter pedagogy, teaching skills, educational theories and so forth, new teachers remain unprepared for life in the "real world" of the classroom. Even some experienced teachers say they have learned more from coteaching a short classroom unit than from several university courses. The problem lies in the nature of theoretical knowledge: no social scientific fact, moral philosophy, teaching method can tell a teacher what to do in particular circumstances. All practical, real-life situations are so complex that any single theory is undermined by the facts at hand. It lies in the nature of theories and generalizations that they are too universal; two very different theories or generalizations could still fit the same situation. What a teacher then would have to do is to find the theory that is most appropriate in that situation. When enacting such a search, however, the teacher automatically encounters trouble: he or she must take time out to reflect, select, plan a course of action, and so on for which the urgency of the unfolding events really leaves no time. Consequently, reflection requires a divergence that results in a lack of synchronicity between the teacher's actions and other classroom events.

My work on coteaching is in response to the problem related to tacit knowledge and teacher education. This work is concerned with the peculiar phenomenological structure of practice and the immediacy that characterizes every minute of the ongoing activity of teaching—an aspect of the teaching experience often omitted in research. This may be one reason why teachers do not identify with traditional, or even qualitative and interpretive, research. My work is also concerned with the induction of new teachers into the field and with finding modes of doing so in the most appropriate way.

Master practitioners in any domain generally know what to do based on a mature and practiced understanding developed in praxis. When they are deeply involved in their work environment, they do not see problems in some detached way and work at solving them; they do not worry about the future and devise plans. Rather, they enter relationality: there is no separation of the subject ("I," me") from its object ("my teaching"). Mastery entails absorption and fluid performance. I do not choose words nor position my feet, I simply talk and walk. Becoming a master teacher is therefore a progression from (a) the analytic behavior of the detached subject in an objectified world, constituted by identifiable parts, to (b) involved skilled behavior based on accumulated experiences in particular settings and the pre-conscious recognition of new situations similar to previously experienced ones.

To understand the nature of masterful practice that does not need reflection prior to action, I draw on the notion of Spielraum (room to maneuver), which I developed in Chapter 4. The range of possibilities currently available to me in my experienced world constitutes Spielraum. As I become familiar with some context, their reality expands, and with it, the Spielraum and therefore the possibilities for acting. "The range of possibilities that Dasein 'knows' without reflection, sets up *the room for maneuver* in the current situation" (Dreyfus 1991: 190, original emphasis). Thus, the existential possibilities open in any *particular* situation can be thought of as a subset of the *general* possibilities that make the world significant and in this way, I achieve a definition of expertise that spans any particular situation in which it might find itself. These possibilities reveal what constitutes sensible, that is, tactful action in a specific situation.

Spielraum and Becoming in the Classroom

There are, therefore, opportunities for learning and growth in praxis. Experience entails Spielraum: Teachers increase the range of virtual actions available to them at any moment, and without reflections, and these provide them with the necessary room to maneuver. For example, in questioning, they have more and more possibilities for asking the right questions in the right way at the right time—a difficult task experienced even by seasoned and competent teachers. From being present (physically) in a classroom, a master teacher emerges as a presence in the classroom. There is a distinction then between the beginner immersed *in* the world and the master operating *on* possibilities that, paradoxically, are introduced by him- or herself in his or her reality. There is an improved distancing without removing ourselves: When we have room to maneuver we can operate at a distance *on* the object without nevertheless being separate from the object. Seizing an opportunity to ask the right question is to operate *on* what has been said by a student. There is no reflection, but there is deep consciousness. This is why master teachers do not have to stop and think in the way that new teachers do. Developing questioning is constructing room to maneuver.

What I have described so far about the lived world of teaching is different from the rational explanations for why teachers do what they do. This poses a dilemma for teacher education: If important aspects of the craft of teaching are ineffable, these aspects cannot be brought into the discourse and therefore cannot be taught in university lecture halls. How, then can teacher education contribute to the development of young teachers in these respects? My answer is, "through coteaching." Developing Spielraum means that new teachers have to learn ways of being and acting, modi operandi, and principles of vision and division. Pierre Bourdieu (1992) noted that there is no way to acquire these ways other than to make people see them in practical operation, to experience each precept applied directly to the particular case at hand. Beginners thereby develop a feel for what is right and what causes us to do what we do at the right moment. Doing what is right does not require thematizing (i.e., reflecting upon) the situation or what has to be done; it requires even less the knowledge of any explicit rule that allows us to describe the formidable practice of doing what is right.

My study was conducted in one of the seventh-grade classes of a local middle school where, with Nadine, I cotaught a four-month unit on water that covered the physical properties of water, the water cycle, and the ecology of a watershed. Domenico Masciotra, who helped us in this study, initially served as a distant and disinterested peer but later spent a two-week period with us. (Being an accomplished karate practitioner, he had obtained an MA in physical education, and a Ph.D. in educational psychology on the topic of the development of Self and Other.) During this time, Domenico attended classes, observed videotapes of other lessons, and reflected with us about the nature of mastery in teaching and relationality. As the unit developed, Nadine and I cotaught this water unit by bringing together our ideas and using them as the starting point for further activities, questioning, and whole-class conversations.

At the time of the study, Nadine was completing a four-month internship with Cam, the regular mathematics, science, and homeroom teacher of the seventh-grade class. She had previously completed a bachelor's degree in child and youth care, and was now at the end of a two-year teacher preparation program that included several practicums and an internship. Nadine had taught in this class for a six-week period during the previous term to complete the student teaching requirement of her program. During the year before Nadine's arrival at the school, I had arranged with Cam to work together. It so happened that this collaboration was to begin when Nadine started her internship. Nadine agreed to take Cam's place and to coteach the water unit with me. She continued to teach Cam's mathematics class, in which she was left largely on her own to figure out appropriate teaching practices. At that point, I had taught for nearly two decades, including twelve years as a science teacher at the elementary- to high-school levels, as well as an instructor of science teacher education courses for elementary- and secondary-school teachers.

LEARNING IN PRAXIS

Coteaching provided Nadine and me with opportunities to see what and how teachers learn when they work together in the same classroom, in praxis, and with the aim of getting the day's job done. This coteaching provides some advantages over other modes of learning, such as reflection on action, which is always removed from action and therefore causes a split between acting and thinking. These advantages arise from the fact that one person may literally step back to engage in a stop-and-think mode required by reflection in action. Here, I illustrate the model of becoming in the classroom and developing Spielraum by tracing out Nadine's trajectory of increasing competence to use questions in a productive way. Her experience of teaching science with me was quite different from that of teaching mathematics where her sponsor teacher Cam left her alone with the class.

Teaching Alone

Similar to many of her preservice peers, Nadine experienced a wide gap between the discourse about teaching at the university and the experience of actually teaching in a classroom. Despite being successful in her university courses, that is, in appropriating a discourse *about* teaching, Nadine found it hard to put the discourse into action:

It was hard, for I remember at the university you're hearing all these ways and methods and these idealistic ways. When you actually get out there it's different, putting it into actions. And I think too, what I didn't really have was any modeling to follow. I don't know what anybody else did, I was sort of stumbling through things myself and so I know, I mean, I know that in September it was a real struggle and a real battle.

Nadine felt that despite doing what she was taught to do, the actual situation in her classroom was not changing: "I'm following all the steps that I've been told to follow, and I'm going a way I'm supposed to be going but things aren't changing." In the mathematics class, she felt that Cam's approach was to "throw me in there and have me figure out what worked and what didn't work." However, she found this frustrating. Even reflecting on her practice with other teachers teaching this class, and considering their practices as an alternative to what she was doing did not seem to lead very far:

I've talked to the other teachers who work with this group, asked them how they deal with the class because they have so many problems. And we all just sort of talk about what we're doing and when it's not working. But I know that one of the teachers right now is just keeping track of things and is just writing down their names and then, there's this process that they go through and it seems to be working but it only works for so long.

Despite reflecting *on* her actions with other teachers of the class, Nadine found that there was a gap between the discourse situation which reflected on teaching and those moments where she had to make decisions in real time, without time-out for reflection. She had no Spielraum, no room to maneuver. She reacted to situations rather than being an active shaper of them. Before my presence, Nadine experienced a strong contrast between what and how she learned both in the science class as well as in the mathematics class where she continued to teach on her own. Yet her mastery of asking productive questions as she cotaught side-by-side with me increased tremendously. I provide three glimpses at different stages along Nadine's trajectory of participation in questioning practice.

In the Beginning

As Nadine cotaught with me, she began to critically examine her questioning. She found that she emphasized right answers. When the students did not respond using the words she was looking for, she immediately provided the answer. Her questions encouraged short answers, filling the blanks in the teacher discourse, and often required only yes or no answers. There was little conceptual development, little time for students to think about answers, or to develop answers as part of the ongoing conversation. The following excerpt was typical for the interactions between Nadine and the students.

In this episode, Nadine attempted to move into a lesson in which students were to build models of water in its solid (ice), liquid (water), and gaseous form (vapor) using as basic components the water molecules they had earlier constructed from small and large marshmallows.

01	Nadine:	How many people can recall on Friday what we made? What we did? And I give you a clue (*Several hands are raised.*), you used marshmallows and toothpicks. (1.6)
02	Tony:	Marshmallows.
03	Nadine:	Chris.
04	Chris:	We made up water molecules.
05	Nadine:	You made up water molecules. So, would you say this is a water molecule and resembles what we did on Friday?
06	Ss:	Yeah.

07	Ss:	No.
08	Nadine:	No?
09	Ss:	Yeah.
10	Ss:	No.
11	Nadine:	What did you do on Friday?
12	Ss:	Yeah, yeah.
13	Nadine:	It is actually a water molecule. And what are these [two little-
14		[(*Points to each "ear."*)
	Ss:	Hydrogen.
15	Nadine:	Hydrogen. And [this big one.
		[(*Points to the "body."*)
16	Ss:	Oxygen!
17	Nadine:	Oxygen. OK, what happens when water, this is only one little tiny water molecule. But when water is in its solid form, what do you notice looking at this? (*Holds up the beaker with ice.*)

At first, students did not seem to remember *what* they had done during the previous lesson despite her clue (line 1). When Nadine spoke again (line 5), it did not seem to matter that a student had uttered the answer she expected. She held up a sample water molecule model to ask whether it resembled what they had previously done. (Within the reality of many students, of course, the object Nadine held up was not a model of a water molecule.) In response, students indiscriminately shouted "yes" and "no" (lines 6–10), and, after a reiteration, several students shouted the sought-for yes answers (line 12). Nadine then stated that she held up a water molecule and asked students to identify the constituent parts. Again, one-word responses (lines 14, 16) moved the lesson along.

I did not use this episode to be ironical about a novice teacher's attempts at becoming in her classroom. Rather, when I compare Nadine's attempts they are characteristic of what many teachers do: ask questions with short answers in noun-phrase form; use an initiation-reply-evaluation pattern; ask questions that socialize students into multiple choice exams and the objectification of knowledge; and break content into discrete topics. Thus, from an enculturation perspective, Nadine was already enacting typical classroom practices that have been targeted for change in recent science and mathematics reform documents. Yet these ways differ considerably from the type of whole-class conversations and teacher questioning that encourage the development of student discourse in the subject matter, deep understanding, and extensive reasoning about scientific matters.

As she experienced me interacting with the students, both in real time and on video during debriefing sessions, Nadine began to reflect on her teaching and, on her own, chose questioning as an important area in which she wanted to improve. She noted that she "was just accepting yes or no as answers, but there were no explanations for them." She recognized mastery in the fact that I appeared to have the questions "on the tip of the tongue," which allowed me to ask the right question at the right time.

I don't always have those questions on the tip of my tongue like you do. But it's really good how you pose these problems for them to figure out and I don't necessarily do that and I'd like to see myself come up with these problems. I mean, I just don't come up with them.

Nadine explicitly addressed the difference in the opportunities for asking questions. She perceived me as having much more Spielraum, a greater range of options for enacting appropriate questions, because these seemed to be at the tip of my tongue. In contrast, she had to think about what to ask next and, under the pressure of the unfolding events, defaulted to emphasizing right answers.

Being with Another Teacher: Coteaching

As Nadine cotaught with me, she had many opportunities to experience mastery in questioning. Sometimes, I taught an entire sequence on my own, conducting a whole-class investigation and conversation. At other times, Nadine engaged in such an activity and, when it seemed appropriate, I moved in (without however disrupting the flow) to ask a few questions that encouraged students to elaborate on, explain, or justify their contributions. Thus, Being with another teacher, coteaching these science lessons in praxis, allowed for modes of learning in which Nadine experienced modes of vision and division, ways of acting, without having to make explicit all of the assumptions and contextual factors (see also the quote on p. 88).

The following episode provides a glimpse at moments of learning to ask productive questions. Nadine had quite explicit intentions with this lesson: "I just wanted to open by showing you this little demonstration to show you that an egg will not float in fresh water, but that it *will* float when you add salt to it." At first, Nadine asked students whether an egg would float in water and salt water. After accepting several one-word answers, Nadine placed an egg in a beaker of water, where it sank to the bottom. She then added salt to the water, but without explication or comment about her actions. Here, after having been asked to make a contribution, I ("teacher") stepped in and requested explanations for students' claims that there should be a difference between water and salt water.

18	Teacher:	Why should salt water make a difference? Why should there be any difference between salt water and fresh water?
19	Tim:	It's like the chemical salt, with all the salts in, with all the salt it changes the thickness.
20	Teacher:	So salt water has a property that makes it float better. Is that what you wanted to say?

21	Tim:	Yes.
22	Nadine:	And what did you (Tony) want to say?
23	Tony:	I wanted to say that the egg floats because the salt is heavier, and therefore the egg is lighter. It's like on the Dead Sea.
24	Nadine:	So salt is heavier and that makes the egg lighter. And what do you think, Stan?
25	Stan:	Well, because we have more salt.
26	Teacher:	(to Tony) Can you repeat, out loud, so that everyone can understand.
27	Tony:	I am not sure, but I thought that the salt would make the egg lighter, so it would float.
28	Teacher:	And did you give an example of some water?
29	Tony:	Yeah, in the Dead Sea, there is lots and lots of salt in there, and when you try to go under the water, it's hard to get in there, and it is pushing you up.

Nadine's intention had been to open the lesson with a little demonstration; as a consequence, students simply guessed whether the egg would float or sink. Each guess was recorded by making a mark on the chalkboard. When she later reflected on such situations, Nadine noted:

I was just accepting yes or no as answers, but there were no explanations for them. So I know that when *you* would get up there and form your questions in a little bit, slightly different way that would ask the students to give more than just a one-word answer, that it would trigger things for me. When I got up there and asked a question, I began to realize, "Oh no that wasn't good enough." I could hear myself asking the close-ended questions.

My own understanding of science lessons was different. As Nadine added the salt, I asked for a speaking turn, and then questioned students why the salt should make a difference (line 18). I did not just accept answers as guesses, but wanted students to elaborate and provide explanations, or, at least, the most plausible hypotheses at that moment. Such situations, in which I entered the conversation and asked questions then and there, helped Nadine to become better at asking questions, for she experienced, in action, what came from the reality of another teacher. As an observer, she experienced another way to ask questions; that experience brought her to think about it, since it seemed to her that it was working better, and then she tried progressively to experience herself, in action, this type of questioning. That is, she experienced questioning in the context of *her* curriculum, but with an opportunity to see it through the eyes of a teacher with considerable expertise in questioning and subject matter. With this change in perspective, Nadine moved from a singular focus on adding salt to the beaker to developing possible answers to my question for the students. Twice she called on students and encouraged them to contribute their reasoning not only to the conversation, but also as an integral part of developing it (lines 22, 24). I, however, had heard something in Tony's answer that needed to be developed. At the next suitable moment, I asked Tony to elaborate both his reasoning and the example of the Dead Sea, which was a natural equivalent of Nadine's experiment. Developing the conversation in this direction showed that the experiment was not just something relevant to a science class, but that there were actual cases of water bodies so salty that some objects that normally sink in water actually float.

In this excerpt, we see how my contribution changed the configuration of the demonstration. Having stood a little to the side in the front of the classroom, I stepped close to the focal place, the egg in the beaker, to which Nadine continued to add salt. I was physically to the side but nevertheless a presence, a Being with and coteacher rather than a detached observer. I asked students to elaborate an explanation for the claim that salt water should make a difference (line 20). I rephrased Tim's answer, and then left the situation to Nadine who took over. By asking two questions that engaged students in constructing explanations, Nadine's reality had changed, and she now continued to operate in this reality of questioning designed to move the conversation to one in which explanations were constructed. We can also see that questioning moved back and forth from Nadine to me. Initially, I stepped in to develop the conversation in ways that Nadine's question did not. Later, we both became so attuned that they contributed in similar ways to the conversation. In this latter form, our coteaching resembled another class in the same school where I cotaught with an experienced science teacher, Laura. Here, the interactions between Laura and myself and our interactions with the class were at a high level, comparable to the improvisations of jazz musicians that Donald Schön (1987) wrote about. Without having to remove themselves from the ongoing action to reflect, we coordinated our actions and developed the unfolding piece.

During our coteaching experience, there were many such situations. Nadine, who had realized that she did not have questions "at the tip of her tongue" in the way she attributed it to me, could then take off and continue. Here, it is as if my contribution to the whole-class interaction changed the conversational context, that is, the conversational reality. All of a sudden, the global possibility of another reality became apparent to Nadine, a reality that would afford new action possibilities. Thus, it was not just that my questions "were good," but more important, they provided a context in which Nadine could now act in new and different ways. My questioning changed the context of the conversations thereby situating or contextualizing the conversation; my questions created a Spielraum where Nadine's developing questioning practices could continue to unfold.

Here, I saw opportunities for taking the conversation in particular directions, opportunities that did not yet exist for Nadine. However, as we talked about it afterward, Nadine noted that she found it interesting to experience questioning which was different from her own. She was learning to feel another way of being and questioning, another way to think about teaching. Nadine entered another reality in which questioning is of a different matter, has a different purpose. She recognized this questioning as useful because it made children think and allowed them to draw on the familiar in elaborating their answers.

With time, Nadine felt that she began framing questions like I did and found it validating to hear them: "I'm learning a lot, and often times, a lot of your questions I am already thinking in my head. So I find it good in validating." She began to create her Spielraum such that she could develop the conversations in the then and there, without having to stop and think about the precepts she had encountered in her university courses. However, when she did ask a close-ended question, she began to notice it and change her actions, "then I tried to make them elaborate further on what they were trying to say. Then I say, 'Explain or elaborate!'"

Developing Competence

Teaching with me provided Nadine with many opportunities to briefly step back, take a time-out from the responsibilities of developing the classroom conversation, and reflect on—but with little delay relative to the action—the questions and interactions of the master teacher. Furthermore, when she was asking the questions, she felt that she learned to master acting in the here and now:

Well I think, I think that it's just the here and now. And I mean, it's easy to think of, well somebody says this to me then I follow this and this and this. But every situation is so different and every student is so different.

The very difficulties of beginning teachers arise from the fact that the here and now tends to be always different and ever changing; becoming a master teacher therefore means to teach masterful in the here and now in the classroom. Thus, working with an experienced teacher allowed this new teacher to develop Spielraum. Working on her own in the mathematics class, she had to use trial and error to find what works for that situation without having to reflect about the next move: "I mean for me it's just all been trial and error. And learning as I go along what works or what doesn't work."

The following whole-class conversation that was recorded about six weeks after the previous episode illustrates Nadine's development, her becoming in the classroom. At this point, I was in the back of the classroom to observe, but I was ready to coteach if Nadine asked me to help out. The lesson topic was acid rain and its origin. In one instance, Nadine asked students how the acid rain formed and where it came from.

30	Stan:	It is like, all the factories.
31	Tony:	The pollution goes up into the air, and then it freezes, and then it unfreezes, in the clouds, and then it comes down as acid rain.
32	Nadine:	But do you guys remember when I did the water cycle demonstration where we had the muddy water?
33	Tony:	No, it doesn't go up with the water, the smoke goes up. Smoke

		from-
34	Nadine:	So you are saying smoke from?
35	Tony:	Factories, from chimneys.
36	Nadine:	Robin?
37	Robin:	It forms bonds, and then acids, the water vapor goes up and then it needs something, it needs something to stick to, and then all the smoke that goes up, so the water vapor is fixed to the smoke and then from the above.
38	Nadine:	Can you explain this a little more clearly?
39	Robin:	Hmm, the water vapor goes up and it needs something to stick to form a cloud, so when the smoke goes up, the water vapor sticks to the smoke and then it forms a cloud.
40	Nadine:	OK, you say it forms a cloud. So what happens after that? So-
41		(4.4) (*Several students raise their hands.*)
42		Bill, you want to explain that?
43	Bill:	Like when the water gets to it, it falls down, and it dissolves in the water, and when it falls down, then we have acidic rain.

Here, Nadine allowed the conversation to develop rather than closing it down to single-word or short answers. Her contributions to this episode encouraged the inclusion of additional ideas (line 32), to encourage a student to develop an idea already started (lines 34, 40), or to invite a student to develop a deeper explanation for his reasoning (line 38). Furthermore, when Robin did not follow the invitation to develop his idea further, Nadine waited more than four seconds before calling on another student (lines 40–42). Thus, although she did not think about wait time research, Nadine enacted wait time I and wait time II in a way consistent with this research: she provided enough time between posing a question and calling on a respondent to allow for the development of answers. That is, without having to consciously implement precepts for wait time, she enacted them because with me, this was the normal thing to do. Furthermore, she allowed students to develop conceptual models of such complex phenomena as acid rain rather than seeking responses that fit into her framework of what the developing conversation ought to cover.

One might be tempted to argue that Nadine "copied" the questioning practices from me. However, when it comes to practices that are enacted, "copying" is a poor metaphor, for there is a gap between describing or seeing an action (even one's own) and enacting it. If it were easy, all of us would be good cooks, athletes, or teachers simply by watching accomplished practitioners. Rather, the coteaching situation allowed Nadine to find appropriate questioning in her actions in a real classroom situation with an experienced practitioner at her side. This experience allowed her, the beginning teacher, to develop her being in the classroom; it allowed her to embark on becoming in the classroom at the elbow of a more experienced peer.

COTEACHING: LEARNING AS PRAXIS

In this chapter, I first developed a phenomenological frame for understanding mastery and its development. I then described and exemplified one beginning teacher's growing competence in asking questions. Contrasting her development with the difficulties in becoming a teacher in other situations (i.e., mathematics class), the beginning teacher attributed much of the rapid development to the fact that she was coteaching with an experienced science teacher. Coteaching, that is, working with someone in accomplishing the lessons as a part of the day's work to be done—as contrasted with faking a lesson under ideal, seldom realizable conditions (e.g., microteaching)—affords many opportunities for learning to teach. Being with, and therefore experiencing classroom events from a similar physical and social vantage point, afforded implicit learning of how to ask particular questions at particular times. Furthermore, being with also led to the development of shared experiences (e.g., during collective reflection on action), and therefore a common ground that served as a communicative basis so important for mutual understanding. Furthermore, being with divides the responsibility for moving along the conversation with students so that at any one point, one of the teachers can step back. This stepping back allows for a crucial time out necessary for reflecting, without retarding the evolution of classroom events. This slight removal afforded reflection in action.

In our daily lives with children, we must often act on the spur of the moment. There is no time to sit back, to stop and think, for deliberating on what to do next. In teaching, we are continuously involved both actively and reflectively. These aspects of teaching are not captured in existing models. Master teachers are characterized by a certain level of mindfulness, a presence in the contingencies of a given situation. Contemporaneous reflection in situations leads one to "stop and think," reflect in action, and differs markedly from the more immediate reflective awareness teachers enact. Teachers need a particular sensitivity for the situation at hand and an understanding of how to operate or intervene in these situations, without necessarily having a theory or set of general principles to describe and explain, after the fact, what they have done. The study of the practice of teaching needs to be sensitive to the experiential quality of practical knowledge, an acknowledgment that much of the instant knowing, enacting in real time, issues from one's body and immediate world. My phenomenological perspective on teaching is sensitive in this way. This view of teaching as practice locates practical knowledge not primarily in the head but rather in the existential situation in which the person finds herself. It is a sense for the way things are. A teacher's practical knowledge, as with Pierre Bourdieu's *sens pratique*, resides in the things that surround him or her, the physical dimensions of the classroom to which the body is adapted. A teacher's practical knowledge is his or her lived experience of *this* classroom, *these* hallways, and *these* staff rooms; it is his or her lived experience as a teacher, felt understanding of the students, felt mastery of the subject matter to be taught, as well as the moods that go with the world at school.

If teaching is so embodied and tied to our experience of being in the world of the classroom, it comes as no surprise that learning to teach requires the personal experience of teaching in classrooms. By coteaching, beginning teachers can observe and imitate the more seasoned peer, how he walks about the classroom, calls on students, waits, feels confident, deals with a difficult situation then and there. The new teacher learns with his or her body, how to feel confident about asking questions. This confidence is not an affective aspect of one's knowing, it is the active knowledge itself, knowing what to do or say, and what to avoid doing and saying.

In being with we develop the fundamental shared experience that is necessary for communication. Because teachers come to experience the same reality, see the classroom and students from the same or similar position, coordinate their decisions with those of the other, they can build a common stock of experiences about which they can communicate. The word communicate derives from the Latin *communis*, meaning "common." As such, we can only communicate that which is common, an understanding that is always rooted in our experiences and precedes reflection. My observations in this and many other studies that I conducted while coteaching showed that it provides an ideal situation because teachers come to build the necessary common ground (and therefore, the necessary intersubjectivity) to construct a viable professional discourse during their reflections on actions. (It goes without saying that there are likely to be pairs of teachers who will find it impossible to coteach with each other, as there are jazz musicians who will find it impossible to create masterful improvisations with each other.) During the ongoing teaching, there are moments for time out in the sense that one teacher can stand back and watch the other in action, there are moments for reflecting on action, but it is done in action. That is, I am not claiming here to abandon the notions of reflection in action and reflection on action. I do suggest that there are times and places where teachers can engage in them, but there are also times, especially in the actions of master teachers, where reflection is not a viable description of teaching *because* it is inconsistent with the experience of teaching.

Why might coteaching be such a powerful learning environment for beginning teachers? Phenomenological answers are based on the fact that being in the world always means to be in a physical and social world. We understand (comprehend) this world because we are part of it (comprehended). We appropriate a knowledge and practical mastery of the social and material spaces because of our bodily inclusion in these spaces and what follows from it, that is, the incorporation of social structures in the form of dispositional structures. Therefore, there is a circular and reflexive relationship of embodied understanding and reflective understanding: comprehending the former kind of understanding requires the latter, which in turn requires the former to be possible.

This work suggests that preservice teachers can learn much from being with a master teacher; but, as my work with Kenneth Tobin has shown, even when two new teachers engage in coteaching/cogenerative dialoguing, a lot of learning occurs (Roth and Tobin 2001). In fact, so much more learning occurs in this way that it by far overcomes possible limitations that arise when coteachers subsequently move on to teach on their own. By enacting collective responsibility for teaching a class (at least for some period of time) and being in the classroom, teachers develop ways of acting tactfully. This is particularly important given that practical mastery ceases to exist as soon as one seeks to express it in the form of rules and formal precepts. Thus, rather than sending new teachers into a classroom where the resident teachers let them work on their own (in a sink or swim model), we should develop school-university relationships that emphasize learning through coteaching. If Nadine and my coteaching experience is transportable to other situations, then we expect that the returns, in terms of developing mastery, would be manifold. Thus far, I have conducted nine studies on coteaching with very similar experiences of learning, even among experienced teachers.

Whereas my studies show that coteaching leads to tremendous teacher learning, some readers may raise the question of whether it is a viable model for inservice teacher education and teacher preparation. Because teacher education and educational financing differ from country to country, and sometimes even within countries, a general answer cannot be provided. However, and without attempting to go beyond what we can learn from the cases studied so far, I sketch some possibilities. In Germany and Denmark, the assignments of beginning teachers are gradually increased over a two-year period. In this situation, coteaching clearly is a viable model. Coteaching is also viable in other contexts if suitable sponsor teachers agree to cooperate. Furthermore, being with a master teacher and coteaching for a period of time may actually be a more appropriate model for inservice teacher education than the current practice of putting on summer workshops with many courses of short duration (as is the practice in many US states).

7

Coteaching

Coteaching and the associated conceptual framework that I present here did not come to me overnight, in a flash of insight. Rather, they developed over many years, as activities of working side-by-side with other teachers, and the learning this affords became understandable in different ways.

Team teaching had been around at least since the 1960s, but it did not have a conceptual grounding other than that opportunities arise when teachers work in the area they know best. Thus, what I sometimes see is teachers who bring their classes together or exchange classes in order to teach "their" subject matter or curriculum unit. In such situations, the teacher-student ratios do not change at all; team teaching simply is a way of organizing work differently. The teachers are still largely on their own, simply enacting a particular division of labor. Learning from one another is, by and large, limited to the moments of exchange when the teachers get together and plan, talk about how to deal with particular students, and so on. More so, learning may actually be impeded in the situation because teachers can rely on working in their specialty areas and are less likely to gain experience in any others, the responsibilities for which are always taken by another person on their team.

Coteaching is fundamentally different. In the previous chapters, I provided a framework for knowing and learning in praxis. As I show in Chapter 6, coteaching is a practical situation in which two or more teachers work together in the same classroom at the same time, thereby changing the teacher-student ratios in significant ways. Being in the same situation and being with another practitioner *explicitly* build learning from one another into praxis and arise from getting the day's work done together. Coteaching therefore is colearning, which does not arise by focusing in learning tasks but by doing a job. (Additional activities are required, and in the next chapter, I introduce my ideas about cogenerative dialoguing, which is intended as an activity by which to learn by reflecting on shared teaching experiences.)

Coteaching as a context for colearning makes sense from a practice perspective. Critiques of the "expert as rational thinker" model have pointed out that what distinguishes expertise from competence resists being captured in formal descriptions. From the large literature on this topic, let me simply make reference to three areas of research. Anthropologists and sociologists of work have shown time and again that scientists and technicians find it hard learn certain activities—doing DNA analysis, building a laser, or repairing photocopiers—just by reading instruction manuals. Rather, they go and engage in these activities with someone else who has already developed a certain level of expertise. That is, the knowledge needed to get the laser to work, to do a DNA analysis, or to do certain photocopier repairs, is not available in printed (explicit) information but somehow is being communicated as the practitioners work with each other. What is really relevant in these situations is a particular disposition for seeing situations and dealing with salient issues at hand. These dispositions, termed habitus, are enacted only in practical situations. That is, the practitioner relates to situations in ways that are only evidenced in that situation. This relationality (see Chapter 5), because it involves the situation and person as a whole, resists description (which is inherently a reduction).

A philosopher and an engineer who were thinking about expertise suggested five levels of knowledge types: novice, advanced beginner, competence, proficiency, and expertise (Dreyfus and Dreyfus 1986). Only Levels 1 to 3 are easily captured in formal statements and therefore learnable in explicit ways. Levels 4 and 5 are those that resist description and are, from my perspective, similar in nature to the levels described by Bourdieu (1980).

In the course of our work on coteaching, Kenneth Tobin and I developed a heuristic for looking at effective coteaching for use in the inner-city schools of Philadelphia in which we are working. This heuristic is available in Table 7.1. As I present a number of case studies of teachers in coteaching episodes, I will refer back to some of the categories that are suitable for describing a particular situation.

COTEACHING INVOLVING OLD-TIMERS

A First-Person Perspective

In spring 1999, Laura and I cotaught for a second time a unit on ecology in a seventh-grade science class. Laura was a seasoned teacher with twenty-six years of experience, an undergraduate science degree, and a master's degree in educational administration. Her own teaching was often direct and, especially in mathematics, centered on textbook–related activities. I had motivated this unit, in which children enacted a research project of a local watershed, by bringing in an article from the local newspaper. This article featured the activities of an environmental activist group and, in the end, invited members of the community to

Table 7.1
Coteaching heuristic

1. Co-planning
2. Respect for the other teacher
3. Rapport with the other teacher
4. Creating space for coparticipation
    4.1. Willingness to step back
    4.2. Step back
    4.3. Willingness to step forward
    4.4. Step forward
    4.5. Tolerance of others' actions
    4.6. Reciprocity
    4.7. Anticipation of what is appropriate
5. Seamless-ness of coparticipation
    5.1. Conductor-less orchestration
    5.2. Compensatory actions
    5.3. Touching base
    5.4. Coordinated action
6. Coparticipation
    6.1. Reciprocal/recursive
    6.2. Upward trajectory
    6.3. Playing off/tossing/parlaying/passing the baton
    6.4. Overlapping talk
    6.5. Finishing one another's sentences
    6.6. Complementarity of action

participate in contributing to the understanding, preservation, and improvement of the watershed. Laura and I invited students to frame their own questions. As they began their research, we intended to scaffold their research practices and therefore their learning by designing particular activities that permitted them to analyze a series of issues.

After the second day in the field, I suggested to Laura that the students appeared to be content to collect a small number of data in support of their claim. The students did not construct a need for collecting more data. In our conversation, Laura and I came to decide not to tell the students to collect more data, but to design and conduct an activity on the basis of which might emerge a discussion about the changes in interpretation when additional information is collected. We brainstormed the outline of the activity: how only partial data were offered for plotting and analysis and how we would subsequently provide additional data that suggested a different trend. I offered to take the lead and prepare the materials for this activity.

As I prepared the materials, I constructed a scenario that closely resembled the activities in an earlier study involving eighth-graders, Elizabeth and Damian, who wanted to find out whether small animals have different activity levels at

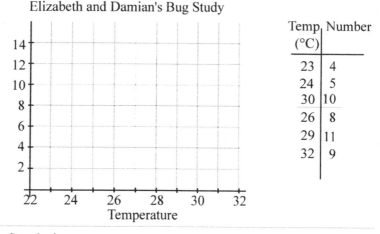

Elizabeth and Damian's Bug Study

Temp (°C)	Number
23	4
24	5
30	10
26	8
29	11
32	9

Conclusion

Figure 7.1. This diagram was part of the planned curriculum and was prepared as acetate.

different temperatures. (Elizabeth and Damian are actually the pseudonyms of students in an earlier study who had conducted such a research project. The data were completely my invention.) They decided to study relationships between temperature and the number of bugs they found under a rotten tree. I prepared a transparency (Figure 7.1) and I thought that, covering up the data table partially, I would get students (in groups of two) to plot the first three data points and write their inferences about a pattern. For this, I would provide a copy of the transparency lacking only the data in the table. The process would allow me to control the data to which students have access. I would then invite the students to a whole-class discussion to talk about their inferences, which I expected might differ. Of course, I knew that we would have to be open in using the students' answers in a generative way.

In the next part of the lesson, I wanted to question whether they were certain about the pattern they constructed between temperature and the number of bugs, and what they would suggest. Students would then plot the additional information and again draw inferences. In the subsequent whole-class discussion, the students would be asked to contribute the answers they had constructed. I would bring this sequence to a close by asking them to identify the most significant thing learned from the activity.

Just as I enter the classroom, the power goes off. I am thinking, "Oh no, now I can't use my acetate!" I begin thinking about my options and wonder whether I should wait for the light to come back on. "But the light might not come on again!" (It did not come on again until we were actually done.) So I reconstruct on the chalkboard the diagram I had prepared. I tell students the story of Elizabeth and Damian, two eighth-grade students who wanted to find out if there was a relationship between the temperature and the number of bugs they could find. I present the story, the table that contains only three data points, and the graph and provide each student pair with a piece of graph paper. I ask the students to plot the data and describe the patterns that they see emerging from their data plots. I use words such as "inference" and "conclusion." From the corner of my eye, I see Laura slightly move forward—I stop to make place for her to speak. Laura asks the students whether they know what I meant by "inference" and "conclusion." She also asks them to think about a graphing activity that they had done in their mathematics class. After a number of students indicate that they understand the connection, she suggests, "Dr. Roth, please continue." (In this part of the world, teachers in schools and professors at the university address another professor formally and with a title when in front of a class or during meetings.)

I invite the students to plot the data. As they engage in their activity, Laura and I circle in the classroom and ask the students questions, correct their plotting, encourage them to think of trends (lines), and so on. I am vaguely aware that Laura is somewhere else as I walk from one group to another but then get absorbed again in the conversation with the group.

Repeatedly, I touch base with Laura while between student groups. I ask her such questions as "How are students doing?" "What difficulties do the students have?" and "Can you help me find an answer to this student's question?" Laura also touches base with me in a similar way. All along, I feel I know how the lesson is going without necessarily having to interact with all the students or be in control of their activities.

At one point, Laura and I touch base and, after communicating our sense that we should go on, decide to move back into a whole-class session. We do so and I plot the data (in black in Figure 7.2). When I ask them about the pattern, many students suggest that the number of bugs increases (linearly), without qualification about what might happen if the temperature might rise even more. I ask, "How certain are you about the pattern you found?" and "What do you recommend we do to be more certain about our conclusions?" One student answers, "Collect more data, it'll show you." I respond, "This is what Elizabeth and Damian did." I walk to the chalkboard and complete the data table. It now features all the data pairs displayed in Figure 7.1.

As if passing a ball back and forth, Laura and I take turns interacting with the students, asking questions and responding to them. We ask them to plot the additional data and we spend some time with each group, especially encouraging them to write down their new inferences. Most of the time, I am simply aware of Laura's presence in the classroom without really thinking about or reflecting on it. She is both there and not there; she is part of the background. At other times, I explicitly seek to interact with her—we touch base to exchange particular observations about student understanding and ask each other to check the understandings of particular students. I then bring the students together for the

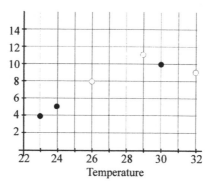

Figure 7.2. The graph as it was drawn on the chalkboard, including the "missing" data points.

second whole-class session related to this activity and I plot the missing data points (circles in Figure 7.2).

The students venture different claims but ultimately come to agree that there is a temperature at which the bugs appeared to be most comfortable. I want them to eventually state explicitly the point that the additional data points were necessary to draw a valid conclusion. I therefore ask the students whether they changed their ideas in the course of the activity. Every now and then, Laura requests a turn, frequently to rephrase one of my questions. I am vaguely noticing—without actually spending time to reflect on it—that Laura begins to talk when I leave a long pause between asking a question and accepting a response.

To conclude the activity, I ask the students what they have learned. There are a variety of answers. Many students remark that bugs like intermediate temperatures, around 29 °C, or that they dislike like the cold. Only after eliciting a range of responses do several students note the desirability of making more than three measurements to get an accurate answer.

After the lesson, Laura and I debrief as we usually do. I note that students were engaged with the activity, that they drew a variety of inferences, and that even those students who were often quiet had contributed to the whole-class conversation. As part of the critical and self-reflective analysis of our lesson, Laura remarked that we should have asked the students to predict how many bugs they would expect at higher temperatures such as 35° or 40° Celsius. I realize that I might have thought of this earlier and agree that this would have been interesting. In this way, we could have opened up further learning opportunities and perhaps made more salient the point we wanted to make with the activity.

When I reflect on the coteaching experience with Laura, the analogy of a jazz jam session always comes to my mind. Teaching with her comes easily, we improvise, toss the lead back and forth, and make space for each other without having to think, "Make space for the other." Teaching with Laura seems to come naturally, even when a surprising event (e.g., a power failure) interferes with the plans we had previously established. There are always action possibilities, always Spielraum, both in the broader sense of where a lesson should go and in a narrower sense of what the most appropriate questions are.

I notice that with time, my questions become more appropriate. Particularly the language I use becomes more appropriate with respect to the language the students currently use. On the one hand, it does not surprise me that I would become more attuned to *these* students and their current language. On the other hand, it is certainly notable that I did not have to spend time to consciously study the students' current discursive competencies.

When we look at the coteaching between Laura and myself, we see two long-time teachers enacting coteaching in such a way that the descriptors in Table 7.1 are fairly accurate descriptors for what is going on. Although one or the other teacher may plan a specific activity, we plan the sequence of activities together (Item #1). We show respect to each other and have an excellent rapport. When we are teaching together, we create space for coparticipation. For example, when I used words that Laura knew students might find difficult ("inference" and "conclusion"), she asked to enter the discussion and thereby showed a willingness to step forward, which she then did (Items #4.3, 4.4). I, in a reciprocal way, willingly stepped back (Items #4.1, 4.2). My account also articulates the seamlessness of our coparticipation. During the whole-class sessions, we both contributed to the unfolding conversation without previously having orchestrated what we would do. As coteachers, we also compensated for each other. For example, when I asked questions that Laura considered too advanced for the students, she stepped in and re-articulated them. On the other hand, when Laura asked close-ended questions, I stepped in and phrased generative questions. During small group activities, we touched base (Item #5.3) and, in a concerted way, enhanced each other's questioning after having become aware of particular student difficulties. That is, as we touched base, we reflected on events that were in the immediate past and attempted to use our insights in enacting better questioning with in the following interactions.

Although we are both very experienced teachers, we recognize and articulate opportunities for learning. By being in the classroom and being with each other, learning occurred as Laura and I worked side-by-side, becoming increasingly attuned to the ways in which we each interacted with the students. Laura began to leave more time before accepting responses and asked fewer questions in the IRE pattern than before. I increasingly used language appropriate for *these* students at *this* time. After the lessons we continuously reflected on our teaching and articulated new and different ways in which activities could be planned to enhance student learning. Thus, out of the collective reflections on our shared coteaching experience, there arose additional opportunities for learning about teaching science in this school.

Differently Located Expertise

In this episode, a trained biologist and science educator (Miles) has agreed to teach a lesson on data analysis in Laura's class. During the previous lesson, he and several other scientists had taken the children to a creek to collect data that would answer the research question that they had posed as a class. In the present case, the question had been, "Is there a relationship between the speed of the water and the number of organisms?" The children had sampled the water and found a number of different types of organism, so there was an opportunity to compare existing relationships for different types.

Although Miles had accompanied the children and Laura to the creek, he had not been in the class for other lessons in which Laura and I introduced students to various types of data analysis techniques. So despite being an "expert" with respect to the subject matter—collecting data and conducting data analysis—Laura was more "expert" along other dimensions, including a knowledge of the curriculum history, what *these* students know at the time and were likely to be able to do. Coteaching with Laura rather than teaching solo therefore came with a range of advantages that coteaching provides.

The following episode begins after Miles has already asked several questions designed to elicit different ways of plotting data. He stands next to the overhead projector, drawing and writing while asking his questions. The transparency is already filled with a bar graph, a pie chart, and the axes of a line graph. Because the goal was to have children look at the correlation of frequency of organisms and stream speed, Miles hopes to elicit a mention to line graphs from them. But his attempts fail. As he realizes this failure while pausing after a question, he makes space for Laura to enter the conversation and thereby provides an opportunity for line graphs to become the topic.

01	Miles:	So you can do a broken line graph that does that kind of thing.
02		But if you got a number, a series of numbers this way, what kind
03		of graph is that called? (*Pause*) I am using the wrong language,
04		Mrs. Ronald?
05	Laura:	No, I think we have just forgotten, because basically Dr. Roth
06		did this with us, and he was kind of showing you what kind of
07		graph to use. We are not doing this (*Points to the graphs on*
08		*projected against the screen.*) kind of graph, for our "Smarties"
09		graphs. (*Graham raises his hand makes noises, indicating that*
10		*he wants to say something.*) We are doing a different graph here
11		this is a whole different thing.
12	Miles:	Does Graham have an idea here?
13	Graham:	A scatter graph, or scatterplot . . .
14	Miles:	Yeah, OK.
15	Johnny:	And it shows you how things relate.
16	Laura:	That's right Johnny.
17	Miles:	If you need to do one of those today, you've got something that
18		you can look back on and make a comparison with. But those
19		are the ones where you get a series of measures, which conform,

20		for instance this dot here (*Points to the x-axis.*) to conform to a
21		measure on this axis (*Points to the y-axis.*), and something that
22		you have measured on this axis as well.
23	Laura:	And then what happens when you get a scatter of points?
24	Jamie:	You draw a line.
25	Ron:	You draw.
26	Sally:	You draw a diagonal line, like an average (*He holds up arm 45°*
27		*to body axis, then "draws" a line with the other hand.*) to show
28		how it changes.
29	Laura:	An average kind of, through [the points-
30	Miles:	[You might get an average plot.
31	Laura:	Right, average plot.

Laura first suggests that students had already done the kind of graph that Miles wants to bring into the conversation. Referring to a particular lesson with me provides a reminder to the students about when and where they encountered the type of graph that is being sought here. She then distinguishes the graph at hand—still unknown to the students—from others that they are currently doing in mathematics—bar graphs to plot the distribution of boxed candy ("Smarties") according to their color. There is an exchange in which Miles acknowledges Graham's answer as correct and Laura acknowledges a contribution Johnny made.

In the subsequent exchange, we see Laura become part of the conversation again as she asks a "necessary" next question, "What do you do once you have plotted your data?" This question follows up on Graham's and Johnny's contributions and links *this* moment to an earlier lesson with me in which drawing "average lines" or "trend lines" had been the topic.

Although Miles has had five years of experience in science teaching, he was stuck in the present situation, in which he had taken the lead. Despite his repeated efforts to have the students add line graphs to the list of graphs that they already had mentioned, the answer was not forthcoming. Because he was *in* the classroom *with* Laura, she could smoothly blend in and get the lesson going again. At first, Miles provided the necessary space by directly inviting Laura to enter the conversation. Likewise, Miles could take the lead again after Laura had mentioned that this kind of graph is different than the ones they were doing with "Smarties." One might have been tempted to say that Miles entered when Laura was finished contributing but at the same time, Laura could be said to have finished when Miles began. Being there *in* the classroom, one could have a sense of two teachers in a relay or tossing a ball back and forth.

Miles asked Graham to contribute in the way he had asked other students earlier. That is, at this point the lesson continued. The conversation continued with Johnny's contribution, which was acknowledged by Laura. Then Miles picked up again talking about the principle underlying the line graph, and when he was finished talking about plotting points, Laura entered again. After three students had called out answers, Laura and Miles completed the sequence in a quick exchange, in which Miles elaborated on Laura's initial comment.

COTEACHING: NEWCOMER AND OLD-TIMER

In the previous examples, I presented two cases in each of which teachers, who already had considerable experience, worked at each other's side. In these cases, we saw coteaching being enacted in ways that allowed all parties involved to learn. Although these teachers exhibited considerable Spielraum, being in and being with another teacher who had had appropriate experiences of the necessary forms and content, afforded them with additional opportunities to learn. Coteaching provided for continued opportunities to learn, all the while accomplishing the day's work, which consists in assisting students to learn. Given these experiences, it was a natural next step for us to ask what might happen if we used coteaching as a context for learning to teach when one of the two (or more) individuals was at the very beginning of his or her career. Here, I want to return to my experience with Nadine, sketched in Chapter 6, and expand on our learning by revisiting the same lesson in which she floated an egg in salt water. This example, including transcripts and drawings of the physical constellation of the teachers, provides a more detailed look at how coteaching unfolds, affords increased learning opportunities for students, and provides learning opportunities as an aspect of praxis. (I provide this example with the understanding that it is not to serve prescriptive purposes, to show how coteaching should be done, but descriptive purposes, to show how one particular pair was teaching at that point in time.)

As a starter activity for the day, Nadine has decided to show how an egg, which will sink in fresh water, will float in salt water (of sufficient concentration). One of her university instructors had shown this activity during the science methods class and she thought that it might fit nicely into the unit on water, particularly into the present section dealing with the physical properties. In our pre-lesson conversation, I had pointed out that it would be important to lead the children through a conversation that had two purposes: engage them in talking science and, in the process, construct one or more explanations. These were "attitudes" toward investigations or demonstrations that Nadine did not bring from her university lessons, which instead had encouraged her to "show" neat phenomena without making the presentation part of an overarching motive of increasing the children's discursive competencies.

Nadine begins her activity standing in the center of the classroom in front of the chalkboard, with a beaker in front of her, on an unoccupied student desk. I am standing to the side toward the left wall (from camera and student perspective). Thus, in this case, Nadine has taken the lead and is on central stage (Figure 7.3a).

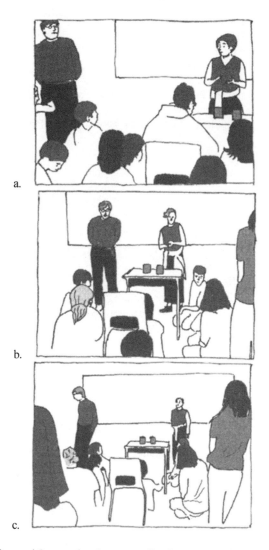

Figure 7.3. Nadine and I coteach a lesson on floating eggs in fresh water and salt water. **a.** Nadine has taken the lead and is at center stage. **b.** When Nadine seems to struggle, I move in to help out. **c.** Nadine transits into a different part of the lesson, while I walk off center stage.

01	Nadine:	What will happen if I put this egg into the water?
02	Tom:	It's gonna float.
03	Stephen:	It's gonna float
04	Nadine:	Lindsey has her hand up?
05	Chris:	A big baby will be formed.
06	Nadine:	Chris, control!

07	Bill:	It's gonna float.
08	Nadine:	Danielle?
09	Danielle:	And does it have salt in it?
10	Nadine:	It has no salt in it.
11	Danielle:	Then it is gonna sink.
12	Nadine:	So you think it's gonna sink. Joanna, what do you think?
13	Joanna:	It's gonna sink.
14	Nadine:	Why do you think it is gonna sink? (Pause) Danielle, why do
15		you think it is gonna sink?
16	Danielle:	Because there is no salt in it.

In this situation, the old habitus is one of asking questions in which students do not have to provide rationales, explanations, or elaborations to their answers. Nadine accepts what the students say without following up or asking them to justify their answers. Nadine does not ask for a justification or elaboration, even when Danielle asks whether there is salt in the water where the egg is to be placed. At this point, a possible question could have been why the salt should make any difference, thereby actively soliciting explanations from the students. Only after another student, Joanna, has provided her guess does Nadine return to Danielle to ask for a justification. But the student's answer, "Because there is no salt in it," does little to move toward further elaboration and justification of students' guesses (hypotheses). At this point, I still stand on the outside perimeter of the classroom (Figure 7.3.a) but sense that this is a good moment to contribute to the conversation. It is perhaps my experience that tells me that the conversation "is going nowhere." I therefore ask a question requiring justification but, without waiting for an answer, I ask a second question, further expanding the context. Both questions open the possibility to either provide a rationale or make a comparison between substances, a comparison that lends itself to a subsequent request for justification should it not be forthcoming immediately. Of course, asking such questions without deliberating comes from a habitus that has developed over years of teaching and leading whole-class conversations. As the subsequent contributions show, students generate further hypotheses including first justifications ("is the opposite . . ." and "is lighter than . . ."). In contrast to Nadine's question, which students could answer by providing one or the other alternative ("sink" or "float"), my question asks for an explanation. Whereas students could say "the egg floats [sinks]" in answering Nadine's question, my question asks for justifications and explanations.

From Nadine's perspective, the question I ask can be heard as coming just in time; it was productive and appropriate for *this* context and *this* conversation. Unlike a decontextualized text about questioning strategies, which might say to use stems like "What happens if . . .?" coteaching affords Nadine to hear questions that allow her to continue a whole-class conversation then and there. That is, although I ask a question, the coteaching situation does not take control away from her, but rather allows her to continue the conversation while affording learning to the students in her class.

Nadine's first contribution in this episode, "I didn't think about that" can be heard as an admission that she had not thought about whether adding sugar to water would be the same or different than adding salt. She then takes over again from me the role of scaffolding a student conversation. Here, rather than asking a question that students could answer by a simple factual statement, she asks what students (e.g., Dave, Tom) thought about the effect of sugar.

17	Teacher:	What kind of differences does the salt make? What would hap-
18		pen if you use sugar? Is it the same?
19	Troy:	No!
20	Christian:	Sugar [is the exact opposite.
21	Chris:	[Sugar is lighter than salt, making it float less.
22	Nadine:	I didn't think about that. Dave, what do you think about that?
23	Dave:	I don't know. I think it will sink, also.
24	Nadine:	Because it has no salt in it? Anybody else have any sugges-
25		tions? Tom?
26	Tom:	It will sink, but very slowly, because when you add salt you
27		gonna make it- (*Gestures upward movement.*)

Nadine places the egg into the water. The egg slowly sinks to the bottom. Nadine then adds salt to the water, constantly stirring. Nothing appears to happen, and she continues to add salt while stirring, but little seems to change in the behavior of the egg.

28	Nadine:	What is going to happen? I am going to add some more salt.
29	Alicia:	It's gonna make it float.
30	Tom:	It's gonna float back up. I don't know why, but like in the Dead
31		Sea, it is hard to go into the water, because there is so much salt
32		in it.
33	Nadine:	Really? Danielle?
34	Danielle:	I think that the salt would make it stay half above the water, half
35		below the water, and so . . .
36	Nadine:	So you think it will be, like, suspended? It won't be quite touch-
37		ing the ground, the bottom, but it won't also be at the top?
38		

Although the students make some interesting points about why the salt should make a difference, Nadine seems to begin to struggle. Being there, I feel that Nadine is missing a "teachable moment" when she fails to follow up on Tom's contribution, in which he shares an example sometimes featured in documentaries on the Dead Sea. Furthermore, she does not follow up by asking Danielle for a justification of her claim that the egg would be suspended.

At that time, the conversation seems to come to a halt Nadine and the students waiting for something to happen as she adds the salt. There is a long pause, only interrupted by student comments not loud enough to distinguish their content. At that point, I move from the side of the classroom to come to stand close to Nadine (Figure 7.3.b). I now have the opportunity to make the conversation productive. This will provide the students with continuing opportunities to learn, while also affording learning opportunities for Nadine, who can thus experience on the spot how to better frame her question and how to get out of an apparent instructional cul de sac.

My contribution occurs in two ways. First, I ask the students a question to get the conversation going again and moving ahead: "Why *should* salt water make a difference?'"

39	Teacher:	So what happened here? At first, it wasn't floating and now it *is*
40		floating? And the only difference [is
41	Chris:	[Salt.
42	Alicia:	[Salt.
43	Tom:	[Salt.
44	Teacher:	is salt. But why *should* there be any difference between salt water
45		and fresh water?
46	Stephen:	Because, it makes a difference.
47	Lindsey:	I don't know, just a difference.
48	Troy:	It's like there is water, and the salt dissolves into it. It may have
49		to do with the thickness or something as the salt dissolves.
50		
51	Teacher:	So salt water has a property that makes it float better?
52	Troy:	Yeah.
53	Nadine:	What do you think about that Tom?
54	Tom:	When you put the salt in the water you make it heavier, because
55		the salt is heavier, and then it makes the egg lighter.
56	Nadine:	Because the salt is heavier and it makes the egg lighter? And
57		what do you think, Steve?
58	Steve:	Because it has more salt in it.

I attempt to frame the question anew in order to afford a further development of the conversation. Three students simultaneously call out "salt" while I make salient the difference between the two situation (floating, sinking), but I reiterate the question, which calls for an explanation of the effect of salt: "Why *should* there by any difference between salt water and fresh water?" (lines 44–45). Two students simply restate that it should make a difference or say that they have no explanation, but Troy then provides a first explanation according to which the dissolving of salt will change the "thickness" of the water. Knowing without reflecting that "thickness" is not part of a scientific discourse about the phenomena, I instantly rephrase Troy's comment in terms of some "property" that brings about the change. (Some science educators prefer to talk about a misconception, but in my research, the notion of a discourse or discursive resource has shown to be more fruitful in understanding students' contributions and promoting learning in classroom communities.) This leaves open the nature of this property, and therefore future opportunities for developing the conversation. (One such opportunity was to arise only three turns later.)

As throughout the lesson, I leave room for Nadine to reenter the conversation. Here, then, Nadine enters the conversation again by asking Tom to venture his ideas in response to the question that I previously raised. Tom adds that the salt makes water "heavier" and therefore makes the egg lighter, relatively speaking. Without pursuing the ideas contained in Tom's contribution, Nadine asks one more student, who reiterates by stating the observation that the amount of salt made the difference. At this point, I realize that the students in this class do not seem to have developed a discourse about floating and sinking in terms of density. Even the most interested students, having developed considerable language for talking about science-related topics, do not use the scientific concept of density. Rather, they use everyday language to talk about the thickness and heaviness (or lightness) of substances.

Again, there appears to be a block. I enter again and pick up on a comment made earlier by Tom but not pursued by Nadine. Tom's comment might encourage other students who had seen documentaries on the Dead Sea to recall their prior experience.

59	Teacher:	(*I orient myself toward and point at Tom.*) Can you repeat but
60		loud enough for everyone to hear?
61	Tom:	I am not sure about it, but I thought because the salt is heavier,
62		so it makes the egg lighter, so it floats.
63	Teacher:	And did you say earlier something about the ocean water?
64	Tom:	Oh, yeah. In the Dead Sea, there is lots and lots of salt. And when
65		you go there, it's hard to go into the water, because it pushes
66		you up.
67	Teacher:	OK, so you have an actual real life example. Has anyone seen im-
68		ages of that on TV before? (8 seconds)
69	Nadine:	Has anyone seen that? (2 seconds) I just wanted to open it up
70		(*I move off to the side as shown in Figure 7.3.c.*)
71		with this little demonstration to show you that an egg will not
72		float in fresh water, but when we add salt to it, then we notice
73		that the egg rises.

Tom begins by stating a hypothesis about the effect of salt on the "heaviness" of water and the heaviness or lightness of the egg relative to the surrounding substance. But I take the conversation in a different direction by asking Tom about his earlier comment relating to the Dead Sea (though I ask about "ocean water" more generally). Tom contributes further observations to the ongoing conversation, namely that the salty water pushes people upward, making it difficult to go "into" the water. My subsequent question then checks whether there are other students who know about the effect of the Dead Sea or other ocean water on the floatation of people. Despite leaving a long pause, no further answers are forthcoming. (Although not thinking about wait time research, I enacted pauses consistent with this research.) Nadine and I realize that the other students either have not seen, or do not remember having seen, a feature on the Dead Sea. Nadine then changes the topic, explaining what she had intended to achieve with this activity, and I walk back to my original position near the left-hand wall (Figure 7.3.c).

Nadine and I subsequently analyze our shared teaching experience. (Although not present in the following transcript, there were two other individuals who had observed the lesson and contributed to our conversation. The presence other individuals helps to mediate relations of power that might be associated with traditional images of the constellation involving an experienced teacher or university professor and a new ["student"] teacher.) In these conversations we attempted to come to a better understanding of our teaching by critically analyzing particular episodes that stood out in our experience. (Sometimes we used videotapes to play back particular episodes as a way of better recalling [re-presenting] a particular event.)

Nadine: I was just accepting yes, no, or, these answers but there are no explanations for it. I can hear myself asking the questions, when I was asking a closed and open-ended question. I really found it helpful when you asked questions that kind of got the lesson going again.

I: What happened for you in this situation, what did you think about? You know, when I asked a question, did you think about me asking a question or did you listen to the question or?

Nadine: No, I was thinking about how you formed that the question or . . .

I: Because at that moment, you didn't have to do, I mean, at least for sort of two seconds or minutes . . .

Nadine: Right, I didn't have to do anything, no I didn't like shut my brain off, I was listening to your question and how you've formatted that question. And that helped me because it triggers in my head. I was thinking, "Oh yeah I should be thinking about that," "I should be asking about that," "that was a good question that really got them going on this tangent or brought them back" or "this got them more focused." Yeah, that was helpful for me to, to hear your questions and listen to your questions and think about how it related and where you were trying to go with that question, too.

I: Did listening to my questioning help you in other ways?

Nadine: Yes, because when you would get up there and form your questions a little bit, slightly different way it would ask the students to give more than just a one word answer. This would trigger things for me when I find, you know, when I would get up there and I asked a question, "Oh no that wasn't good enough, explain, or elaborate and then."

I: You mentioned that in the middle of asking questions, you become aware of the type of questions you ask?

Nadine: When I asked a close-ended question, I think "Oh" and then I try, make them elaborate further on what they were trying to say.

I: So what do you think we, at the university, could do to better prepare you for teaching a lesson as we did today?

Nadine: I realized that I didn't know the science involved in the demonstration, like I could feel in your questioning that you know the science. So I am thinking that I would have liked to have another science course. I think that I would have benefited more than from taking so many subjects that are not important in schools, like art, music, and PE [physical education]. When we're getting to the classroom those were the three subjects that we probably spent the least amount of time actually doing and learning about.

Deepening the Analysis

Let us take a step back and look at the entire episode for a moment. At a macro-level, I initially stood somewhat to the side, off center stage. During the episode, I moved in, participated in the conversation by passing the baton back and forth to Nadine, and finally moved off stage again. Associated with this physical movement was a change in the manner in which I participated. Initially I was simply there (Figure 7.3.a), taking only one turn, during which I asked three related questions (lines 17–18). Later, after moving on center stage and next to Nadine (Figure 7.3b), I increased my participation in the conversation. Through several turns, I guided students to elaborate on their descriptions of the phenomena and begin constructing explanations (lines 39–52, 59–68). But I did not monopolize the teacher role in the conversation. Rather, in the same way as Nadine had shown willingness to step back to provide a space for me to step forward (literally), I also stepped back to allow Nadine to continue on with the conversation (lines 53–58). Thus, there is reciprocity in the way we teach. We have good rapport and respect for one other, while recognizing our different levels of competencies with respect to science content.

Central to the approach that Nadine and I chose is a concern for student learning, a system of activities in which teachers are involved. We conceived of teaching as a matter of facilitating students' learning about the physical world, that is, in mediating their relationship with the world (Figure 7.4). In the process, we saw opportunities for our own learning through participating in the job to be done. In the present episode, we had decided to introduce students to a new phenomenon and, in the process, allow them to develop new discursive tools to describe and explain about floating and sinking (Figure 7.4). We both already had available the tools (discourse) for describing and explaining the phenomena. These two mediated relations provided the context in which students could develop a new relation to the world and the tools that mediate this relation. This is the context also for Nadine's learning, as she worked at my side and, in praxis, experienced how another practitioner mediated student access to the world and the discourse that I employed in the process.

Unless Nadine explicitly had stepped back and looked at the situation by removing herself from the action, her learning was implicit in getting the job done. She was aware of what was going on, but she did not look at the situation. She experienced the questions but did not generally think of questions *as* questions. When she did so, she took herself momentarily out of praxis and became aware of the questions. I suggest that this is made possible because of the

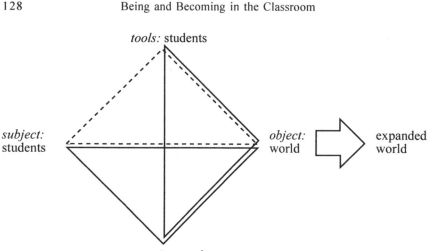

Figure 7.4. Teachers mediate students' access to the world, here by providing a new phenomenon. Teachers already have a tool that mediates their own access to this phenomenon (discourse). The purpose of the lesson is to allow students to construct the object and a discourse that mediates their relationship to this object.

division of labor that coteaching brings about. The ongoing process of teaching and awareness of teaching are distributed across the two teachers, in itself constituting a division of labor of praxis and awareness from praxis.

Sometimes we planned small-group activities. In this case, Nadine often began by following me to one or two groups, listening to my ensuing interactions with the students. Then she would walk to another group and interact with the students on her own. Periodically, Nadine and I touched base with one other to see how things were going, particular concerning difficulties students seemed to have, and to make further plans regarding the length of the activity, how to conclude it in a whole-class forum, and so on.

In the second part of the episode, Nadine and I talk about the moments shared during the teaching experience. These conversations constitute a vital part of learning about teaching in that they are contexts where teachers develop ways of talking (Gr. *logos*, "talk") about praxis—I call the resulting understanding "praxeology." Praxeology goes beyond the primary understanding that arises with a first-person experience in that it is the result of critical hermeneutic analysis and a generalization of understanding at the level of the participants. In Chapter 8, I focus on the nature of these conversations. Here I include our conversation to show how Nadine's understanding did not only arise from sharing the primary experience but also from the experience of talk about praxis. In my view, these two interrelated activity systems form one unit praxis/praxeology, though this is a dialectical relationship, given the contradictory nature of praxis and talk about praxis.

Reflection on Action during the Lesson

There are moments in coteaching when we are not completely absorbed in the conversation but rather take a more reflexive stance. That is, there are moments when we can reflect as the lesson continues—though our own activity is different at that moment because it has a different object (e.g., Leont'ev 1978). Because there are situations during which one teacher takes the lead, the other can, with a slight delay, reflect on the events that have just passed. There is therefore a "division of labor" in two senses of the word. First, the teachers co-participate in the practice of teaching and therefore take different or alternating roles. Second, because one individual can actually think about the events as they unfold, there is a division of labor distinguishing "praxis" and "reflecting on praxis." That is, there is an opportunity for learning through reflection when the situation has not changed very much so that its potentially salient and important aspects can be articulated with very little delay, a first form of abstraction. Neither Nadine nor I engaged in reflection in action. Nadine was reflecting on events, but these were events that had just passed and these were events that she observed rather than events that she enacted. I drew on my room to maneuver, my Spielraum, which I had developed during many years of teaching science and analyzing my own teaching.

In the following vignette from our coteaching research, I represent in parallel the events as they are available from the videotape and the elicited commentary that Nadine provided later on in the day, after watching a videotape of our joint lesson.

I had offered to do a demonstration with an associated whole-class exchange to get the students talk about the properties of water and how they change when other substances are added. I stood in the front of the classroom with two beakers next to me on a student desk, one containing salt and the other, water. There were also a battery, wires, and a light bulb on the desk. I connected the wires, bulb, and battery to show that a current was flowing as shown by the lit bulb. I then broke the circuit in one spot and placed the two leads into the water. Now there was no light. Nadine stood slightly to the side of me, watching the events and listening.

Teacher: Nothing, OK, so, there is no light coming on, this is amazing because they- Aren't they telling us on TV that water is conductive?

Bill: But we need to add salt!

Jon: May be it's the wire?

Teacher: OK, someone said salt, someone talked about salt.

Bran: I did.

Teacher: What do you think happens if I put that (*I hold two leads.*) in the salt here?

Bill: Well, nothing.

Stan: You got to add the water also.

Nadine: I was listening to your questions and how you've formatted that question at that moment. And that helped me then and there, because it triggered something in my head, I go, "Oh yeah I should be thinking about doing the substances differently before actually testing

Arlene: Try it!
Teacher: OK, we'll try it. (*I put two leads into the salt.*) Nothing is happening!
Bill: You need salt in the water for the whole, it'd give you more of a chem- I think it'll . . .
Carl: We'll have a chemical reaction
Teacher: OK, What happens if? What happens if we had some of the salt in here (*I point to a beaker with water.*)?
Bill: Mix it, mix it around!
Teacher: We have to, we have to mix it. (*I mix the salt and water in the beaker.*) What happens if I put the wires in there *now*?
Tory: It'll work.
Stan: Chemical reaction!
Tory: It'll work.
Teacher: Why would it? Explain! Who has an explanation?

the salt water," or "I should be asking them to explain their answers," or "That was a good question that really got them thinking about what might happen if you did not add the water." This is helpful for me to, to listen to your questions and hear your questions then and there, as they happen. And then you ask them, "What happens if you put the wire in the solution?" And that got them thinking again.

In this episode, one can see me enact the lesson with students, whereas Nadine stayed slightly back. This physical removal was paralleled by the removal from teaching activity and an enactment of reflective activity. While there and still part of the classroom, Nadine was enabled to take a reflexive stance: for example, to take a question that I just asked as the object of a situated inquiry. In this, she could not pursue her reflection too far, for she would no longer have followed the lesson as such and would have missed much of the way in which the questions assisted in unfolding the conversation. ("Fly on the wall" observers get detached in this way and therefore construct a very different understanding of the lesson, how it unfolded, the constraints that mediated teacher and student actions, etc.) Rather, the removal was just sufficient to note that a particular question was good, to perceive how it had unstuck the conversation or facilitated the emergence of student explanations. But then Nadine immediately gave up her position and readied herself to enter the conversation at the next opportune moment.

Teaching and reflecting on teaching—in the same way as for any other praxis—are part of two distinct activity systems. These are neighboring and related systems, but they cannot be accomplished simultaneously by the same person. But in coteaching, the division of labor that is embodied in the process of teaching also allows a second process of reflecting on practice—which historically is embodied in the division of labor between university professors (theory) and teachers (practice). In their coteaching, Nadine and I take turns at being the lead person. This allows us to increase the learning opportunities for students because, from a learner perspective, the Spielraum of teacher actions is combined. Working collectively, we have more action possibilities. We can also say that a zone of proximal development is created between the actions of individuals (Nadine or I) and the new form of collectively generated activity. In this zone, one teacher also has the possibility to reflect on the ongoing events.

The situation is quite different when a beginning teacher is alone in a classroom. First, because of his or her limited experience, there is less Spielraum available for dealing with the unfolding events in the classroom. Second, because of the all-consuming activity of teaching, there is no time to reflect on a particular event and how a more experienced practitioner would have dealt with it *then and there*. Because Nadine also taught mathematics, but all by herself, we were afforded an opportunity to come to better understand—through Nadine's reflections—the differences between the traditional process of teacher induction and coteaching.

In my research with Nadine, I was able to see the difference of learning to teach in the traditional way—student teaching or internship, where students first observe and then take over—and in the coteaching method. Whereas Nadine was coteaching science with me, she taught mathematics by herself. Her supervising teacher, Cam, wanted her to "learn to stand on her own two feet," and therefore left her to herself in the classroom—though in moments of trouble (mostly discipline), he was willing to come in and help out. Nevertheless, Nadine had two considerably different experiences of learning to teach. In this section, we take a look at the experience of learning to teach on her own—mostly drawing on the resources that the university had bequeathed her. My account will show that this experience, though it was happening in parallel to the science lessons, was very different. In the next section, I draw on my recorded conversations with Nadine to allow readers to hear through her voice what this different experience was like.

A NEW TEACHER TALKS ABOUT TEACHING

"I Was Sort of Stumbling through Things [by] Myself"

I felt like just thrown into it right away. I think Cam just wanted to throw me in there and have me figure out what worked and what didn't work. I find that frustrating that I didn't have any modeling because I know there's other ways, I know there's other things out there and I know that it works but I haven't seen it.

The seventh grade that I was assigned to was a difficult class to deal with. Students did not easily focus on their assigned tasks and the strategies I learned at the university for making students accountable for their behavior did not work. These included removing students temporarily from the interactions by asking them to step out, talking to students away from others so that they could not make a big issue out of the pertinent situation, or making students stay behind during lunch and after school did not seem to work. The only person who seemed to have any significant impact on controlling student behavior was Cam, the regular teacher in this class. Yet he was notably absent for most of the time, which made it difficult for me to learn in the way, for example, I had learned about questioning by working with you. To complicate the matter, you [Michael Roth] could not be a role model, for you were a visitor, constrained by his own research ethics, and therefore felt disempowered even with respect to me. You told me that I was doing a better job than many teachers with several years of experience. Yet throughout my student teaching and internship experiences in this classroom, I struggled with the issues of classroom control. After many unsuccessful attempts in bringing what I had learned at the university about classroom control to action, I gave up and attempted to get a feel for what is right in each individual situation, with each student.

I remember, at the university we were hearing all these ways and methods and these idealistic ways but when I actually get out there it was different putting, everything into actions. I am following all the steps that I have been taught to follow, and I am going in ways that I am supposed to be going. But things aren't changing. I don't know what anybody else in my program did, but I was sort of stumbling through things myself. I am constantly battling with and learning and trying to find new ways or new things. I do not feel like I figured it all out because what I see happening is that those students who should not get disciplined are getting disciplined in my class.

I might have been able to learn more about keeping an orderly classroom while working with you, which I could then have transferred into my mathematics class. Unfortunately, I could not learn from you with respect to discipline what I learned relative to questioning. You told me about a study you had conducted where you showed that positioning with respect to individual students changed the ways in which students interacted with each other [Roth, McGinn, Woszczyna, and Boutonné 1999]. That is, you had positioned yourself such that students who interrupted the lesson quieted down, inattentive students were drawn back into the conversations, and locus of the conversations changed from groups of students in one area of the classroom to those in another. But in this classroom, you were a visitor. I was much more at home than you were, because I was also teaching them mathematics, was the homeroom teacher, and responsible for some of their sports activities. Thus, although you were more senior to me in terms of your understanding of subject matter and subject matter pedagogy, you felt junior to me in this classroom with respect to disciplinary issues and silently expected me to deal with any issues arising. Without a coteaching peer who could have played the part you did with respect to my questioning, I had to manage by stumbling through.

Learning in Situation: Particulars

We learned a lot in university classes, but I think that that which we really needed to know, we did not get. I think that a lot has to do with the "here and now." It is easy to think of, "Well somebody does this to me, then I follow this and this and this." But every situation is so different and every student is so different. So what I learned in the abstract does not seem to fit any particular case.

I mean for me, as far as classroom control, it has just all been trial and error. That is, I was learning as I went along finding what works or what does not work. I mean, this class is the way this class is because of the individuals that are in there.

So I learned that there is a considerable gap between generalizations about teaching made by others and my own lived experience. Theories, in the way I understand them, really do not deal with the complexity of what I was living in the classroom and there were always several theories that seemed to fit a singular event. And different events seem to be compatible with the same theory. In the mathematics classes, I was on my own, there was not another person that I could draw on or who could participate in making the best of a situation. Also, teaching on my own, I did not have opportunities to think about "best action" while the lesson was going on. So, when nothing of what I had learned seemed to work, I resorted to trial and error. I tinkered with different ways of dealing with discipline and thereby found what works best for me in this classroom with these students.

Tinkering, though it was very time-consuming, allowed me to get a feel for acting appropriately in the here and now of the classroom. The practices I developed worked, and I knew them without having to think about them in the way I had set out to approach finding the best method of establishing and maintaining classroom discipline. It may sound trivial to say, "This class is the way this class is because of the individuals that are in there." As I learned to teach, however, I thought that such a statement is actually very profound when I compare it with the broad generalizations of the theories I had to learn but that do not describe any particular situation. As a teacher, I never acted in hypothetical and contextually impoverished situations but always in the here and now and with a particular student, class, or physical context.

The more time I spent in this seventh-grade classroom and as my experience grew, I developed ways of dealing with each situation as a particular. For example, I frequently ran into trouble with Troy. I found it worked best when I was not always down on him, on his back, or asking to speak to him in the hallway, at lunch time, or after school. When I let go in particular situations, things turned for the better. He finally took a step back. I found that when I did that with Troy, it really worked and he just sort of did his thing. When he needs help he asks for help. He no longer felt as if he is singled out as the one that is in the wrong all the time.

In my experience of teaching with you, it seems that your knowledge has a lot to do with knowing particulars. You say and do the right things at the right moment whatever the particulars of the situation. I learned that each lived situation, each experience, increases my understanding of teaching and changes my ways of being in the classroom. Sometimes my emerging understandings are silently embodied and unarticulated, sometimes remarkable by others in the ways I comport myself; at other times my understandings are framed in the form of narratives. Thus, as teachers we are not only beings in classrooms, but more importantly, we are always becoming . . . more experienced, better questioners, more spontaneously tactful. I am becoming an old-timer in and through praxis by participating. The present study shows that this becoming is less painful, more efficient, when I coteach with you, a more experienced peer. In this situation, I come to understand myself through understanding another person; but to understand the other I also need to understand myself. It is through this dialectic of understanding oneself as another that I understand myself and you.

Reflecting on Action with Others

At first, I had attempted to deal with discipline on my own. I was thinking about what I heard in my classroom management class and in the textbook. When things do not go as orderly as I wish them to, I feel like I am pushed up against these walls. I needed to find ways of solving the problems here and now without disrupting the rest of the class. I began asking students to see me during recess, lunch, or after school. I thought students would eventually experience seeing me as a form of punishment and stop misbehaving. However, as I never taught the students just prior to these breaks I found it difficult to make students actually show up. Eventually, I had to develop new ways of dealing with the discipline problems. I thought that I might learn how to best deal with discipline by interacting with other teachers after school or during recess.

I attempted to bring about changes by talking to those teachers also teaching this class, who were familiar with the particulars of each student, and in this way arrive at a better set of strategies. That is, we talked about problems that occurred in class, but we did so in the remove from actually teaching, allowing them time to reflect, in the time out from actual teaching. I have talked a lot to the other teachers who work with this group, about how they deal with them, because they have so many problems. We all just sort of talked about what we were doing and when it was not working. For example, one of the teachers was keeping track of things and was writing down their names. Then, she had this process that they went through and it seemed to be working. But from what I learned, whatever we did it only worked for so long.

For me, learning from other teachers was different than learning from books. But there was still that gap between what we said we would do and then doing it in the classroom. Really, there were two gaps. First, we did not share the experience in the classroom so we never really knew how the other teacher would have reacted in my situation. We did not have shared experiences in the way that you and I had. You and I we were actually able to refer to the same situation, which we sometimes saw in similar ways, sometimes in different ways. Nevertheless, there was something that we took as shared and that helped me to learn. There was also a second gap between talking about what to do and actually doing it in the here and now of the classroom. Nevertheless, talking with the other teachers who taught in the classroom helped more than learning from textbooks or in university classes. In effect, we sort of built local theory and plans of action, just for this class, so that we all could learn how to handle the students. Hearing the stories others told allowed me to make sense of the class as an entity. For example, it turned out that the same students seemed to be causing the problems for all the teachers. While this did not automatically lead to change in what I did, it nevertheless gave me a different understanding: there was a problem that was more endemic to the situation and not just my personal problem.

CONCLUSION

Nadine concluded this experience by noting that coteaching had allowed her to learn tremendously. By working alongside an experienced teacher—rather than just being observed on occasions by a sponsoring teacher and her university supervisor (some other professor than me)—she experienced and participated in praxis, in addition to having the opportunity to engage with experienced teachers in reflection on action and curriculum planning. Every instant that the Other asks an unexpected question, deals with a situation differently than she herself would have done, became an opportunity to embody new ways, for reflecting in action on possible consequences, and reflecting on action concerning possible means for organizing lessons in a different way.

When we both felt ill at ease, our learning was constrained. In this case, we felt it would have helped us tremendously to coteach with Cam, who seemed to be in his element when it came to organizing and capturing the attention of this class during whole-class activities. In Nadine's teaching, and without the experience of coparticipating with a more experienced teacher, her learning was constrained and involved a great deal of trial-and-error testing of ways to control the class. In my case, coteaching with Cam may likely have provided more opportunities for all students to coparticipate in, and therefore colearn from, the ongoing conversations related to the physical, biological, and environmental properties of water. I recently taught in a similar situation including a new teacher, her cooperating teacher, and my friend and colleague Ken Tobin. In this instance, the presence of the cooperating teacher allowed us to learn tremendously.

Coteaching may therefore be an ideal vehicle, not only for professional training, but also for in-service teacher professional development. One can easily envision in-service efforts in which a competent science teacher might coteach with two or three elementary teachers at a time. Such coteaching would come with an additional benefit of overcoming the deleterious effects of professional isolation that relegates teachers to "their" classrooms, with few opportunities to coparticipate with peers as part of doing their work.

Because we find ourselves *first of all* in a world to which we belong, physically and socially, and in which we cannot but participate, that we are *subsequently* able, to set up objects in opposition to ourselves, objects that we reclaim as knowable. There is consequently no self-understanding that is *not* mediated by signs, symbols, and texts. Because of the fundamental condition of existence, being in the world and being with another, the way we normally exist and act in our world, we should not separate and individualize competence as silent and implicit knowledge, theories enclosed by our skulls. Rather, when we are interacting with students, then we are part of this classroom, filled with these students, at this time, teaching this subject matter, on this day. As teachers, we engage in a relation with the situation, which I described in Chapter 5 with the term *relationality*. What happened to Nadine in our collaboration was that she developed relationality as a matter of course, by coteaching.

Because teaching is so embodied and tied to our experience of being in the classroom, it comes as no surprise that learning to teach requires the personal experience of teaching in classrooms. By coteaching, new teachers can observe and imitate how a more seasoned peer walks about the classroom, calls on students, waits, feels confident, and deals with a difficult situation, always right then and there. The student teacher learns with his or her body to feel confident about asking questions, to call on students, to wait, and to deal with different answers from the students. This confidence is *not* an affective aspect of one's knowing; it *is* active knowledgeability itself, knowing what to do or say and what to avoid doing and saying. As other studies of mine have also shown, this knowledgeability is a form of embodied knowing acquired in praxis. The present study shows that such knowledgeability comes to be embodied with much greater ease through coteaching, which is colearning, in praxis.

I conclude this chapter by suggesting that the study of teaching praxis needs to be sensitive to the experiential quality of practical knowledge, an acknowledgment that much of the instant knowing, enacting in real time issues from one's body and the immediate world. Our work together as teachers allows us to evolve understandings from the continuous interplay of two activities. First, we develop shared understanding of praxis, which arises from being in the classroom, enacting caring relationships with an Other. Second, we enact a critical and rigorous inquiry in the tradition of a hermeneutics of text and action, which is informed by past research on teaching. My ongoing work suggests that in coteaching, all participants (newcomers, old-timers, supervisors, and researchers) are afforded tremendous learning experiences.

8

Cogenerative Dialoguing

In my use, praxeology is knowledge of teaching that has been developed out of teaching praxis; praxeology literally means "talk" (logos) about praxis. I use praxeology to focus on the importance of teachers' local knowledge to understanding and developing their practice. Theories are usually developed as systems of knowing that hold across a variety of situations: theories articulate what is generalizable across often rather different situations. However, in this way, much of what characterizes teaching—the familiarity with the setting, the aspects of the unfolding events of which we teachers are aware but do not necessarily articulate—are drained from these "abstract" frameworks. Praxeology (talk about teaching) is inherently different from praxis (teaching). In praxeology we find symbolic mastery; in praxis we find practical mastery. Many have pointed out that the two constitute different forms of knowing, and even the most accomplished practitioners stand no better chance to articulate in words the essence of practice than any observer watching them (Bourdieu 1980). Practical mastery can only be acquired in praxis; symbolic mastery is acquired by talking about practice. But symbolic mastery does not guarantee practical mastery—as many students of teaching have found when they move from their university classes into the classroom. This is often conceptualized as the theory-praxis gap. But rather than valuing one type of mastery over the other, I propose to understand the relationship of praxis and praxeology as a dialectical one. Praxis/praxeology is a dialectical unit, whereby the contradictions inherent in the unit constitute the possibility for growth and change (Il'enkov 1977). In this chapter, I describe the opportunities that arise for understanding teaching when those who have co-taught get together to articulate and theorize their experiences. The new understanding may give rise to an expansion of practical (rather than theoretical) possibilities, which teachers enact to promote change.

ARTICULATING AND ANALYZING SHARED EXPERIENCE

Coteaching, that is, working together side-by-side, provides teachers with opportunities to experience lessons from similar locations. The experiences that are salient for one or the other teacher can subsequently become the topic of their professional conversations, which themselves lead to a further understanding of teaching and learning. That is, out of their shared experience of working side by side, being in the same classroom and being with each other, teachers develop an understanding of praxis that becomes the basis for their subsequent efforts of articulating what had happened. I begin by analyzing several episodes from one of my studies on coteaching (involving Birgit, Chris, and, in the present case, several other teachers who cotaught with them). I then articulate in more abstract form what is going on in these situations, before providing an example from my recent research where students participated in the sharing, negotiating, and explaining of shared experiences and in developing action alternatives.

Before actually moving to the first example, I want to point out that in these sessions, traditional hierarchical relationships are removed. As all teachers are involved in teaching the children and blame cannot be placed because of our principle of "If you can't or didn't make a change, don't blame others," the general concern is with mutual learning. In the course of the work on coteaching, Kenneth Tobin and I developed a heuristic that allows us to check whether our process is unfolding appropriately while we conduct the session or as we reflect back on what had happened during the session (Table 8.1). Readers will easily recognize that our intent is to ensure an equitable conversation, that is, opportunities for all stakeholders to talk, contribute to understandings and explanations, and participate in multiple ways.

The design of these conversations about praxis follows the example of *cogenerative dialogue* used particularly in the democratic workplaces of northern Europe. The northern European labor context is very concerned with equitable and democratic participation of all those working in the same company. In cogenerative-dialogue sessions, all participants operate out of their own initial frames, or primary discourses, but communicate at a level where frames can be analyzed, and altered and new frames can be generated. Freire suggested the need for dialogic relations within a community, thus providing its members with an opportunity "to name the world in order to transform it" (Freire 1972: 136). In a sense, cogenerative dialogue in the way I use it here leads to "local theory." To avoid the connotations associated with the term "theory" I adopted the notion of "praxeology" to signify the understanding arising from the dialectic of praxis and cogenerative dialogue.

Let us look at some of our sessions to see what and how teachers learn to articulate their shared practice and what we can learn from these conversations about the relationship between praxeology and praxis.

Table 8.1
Heuristics for Cogenerative Dialogue

1. Respect: Do participants "respect" each other?
2. Rapport: Does a rapport exist between participants?
3. Inclusion of stakeholders: Are all stakeholders (student teachers, students, school personnel, high school students, university personnel) included in the dialogue?
4. Ways to participate: Do participants engage in the following?
   4.1. Coordinate discussion?
   4.2. Listen attentively?
   4.3. Initiate dialogue/ideas?
   4.4. Ask critical questions?
   4.5. Provide evidence?
   4.6. Express an opinion (agree/disagree)?
   4.7. Speak freely?
   4.8. Clarify and elaborate on ideas?
   4.9. Suggest alternatives?
   4.10. Evaluate ideas and practices?
5. Opportunities to participate: Are the following enacted in order to make opportunities for participation? That is, do participants:
   5.1. Allow equitable participation irrespective of traditional distinctions including gender, race, social status, and level of experience?
   5.2. Provide space to participate?
   5.3. Show willingness to participate?
   5.4. Tend invitations to participate?
6. Discussion topics: Are the following teaching- and learning-relevant topics raised?
   6.1. Learning to teach?
   6.2. Teaching and learning?
   6.3. Planned and enacted curriculum?
   6.4. Teaching kids like us?
   6.5. Coteaching?
   6.6. Transformative potential of activities/curriculum?
   6.7. Particular events that stand out in the experience of individuals or the collective?
   6.8. Quality of the learning environment?

DEVELOPING AN UNDERSTANDING OF STUDENT-CENTERED TEACHING

Birgit and Chris had been coteaching a unit on civil engineering for nearly two months when Nancy, Janice (from a different elementary school), and Wendy visited their classroom to see how the lessons unfolded and to learn how one might teach the engineering curriculum. However, our idea was that these "visitors" would learn much more if they actually participated in the lesson as teachers or learners. We suggested that they might begin by following one of the regular teachers (Birgit, Chris) around, and then interact with the children on their own. After the lesson was over, the teachers met to talk about their shared experience and, to arrive at some level of explanation (which is always associated with some form of abstraction) for what was going on.

Nancy: We also noted they were very articulate, the children were able to express their ideas so well in such a sophisticated manner. Now, is this again a normal thing for that crowd, is it because . . .?

Wendy: Well, not really knowing the class, I don't know Chris' class that well, but generally I found that our school is, it is mixed. Within my own class, how many students say exactly what they want to say, and others have a lot of difficulties. They might have the ideas, but just can't get it out.

Nancy: It's just that these are so many and all of them that I listened to were able to talk about engineering.

Janice: You obviously put a lot of work in to have articulate children but also you put a lot of background knowledge in.

Nancy: Well this is what I was wondering, there is so much background knowledge that the children seem to have, which they probably did not develop on their own but was introduced by you.

Janice: Because the kids were able, talking about the beams and supports and stays, and I thought I was having a difficult time when I wanted to speak to them about their bridges, because I didn't have the vocabulary that they did.

Birgit: Well, I can comment on that. It's important for you to know that we didn't give them that vocabulary. The vocabulary came from the kids. But the way it came was through questioning and letting them find their own voice to describe what they have done by sharing with each other. They came up with the words "stay," "beam," "column," and "reinforce." The only word that we had inserted in that was "catastrophic failure." And that was purposefully done to celebrate when a bridge fell down in the planning process and that it is better than falling down after it has been built.

In this excerpt, the teachers attempt to articulate an explanation for the source of the fourth- and fifth-grade children's remarkable competency to talk about engineering. Nancy, who had interacted with different children and subsequently with her fellow teacher Janice, notes that the children in this class were very articulate about engineering ("I was having a difficult time when I wanted to speak to them . . ."). Wendy, one of the teachers at the school, suggests, based on her own class, that the school was composed of students with mixed abilities. This comment, in the context of Nancy and Janice's observation that so many students were very articulate implies that much of the discursive competence developed as a result of the curriculum and the teaching of the two teachers (Birgit, Chris). Taking turns, Nancy and Janice provide a description (beams, support, and stays) of the children's discursive competence and hypothesize that the teachers must have introduced much of the terminology ("background"). Thus, the visiting teachers realize that in this community of engineering practice, they were in many ways less central than the children as far as talking engineering design was concerned. Speaking at the end of the episode, Birgit suggests that the children introduced much of the engineering vocabulary themselves. However, this introduction was not spontaneous but occurred as part of the questioning strategy, intended to allow children to describe their engineering experience in their own voice. During the "sharing" sessions, children presented new words, which were subsequently explained so that other children could also begin to use these words in their own descriptions and explanations of engineering design.

In this situation, then, teachers engage in the attempt to build explanations for how to teach this engineering unit that it allows children to develop their own language. The new teachers, on their part, highlight the tremendous achievement, whereas Birgit provides an explanation of how such competence came about without the teacher having to introduce background.

As the conversation continues, the three teachers further theorize the origin of the children's discursive competence. This time, Nancy and Janice draw on their observations of Birgit and Chris's teaching, which they had made from the perspective of coteaching rather than from the position of the proverbial "fly on the wall."

Nancy: A large part of your role was giving support to each other. What I noticed with Chris was that she asked a question or an answer was given to her, she would look at you when she answered the child. She was really getting a lot of support. And you did the same to her actually too, when there was a question you didn't understand, so is the plan, are you testing if this is working with one teacher as well as seeing how it works for the two.

Janice: So much a big part of what you two were doing was helping each other with the questioning with the fine details, with the reinforcing of the children's ideas. If you don't learn that then the lesson is one-dimensional. But If you learn all those other skills that draw out thinking and creativity, and really encourage excellence and encourage children to reach their potentials that's what makes a unit valuable. And you can't get that by yourself. Unless you have someone—someone has to give you those skills—someone has to have developed those skills to give, to be for the benefit of the children.

Birgit: I said that to Michael that my teaching practice has improved so much this fall, but just watching myself and Chris interact, by seeing what she does, things that I would never have thought of doing. But that are so useful in setting up the unit. And these are more things that have to do with the classroom cooperation and management. Like we had a big session on how do you encourage the participation from each other. And it was wonderful, and I think it has really enhanced the unit from when I taught it separately. I know the content but I am a little rusty on teaching. I haven't been teaching for a couple years. It's just been wonderful, like as a teacher I never had the opportunity to go in—except when I was student teaching and that was completely different—and watch a master teacher at work all the while teaching with her.

In this episode, the teachers construct observations and explanations for the tremendous success (children's remarkable discursive competence) of this engineering unit. Nancy begins by describing that the two teachers supported each other's teaching during the ongoing lesson, for example, by mediating when one of them had misunderstood what a child had contributed. Nancy also noted that Birgit and Chris had constantly checked visually with the other person. Janice contributes in two ways. First she reaffirms Nancy's observation, and then she moves on to point out what the two teachers had been doing together, working "to draw out thinking and creativity and encourage excellence," which are essential teaching skills. She concludes that teachers have to be introduced to these skills, because "you can't get that by yourself." Birgit elaborates these descriptions, noting that she had learned tremendously by coteaching with Chris and that the unit was thereby enhanced. In the context of Chris's comment that this unit was so much better than when she had taught it on her own (made elsewhere in the conversation), the value of coteaching as the source of professional development was highlighted.

This episode shows how the cogenerative dialogue allows teachers to articulate their teaching and to theorize it. Here, Janice and Nancy are visiting teachers, who intended to teach the unit somewhat later in the year. Their participation in the lesson led by Birgit and Chris allowed them to experience what all participants in the classroom on that day came to call an excellent lesson. Their participation in the cogenerative-dialogue session allowed them to frame their observations and elaborate emerging praxeology that explains what had happened.

In this episode, the teachers talked in largely positive terms about their teaching. Some university-based educators may feel that teachers talking about praxis will not be critical enough of their own teaching. In my experience of cogenerative dialogue that follows coteaching, this is not the case. Over a period of eight years, all teachers involved in the coteaching experiences and the following cogenerative dialogue sessions also critiqued their own teaching, which became a driving force for change. That is, they experienced themselves enacting practice in ways that did not conform to their desired images of the practice. This contradiction between practice and desired image then became a driving force for change.

DANIEL'S BRIDGE: KNOWING WHEN TO STOP

In this conversation, Chris and Birgit critically analyze one classroom episode that they had experienced together, though from differently located positions. Birgit had questioned Dan, a child labeled and treated as "learning disabled" by the school district services. As always, Birgit attempted to encourage children to extend what they had done. Dan had quickly finished the bridge that he had wanted to build, whereas Birgit wanted him to continue—by strengthening the existing bridge or building a new one. In part, she wanted Dan to continue because this would allow him to learn more; in part, she wanted him to continue designing bridges rather than simply moving around the classroom and talking to other students. At one point, Chris joined Birgit and Dan and suggested that the boy did not have to make another bridge. This, therefore, brought the interaction between Birgit and Dan to a stop. During our cogenerative-dialogue session, we attempted to understand what had happened. (Although there were five teachers present during this session, only Chris and Birgit talked during the following excerpt.)

Chris begins this excerpt by first providing a description of the classroom situation followed by an explanation in which Dan's special needs became the reasons for her actions. She suggests that because of her knowledge of the child (and school), she is more aware of these special needs. She ends setting this episode in the context of the engineering unit, by weighing the intention to extend children's thinking against the needs of this child to experience success.

Chris: Birgit had asked Dan some questions and he had changed something underneath to make his bridge stronger. I sort of came in and didn't know what she had talked about. And she was trying to get him to think about building a top on the bridge. Because I knew the kid better than Birgit did I wanted to stop, because I thought this was enough for that kid. I thought he had done this magnificent thing. I didn't think he should do another thing to it, he is really proud of it, it carried weight, that's what we asked them to make it to do. And it just needed to stop then, and I probably could judge that way quicker because I know the kid so much better than you do. But on the other hand, what we have been trying so hard to do is to extend that thinking, and it is hard to draw a fine line between extending the thinking and putting them down almost because, you are this powerful person you are the authority figure.

Birgit: Well what was interesting for me out of this situation, I have been working really hard at my questioning. But I think sometimes, I am taking it too far, in other words, just stopping and making a balance, between what they had done and how far they can go. He had used a number of wonderful techniques in this bridge. Just because he had built it quickly, why should he have to go on?

Chris: You felt that you needed to bring out more and to encourage him to go further?

Birgit: Why does it have to be more? I guess I was trying to feel out whether he was interested in taking his bridge further. Because sometimes they are interested and just not sure whether they want to take a risk by taking their project further.

Chris: Yeah, if I had not come, you probably would have done the same thing, just not so quickly.

Birgit: Yeah that's right . . .

Chris: And I sort of barged in and did it.

Birgit: I really feel that it is important not to force it; if they really don't want to build a bigger or whatever, that's fine; what I learned from you is that sometimes I did have too high of an expectation about where to take it.

You know, like sometimes, especially for a kid like Dan that you did know is struggling you know in some other areas, being really in tune with that, and celebrating the small successes they have made, like the successes he's made might be different than someone else in the class. And he did have a cantilever in that bridge, which is a rare concept that not a lot of kids get . . .

Chris: And the braces, not the braces underneath, but the braces sideways, I mean, it was a lot of thought.

Birgit: . . . and when I questioned him about which part he thought would go first if it was tested, he was right on. Like he knew that those foundations on the side would give out first, so I asked, "how might you prevent that from happening so we can make it longer?" But he wasn't really interested in doing that at that point. You know, you said you would say to him he would have another opportunity to do another bridge rather than to mod-ify that one . . .

Chris: And he really took off with that too . . .

Birgit: He was really exited. Oh, and he didn't want to have any other materials, he loved the picks and tape.

Following Chris, Birgit attempts to build an explanation for what had hap-pened. She suggests that her questioning might push the children too far or too hard. In her view, she needs to find a balance between a child's needs to experi-ence the success that comes with having successfully achieved an activity, and her own need, to foster a child's continuous development. Both continue to elaborate the special circumstances that mediate questioning sequences with stu-dents such as Dan. They build a description of all of Dan's accomplishments, and thereby construct evidence in support of the Chris's decision that Dan should not be pushed further.

In this situation, Chris and Birgit constructed praxeology about when it is appropriate to push children's development by means of questioning and when one should stop. Both recognized the general need to assist children in their de-velopment and the tremendous contribution the practice of asking challenging questions makes in this development. However, they also constructed factors that mediate the interactions in situations with children such as Dan. Here, there is no need to abstract theory from the particular child. Dan stands for children with particular disabilities and both teachers know that they would recognize these disabilities in other children. In this way, the two teachers not only learned how to ask productive, development-fostering questions but also when to stop asking such questions because they may actually interfere. In the follow-ing section, I elaborate more on the development of Birgit and Chris, which arose from their coteaching experience in general, and their cogenerative dialogue in particular.

VIDEOTAPES FOR CRITICAL INQUIRY

Whenever possible, we all met to talk about teaching: Birgit and Chris who cotaught the lessons, Sylvie (research assistant) who focused on videotaping, interviewing children, and collecting other data, Alain (professor) who joined the others more infrequently, and myself. Together, we talked about teaching and about specific events in this classroom to develop our understanding of learning about engineering (students, teachers), teaching, and learning to teach. An important focal point for our meetings were episodes from the videotapes, which Birgit or Chris had already selected as providing some interesting event from which we could learn. At other moments, I selected one or more episodes featuring a particular aspect of teaching such as questioning. My interest lay in learning to ask questions, a topic that had emerged both from my own teaching as well as between Birgit and Chris in the present study. As a researcher, I was interested in providing them with ways of developing their understanding.

The episode we observe comes from a lesson during which students are designing towers. Each group was asked to design a particular feature such as being earthquake-proof, carrying high loads, and so on. While the children design their towers, Birgit and Chris spend time with each group, engaging them in conversations that allow them in articulating the process and products of their engineering design activities. In this particular episode, Birgit approaches the group consisting of Andy, Simon, and Tim. They are working on a tower that was to withstand earthquakes, a capability that they would test with the "shaker table," a desk on which the tower was to rest and which was then moved quickly back and forth. The tape shows how Birgit sits down and engages the three boys in a conversation about their tower (Figure 8.1).

Birgit:	OK, good, I am interested in asking more. Now, I like the lightening rod on the top.
Tim:	You won't get hit by lightening.
Birgit:	One of the things about your tower that is kind of interesting is that it has a leaning effect. What is the purpose of that?
Simon:	This is how we build it.
Tim:	It was like the leaning tower . . .
Birgit:	Oh I see.
Simon:	The leaning tower of Pisa.
Birgit:	So actually, your tower, you're trying to tell me that it's unique and actually want to buy it because it's different than boring old straight ones. Is that right?
Tim:	Yeah, I don't want to be selling it.
Birgit:	So what might be a benefit to me if I bought this kind of tower?
Simon:	Hmm, well we'd have to work on it.
Andy:	Lightening wouldn't hurt you.
Birgit:	OK, well I could make some money on tourism if people want to come and see it, couldn't I?
Tim:	Yeah, because it's the lightening tower of Tim and Simon and Andy.

Figure 8.1. Birgit engages (from left) Simon, Tim, and Andy in a conversation about their tower. Her questioning during this episode later becomes the focal point of a professional conversation to come to a better understanding of questioning in the context of this unit and to articulate learning so as to ask appropriate questions with the right timing.

Throughout the lessons and our conversations, Birgit's great competence in asking productive questions was noted time and again. A detailed analysis of Birgit's questioning showed the broad content domain that her questions covered (Roth 1996). The analysis provides evidence for the complexity of questioning that is characterized by the interactions of context and content of, and responses and reactions to questions. Birgit's competence in questioning was related to her discursive competence in the subject matter domain. For example, she covered nearly all of the domain-specific knowledge categories that a sociological study had revealed. But the question content was always mediated by the contingencies of discourse context and response/reaction patterns. Questioning ultimately scaffolded students' discursive competence.

In this episode, we notice how Birgit asks questions of the students that are unlike those that characterize school questioning sequences. Teacher questions are normally formatted: all participants in an exchange already know that the teacher's question is rhetorical, and that he or she already has the answer. Birgit's questions are open: she does not and cannot know the answer that students will provide. For example, she asks the three students about the purpose of the "leaning effect" exhibited by their tower or what the benefit would be to her if she bought their tower.

During one of our meetings, I asked if, as a collective, they could talk about this episode, what happened, and what could be learned from it.

Chris: So much positive you've got out of that, like I would go, "Why is it leaning?" Like I would be much more negative about that. That was really neat.

Birgit: I am realizing too that I might have stopped questioning a little earlier . . .
Chris: Well because of everything else that is going on in the classroom, and-
Birgit: But I thought they did really well anyway in answering the questions.
Chris: Yeah, but you were leading them along in a way that was positive. I know I tend to not give kids credit for having done it. They have worked on this, may be they have talked about football the whole time, but their thought has been in what they are doing, and I tend to down, I don't give them enough credit sometimes.
Birgit::   Well I think why I got into the "leaning" a bit, there, I have seen a lot of towers lean, it is easier to do that, and a lot of times people are really down on themselves because . . .
Chris: Oh, may be that is how I would feel, you know, I want my tower to be straight, that's good . . .
Birgit: But there may be some positive aspects, too.
I: You wanted to say something about one of the questions that Birgit was talking about.
Chris: Oh, I just mentioned to Alain that I was impressed with the questions you asked, right in the beginning, if I was to buy it . . .

Knowing the videotapes, I had wound the present one ahead to another situation in which Birgit interacted with children. That is, I created opportunities for teachers to talk about another, similar teaching episode and thereby "generalize" their understanding (though this is still local knowledge developed by the teachers).

I: This one here is a longer piece, this is one question that you used about twenty minutes later . . .
Chris: Oh, I did, because I really liked it, it was a great question. Yeah, thanks, but that put it into my being, instead of seeing it in the book, where I'd never use it. It made it become part of me, which is just that tremendously incredible fact . . .
Birgit: One example of the way it worked the opposite, it was really odd when you showed your little sheet of questions you used. Like the reminders about when you are questioning not to judge when you say "Good," that is something that I do all the time, and I really consciously I have taken this out . . .

Here, Birgit articulates how she had eliminated one aspect of her practice that she had come to note in this classroom, and in particular by watching herself on videotape interact with students. She had frequently responded to students' work with "Good," thereby working against her own attempts in challenging them.

Chris: Remember even when you first started you did that more than you do now, in total . . .?
Birgit: But also, the second thing was how to say, like how to get kids explain why they said something.

Chris: Yeah, I don't do *that* yet, I am not very good at that. You are way better,
           you started to draw out more the explanations the "Why are we doing
           that?" Remember in physical education yesterday, you asked "Why are we
           doing *this* this morning?" "Why do we want to know?" Like I asked the
           question "What is the, where is your tower gonna break?" and Birgit asked
           the question, "Why is it going to break?"

DIALECTIC OF UNDERSTANDING AND EXPLAINING

Understanding and explaining praxis are opposites and mutually constitute
each other; they form a unity even though they are exclusive opposites. That is,
primary understanding and distancing explanation stand in a dialectical relationship. But from this apparent contradiction of the unity of mutually exclusive
opposites, there is a tremendous potential for change and development. Let us
develop the two concepts and their relation for a moment following the work of
the philosopher Paul Ricœur (1991) and similar work by the critical psychologist Klaus Holzkamp (1991a).

Fundamental to these approaches is that understanding of praxis can only
arise from lived experience. Here understanding is used as knowing how rather
than knowing about. Knowing about praxis allows us to explain, in verbal and
other descriptions, salient elements and events of some situation. Knowing
about is always knowledge mediated by signs (psychologists used to say "representations"), whereas knowing how is the unmediated and absorbed coping in
the world as it presents itself in and through activities. Knowing about always
requires understanding of the situation that it is about. But to be significantly
enhanced, knowing how requires knowing about. That is, reflecting on praxis,
while it distances us from our experience, it allows us to objectify and analyze
it. But as we make this distancing move, our understanding is still there, providing the background sense that makes knowing about possible. Articulating
praxis in part by drawing on cultural knowledge developed in some domain allows us to increase our understanding, itself being tied to the lived experience of
praxis.

The notion of praxeology maintains the tie between lived experience and
analysis, between understanding and explaining. Praxeology replaces theory,
which was always considered as something separate from praxis. Praxeology is
an articulation of praxis out of the experience of praxis, by engaging in the dialectical process that links understanding and explaining. That is, the praxis of
coteaching/cogenerative dialoguing engages teachers in both phenomenological
and hermeneutic processes of delving into lived experience of teaching and articulating teaching through retrospection of events or by observing recorded
events made present again in the form of video images. In my way of conceiv-
ing of teaching, *praxeology* is more appropriate than "theory." Praxeology is
still talk *about* praxis and therefore removed from practical action. But praxeology is rooted in, and emergent from, praxis, involving practitioners who create

knowing about, through articulation of what they are doing, out of their experience of knowing how.

We therefore end up with a unity of two contradictory poles: the teacher's knowing in action as her or she is engaged in the praxis of teaching and his or her own ways of talking about this experience. However, contradictory poles that form a unity are a problem only to classical logic. They are not a problem at all to dialectical reasoning. In fact, contradictions within an entity can be driving forces for change. This then has tremendous implications for teacher training and development. Rather than having praxis follow theory (the currently dominant approach) or theory follow praxis (traditional) we have a unity that includes both. Rather than "removing" or "diminishing" the gap between lived experience and its explanation (praxeology) we exploit its positive potential for bringing about change in a dialectical fashion.

Many teaching practices are unarticulated. They remain as such unless, for various reasons, they are made conscious, that is, framed or articulated as practice. Their coteaching provided Chris and Birgit with many opportunities to make conscious aspects of their teaching. Once explicit, these aspects contributed to a change in their professional discourse in which they made sense of the classroom events. That is, cogenerative dialoguing allowed them to bring new elements into their discourse and with it, to understand what they are doing in new terms. In some instances, this articulation allowed them to link their practice to previously irrelevant theoretical knowledge; that is, they made sense of a theoretical statement based on their articulation of learning-in-practice. While the discourse of researchers who look into teaching from the outside is often characterized by distance, detachment, abstraction, and reflexive stance, the teachers in this study accounted for their knowing in practice and learning in practice by describing their actions in specific classroom episodes. These accounts were more like narratives rather than theoretical frames of practice.

In the course of their professional life, teachers develop practices of which they are not aware, but that constitute effective means of dealing with the complexities of classroom life. For Chris and Birgit, their lived experience of coteaching and watching videotaped classroom events became important settings for articulating aspects of their practice. For example, Chris notes "It was really neat with the videotape, to be able to see how there are things happening in the classroom that I can't see, that I don't know that they are happening." In her case, smiling at specific students while asking them to answer a question constituted one of her previously unarticulated practices. After watching a videotaped lesson, she remarks:

I didn't realize I smiled a lot. You know who I smile a lot at? Jeff. I noticed- that was one thing that went through my mind after I watched myself last night (on videotape). I thought I am always smiling at Jeff. I mean, I might ask a kid a question. But when I ask Jeff a question, I smile at him just to get us on a better footing, just right off the start. And another boy I do it with is . . .

Here, Chris notices for the first time that she smiled a lot, particularly at Jeff and several other boys. In the period between watching the videotape and talking about her observation, Chris had already constructed an explanation of her practice. Accordingly, she smiles a lot at these boys to provide a good start to the interaction. Her claim gains support in her description of Jeff, who "is extremely obstinate and reticent to do what he is told, loves to get into a power struggles, and seeks to antagonize teachers." Thus, after she made "smiling" a part of her professional discourse, she reconstructed a range of classroom events and interactions. The concomitant changes in her language and perceptions mutually constituted each other.

Chris and Birgit used the videotapes to analyze their teaching in specific terms, according to categories that became salient and of particular interest to them. This allowed them then to take a more "objective" look at their practices to monitor change. For example, after they had become aware of the gender issue in their class, Birgit took on the task to monitor their progress in this domain by "look[ing] at other videotapes, with that question in mind." Beside watching videotapes individually or together, Chris and Birgit began to articulate their own and each other's practices when they approached the same classroom event in different ways. In one instance, Chris had intervened in an interaction between Birgit and the class. Chris's unexpected actions encouraged Birgit to articulate, "I thought it was interesting because I would not have thought of it." Especially fruitful learning experiences arose when Chris and Birgit could talk about their practices immediately after the lesson, while still in the classroom. Often, these conversations developed over and about student-produced artifacts or in the presence of the concerned students. This presence gave these conversations, the reconstruction of classroom events, and associated construction of explanations an additional aspect of authenticity. Here, the immediacy of the experience, the availability of relevant artifacts, and the presence of another practitioner who had shared the experience, allowed Chris and Birgit to make conscious aspects of their questioning practices and to engage in a pedagogically useful reflection on action.

After having brought a particular practice into their discourse, Chris or Birgit could link it to a rule or theory which they had previously learned at university, but which did not yet describe an aspect of their practice. That is, they had "known" some proposition or theory, but it had had no significance in their practice. In their joint work, there were opportunities for making a link from practice to theory; that is, theoretical knowledge became meaningful as they constructed a practical equivalent or mapped their experience onto a previously meaningless (theoretical) language. One such opportunity arose from Birgit's practice to ask students questions such as, "Why are we asking you to make it that big [30 cm] span for bridge?" "Why do we ask you to hang the bucket in the center rather than elsewhere on the bridge?" or "Can you think of why we would set it up that way?" Chris spontaneously recognized the questions' value by commenting to the class, "Birgit's got great questions, right?" While reflecting on Birgit's practice, Chris recognized a link to something she had "known" (theoretically) before:

You just asked the kids, "Why are we doing that?" And I thought, "God damn, why didn't I ask that?" You know, that old Madeline Hunter, "Give the reason why you are doing it, model what you are doing, tell them to do it, and recap at the end." (Madeline Hunter's *Elements of Effective Instruction* was a popular program designed to help teachers teach better lessons, increase student involvement during learning, and increase achievement.)

However, although it was familiar (theoretical) knowledge that she had learned previously, this rule has not had an equivalent in her practice. A few days later, I observed that Chris began to ask similar questions. After two groups had "shared" their bridge constructions and responded to questions from their peers and teachers alike, Chris asked the students, "Why might it be important to share the bridges?" and "Why might it be important to share?"

When teachers talk about their work, they use their everyday discourse to describe events. Their talk lacks the distance, detachment, abstraction, or reflexive stance that characterize the discourse of most researchers and analysts. When they talk about their knowing or learning-in-action, Chris and Birgit do not talk in universals, but they provide accounts of specific events. These accounts stand as a whole, and it is for the listeners to draw a lesson about just what Chris or Birgit had learned. That is, their own biographical accounts are much closer to the lived experience than more removed descriptions such as those that characterize journal articles, and even more so those that use numbers to stand for the world of teaching.

When Chris and Birgit talked to each other, the slightest index is often sufficient to evoke an understanding how knowing in action had operated or how learning in action had come about. When I wanted to know about it, I had to ask the two to "tell the whole story." For example, when Birgit explained to a visitor what she had learned about timing, she immediately referred to the (earlier cited) event that had involved Dan. Chris knew immediately what Birgit referred to. By that time, after two months of coteaching, the two were so much in tune that such a reference sufficed to know what the other meant. When asked, they jointly constructed an account (narrative) of the event without being able to say what constituted the fine line between "extending Dan's thinking" and "putting him down," which Chris, but not Birgit, had recognized. All they could say was that in *that* situation, Chris had recognized it, and for Birgit it had constituted one aspect of her overall learning to time productive questions.

Over time, Birgit began to know the classroom in ways characteristic of Chris. Together they build up a repertoire of shared narratives growing out of their coteaching experience. Both used these narratives to respond to questions about their knowing in practice and learning in practice. While in their conversations it was often sufficient to reference an event in broadest strokes ("like with Dan") to communicate what they had learned, their narratives left unsaid exactly what had helped Birgit to get her timing right. The important aspect of the practice was implicit in the narrative and could be fully understood only if one had experienced the same situation. Even the enumeration of relevant background information only hinted at Chris's sense still absent from Birgit's practice. That is, knowing about Dan's learning disability, his impending departure for a special program, the many engineering techniques in his bridge, the extent of shared knowledge in the classroom community, and so on could not overcome the inherently indexical nature of their knowing in practice.

In the case of a particularly problematic issue in their teaching, providing equal learning opportunities for boys and girls, Chris and Birgit provided many accounts of specific events to talk about their praxis. They reconstructed events involving Patricia or Renata to illustrate that an increasing number of girls contributed to class discussions. They talked about the "keeners," Jeff, Tim, and Tom. They related situations in their own biographies to Carla, Kathy, and Renata to help me understand the conflicts they felt when asking girls to respond. Or they referred to a specific instance in which Chris had told Dan to "shut up" as part of her attempt to provide a safe environment for girls to engage in "risky" responses. Much of my learning about practice arose from participating in these classroom events. All participants in the classroom automatically knew all of that which Chris and Birgit's narratives left unsaid and provided the ground against which all their activities happened and made sense.

When Chris and Birgit actually made general statements about their practices, they usually followed up by describing concrete situations in which their practice differed. When they made a general statement such as "I (always) do this . . ." they invariably cited an instance that was not covered by their blanket statement or was contradicting it such as "one example where it worked the opposite . . ." Chris stated that she never asked that student to respond who put his or her hand up first, only to add, "but sometimes I do," and then provided descriptions of situations where it was appropriate to ask the first person. She said that she followed the rule, be consistent (e.g., following up on what she told students), but modified the strength of this assertion by providing the narrative of a situation in which she felt uncomfortable with this rule and did not apply it.

In these early stages, students had not been part of the cogenerative-dialoguing sessions. However, the need to include students emerged while I collaborated with Kenneth Tobin, who had instituted coteaching/cogenerative dialoguing as the paradigm for science teacher education at the University of Pennsylvania. It turned out that unless students participated in taking an active part in making sense and in collective responsibility, changes made to the classroom context would always be experienced as an imposition. This was a contradiction that led us to change our practice of cogenerative dialoguing, for if we wanted change to occur, students had to be part of designing it. We therefore began to invite student representatives.

COGENERATIVE DIALOGUING WITH STUDENTS

True transformation of the classroom cannot happen without also involving students. Trying different ways of arranging these cogenerative dialogue sessions, we ended up feeling that those situations involving two student representatives turned out to be the most productive sessions. We know neither why this would be the case nor have we worked out all the kinks in the system. For example, on the one hand we think that different students should be involved over the course of several weeks and months. On the other hand, changing students continuously does not allow for an "institutional memory" and the associated practices that go with it to build up within the group.

The following episode comes from one of our research projects in an urban school (almost all African-American students, from areas with high rates of poverty, unemployment, and crime). Four of us had taught a science lesson involving two parts: a student-centered inquiry and a whole-class session on genetics. At the moment of this episode, Tania is a teacher in training with some previous teaching experience in a private school; Tony, a thirty-year veteran teacher in urban schools is her supervising teacher. Peter is a university professor and Tania's methods professor, who also supervises her in the field. My role is that of coteacher and researcher, spending time at the high school to learn about teaching in urban schools employing the coteaching methodology. Sandy and Sally are two students from the tenth-grade class. All of use had been present in the same lesson. One of the issues raised was the problem of students not getting enough attention, falling behind. Coteaching was being discussed as one of the approaches in which the problem could be addressed. This episode, which is only part of the entire dialogue on this topic, is rather typical for the way these sessions have been enacted by us in that context.

Tania begins this episode asking the two students whether they prefer one class with several teachers or breaking the class so that each group (in separate rooms) works with a different teacher.

Tania: Do you like the change, how does it make feel you when there are multiple teachers teaching together?
Sandy: This is more helpful.
Peter: Is it good to divide the class, one teacher on each side or is it better all three teaching the combined class?
Sandy: That's what I think, I think the combined class, because the whole class would just be together.
Sally: All do the same . . . experiment, because . . .
Sandy: Yeah, because people . . .
Sally: from Miss Lee's class go, "Oh, we don't get to do stuff like that." "Yeah, they get to do that stuff but we don't."
Sandy: Like they get to throw sandwiches but we don't, because their teacher don't give them as many activities. So I think if the combined class was, you never know, like it might more people like the thing and they catch on.

Sally: And then we could move to different groups, only in one class.
Tania: Sort of on a lesson by lesson basis?
Sally: Yeah.

In this situation, Sandy and Sally carry much of the development of the topic. Sandy and Sally, as other students in our research, agree that having all students in the same class leads to less differentiation and gives rise to more learning opportunities. All students would engage in the same type of activities and yet have multiple opportunities of interacting with various teachers. In a sense, what the students suggest is contrary to the ideology of "decreasing class size." Rather, in this context, students are comfortable with larger classes, on the one hand, and appreciate multiple learning opportunities that arise when there are multiple teachers available for interacting with them.

The conversation continues to unfold and the participants provide each other with the space to talk. Here in this case, it was evident that the student wanted to develop their ideas about the different proposals made by them or others, and arrive at possible alternatives for teaching in a different way, making different structural arrangements that benefit all students. Peter, fully subscribing to the notion of learning by being with and coteaching, then suggests that he is in favor of all students and teachers being in the same room.

Peter: This is my opinion, too, especially if we pushed back the partition, then, if we had more people like you (Sally), and you have three teachers who can deal with those who are not catching on . . .
Sandy: Yeah.
Peter: . . . and sometimes Tony's got the best explanation, sometimes Tania has the best explanation. But sometimes, for some people, another teacher will have the best explanation. So I kind of like to have more people together. But, we scientists, we don't have proof to say this is better than that. So what do you think, Tony, that you just had their input?
Tony: I still like really small groups. You know.
I: From your perspective why would that be?
Tony: Get more attention to the kids.
Sally: Yeah.
Tony: I am just afraid that in a large group of thirty that you know, that they don't get the needed attention (*Makes a gesture that indicates "separation" or "segregation."*) I mean, that is what my fear is. It may not materialize but when I have a group of fifteen and one, you know, the one teacher is going to know what is going on with everyone of those fifteen kids.
Sally: It's just like having a big class with three teachers.
Tony: That's true.
Sally: It's basically the same thing.
Sandy: It has the kids divided in the whole group, like Miss Tania says, like me I like the reports, that's easy to me, she (Sally) likes the DNA and similar things. And I think that if everybody likes something, sit together in a group. And the people, who catch on fast to what she likes, sit with her, and she can help them and not only y'all (teachers and professors).

Tony: Yeah, if you had the one large class and with three teachers, then we would basically break down into groups. Like that's what you are asking?

Sally: Yeah, yeah.

Tony: So you want to get more groups there?

Sally: Yeah.

Peter: And if two or three groups are working ok, then the teachers can put their resources over into the groups that are not. And I suppose there is a chance to have "wandering experts," who catch on quickly, and you (Sandy) might be the wandering expert on the report writing, and so . . .

Let us take a brief look on what happened in this situation, because I think it is remarkable given the historically different locations that students, teachers, and university professors take when they interact. Here, the teacher Tony declares a preference that is opposite to the one earlier espoused by the students and subsequently the professor Peter. I served here as a facilitator to elicit a further elaboration from Tony—an elaboration with which Sally whole-heartedly agreed. Sally later suggested that in terms of student to teacher ratio, there was really no difference between having each teacher take a small group or all teachers teaching one large class. In this situation, there is not only space for Sally to disagree with her teacher in an open way, but there is also room for Sandy to develop an alternative approach in which students like Sally or herself participate in teaching. Tony begins to realize that at least those students present have a preference for large groups with several teachers. This and many other suggestions made by students contributed to the changes that were brought about by teachers and students in *this* classroom. This change is all the more remarkable as Tony had been teaching for thirty years and learned, despite the adage that "you don't teach an old dog new tricks" or a common conception of longtime teachers as resisting change.

The fact that students participated did not change the way we used the heuristics. In fact, after we introduced the heuristics students like Sally and Sandy immediately noted that they while they were enacting many of the items on the list, they were not asking critical questions (Table 8.1, item #4.4). The heuristics therefore became a tool for us to allow students to interact in different ways with other stakeholders in the classroom and to make the cogenerative dialogue sessions even more fruitful.

EPILOGUE

In this chapter, I presented the second aspect of coteaching, cogenerative-dialogue sessions as a space in which teachers and students can develop their primary understanding of praxis by critically interrogating shared—though from different positions—experience. The generalizations arising out of these experiences by means of critical (hermeneutic) analysis stand in a dialectical relationship to the lived experience that is the topic of talk. In the following chapter, I focus on the opportunities for becoming in the classroom as a result of the dynamic of development that arises from contradictory unity of praxis and praxeology.

Qualitative researchers often use negotiation and triangulation procedures to establish common understandings of certain events. In cogenerative dialoguing as I practice it with my collaborators, the goal is not to arrive at a common understanding and to attempt to negotiate until everyone agrees with a particular understanding. What is more important to us is to understand different ways of viewing events as a result of the different ways in which participants are positioned and as a function of their different experiences. This means, we take different understandings as arising from a structural (explanatory) analysis rather than as opposite viewpoints that are somehow psychological characteristics. For example, it makes little sense to presuppose that a female African American tenth-grade student should see and experience the events in a biology classroom in the same way as a white middle-class professor of education. Furthermore, it makes little sense to presuppose that the experiences of the former are any less authentic than the experiences of the latter. For me, the way out of the quagmire is to approach each understanding as the result of a dialectical relation of cultural-historical process and individual development.

Teacher development can be understood in the same way. At any moment, the teacher Self is the product of previous tensions of individual development and cultural-historical processes. In this, opportunities for teacher development arise from another dialectical tension that opposes knowledge arising from coteaching and knowledge arising from cogenerative dialoguing. Coteaching/cogenerative dialoguing and the associated dialectical unit of Praxis/praxeology provides some useful tools for rethinking the theory-praxis gap. I attend to this task in the next chapter.

9

Praxis and Praxeology

> Identity is merely the determination of the simple immediate, of dead being; but contradiction is the root of all movement and life, and it is only in so far as it contains a contradiction that anything moves and has impulse and activity. (Hegel 1969: 67)
>
> The philosophers have only interpreted the world in various ways; the point is to change it. (Marx and Engels 1970: 123)

Scientific research and the expectation to use scientific knowledge for improving living conditions and changing human practices have gone hand in hand; how this knowledge will help has become more complicated and problematic (Chaiklin 1993). As my second opening quote shows, some have characterized science (philosophy) as interpretive work that neglects to change social practice—even today, practitioners often deplore the uselessness of university-based research. Seth Chaiklin also pointed to an increasingly complex gap between knowledge and the practices it is supposed to describe. In this chapter, I propose a new (to teacher education) approach to the theory-practice gap that has riddled educational theorizing. Taking a different route to understanding than classical logic, the dialectical approach embodies contradictions, which as Hegel pointed out, "is the root of all movement and life." I propose praxis/praxeology as a dialectical category that can actually drive teacher development, which I conceive of in terms of "legitimate peripheral participation" that begins when an individual decides to become a teacher. To lay the groundwork for my argument, I begin, consistent with the cultural-historical tradition, by analyzing how the split between theory and praxis of teaching has come about. I argue that there is no way out of the contradictions embodied in current forms of teacher education. A different way of understanding the relationship between knowing to teach and knowing about teaching is necessary, leading to a different conception of learn-

ing to teach, which we portray as an ongoing process of development and
change in praxis.

BRIEF HISTORY OF THE SEPARATION OF
PRAXIS AND THEORY OF TEACHING

Before the mid-1800s no particular preparation was thought necessary to
prepare an individual to teach. Individuals should be able to teach up to the
level that they had themselves attained. Until that time, children learned by participating in family life and sometimes were taught by their older siblings. In
colonial America teacher ability ranged from bare literacy to college education.
Female teenagers adept at academic subjects were customarily appointed to supervise a classroom because women were thought to possess innate abilities and
dispositions that were ideally suited to care and raise the young. Young men,
frequently having attended schools for a longer period, were often appointed to
teach the higher grades. In these initial stages, teaching was a craft without formal craft knowledge. Praxis existed without theory and therefore predated theory. Before any theories of education began to develop, there already existed
considerable lived experience of teaching and practical knowledge produced and
reproduced in concrete situations where new teachers learned from old-timers in
the field. These early forms of praxis provided the ground for subsequent theorization to evolve.

The development of parochial schools, the increasing number of their students, the absence of methods that allow a regulation of whole-class activities,
and the associated confusion and disorder all demanded assistance for the
teacher. The best students in a class, among whom various tasks related to
teaching were divided, provided such assistance. This organization was also apparent in the Lancastrian monitorial system, characterized by the presence of a
master teacher aided by monitors in the instruction of students. The creation of
such systems entailed more than a mere division of labor to facilitate the task of
the teacher; it also permitted some students to become familiar with teaching
practices. This division of labor is very similar to that which had occurred in the
shops of master craftsmen, where apprentices and journeymen both learned the
essential practices and contributed to the work that had to be done. It also came
with economic advantages because the helpers constituted cheap labor.

In the nineteenth century, changes in teacher education became more rapid.
The number and popularity of common schools grew and, with it, the need for
qualified teachers. In the early part of the century, emerged the need to produce
more teachers to staff the schools and the belief that teachers needed to be prepared differently. Simultaneously, American educators became familiar with the
Prussian seminaries, where students were familiarized with principles of education and were given the opportunity to practice teaching. Based on the Prussian
seminary principle, normal schools emerged where teaching was regarded as a
profession that required specialized preparation not obtainable elsewhere. Normal

schools also met the need to change the general perception that teaching was a lesser occupation and teachers were cheaper, more replaceable, and less knowledgeable than were other professionals. Normal schools frequently were associated with "practice" or "model" schools, where prospective teachers got their first teaching experiences. Many graduates of leading normal schools became teachers at other normal schools. Although this separation of praxis and learning about praxis constitutes a form of division of labor, the fact that normal school teachers most frequently were experienced teachers did not lead to a strong separation of theory and praxis. Knowledge about teaching retained its strong ties to teaching praxis, as those who taught embodied the knowledge they were teaching about.

In normal schools, practice teaching occurred prior to formal training. Implicitly, normal schools followed a materialist epistemology in which (abstract) knowledge followed lived experience (Engels 1970). However, in the context of a rising industrialism, normal schools found themselves in a precarious situation. They were criticized for a lack of theoretical foundations and rigor. Increasingly, the industrialization of society demanded a trained labor force suitable to fill the jobs in an ever-expanding market place. Educators began to adopt principles that paralleled the laws of scientific management designed to increase work efficiency through orderly behavior and scientific decision making. Associated with this adoption was a shift in the relative importance that knowing to teach and knowing about teaching. The division of labor between school-based teachers and university-based teacher educators and associated struggles for the primacy of formal and practical knowledge led to a separation of practical mastery and symbolic mastery, which also characterized other professions. This separation of praxis and knowledge about praxis into different professions is the result of a division of labor made possible by the shift from the environment as the determinant of individual development to society as the primary unit that needed to be maintained, preserved, and developed.

The principles of scientific management were eventually applied to education, and a need was recognized for teacher training. Teachers needed to understand and carry out the instructions of the school administrators; scientific management became a means to effect curriculum and teaching. Lesson plans became important instructional tools that could be taught to prospective teachers in a recipe-like fashion that were subsequently to be turned into practice by the individual. The emerging field of psychology also laid claims to providing theoretical knowledge foundational to education. For example, Edward Lee Thorndike (1912) suggested that correct habits could be built through exercise and drill—teaching was seen as supervision of this process. He viewed teaching as a science concerned with the control of human behavior and that it was possible to make scientific measurements of the results.

Many believed that teaching needed to be made more scientific and teachers needed to employ methods that were shown to be effective. Normal schools were associated with an unscientific approach to education and were too strongly associated with local community control. Under this pressure, teacher-training institutions evolved throughout the twentieth century. In the 1920s, state teacher colleges emerged from normal schools, and subsequently transformed into state colleges and state universities. Associated with this shift was another one in the relative importance of theory and praxis of teaching. For example, the field experience part of teacher training decreased from thirty-three percent to fifteen percent at Keene Normal School from 1915 to 1944. Following the model of Teachers College at Columbia University, the practical and theoretical components of college- and university-based teacher-education curriculum changed. Whereas field experience preceded the acquisition of theoretical knowledge during the normal-school years, it became an appendix after the universities took over the training of teachers. University-based teacher education now embodies an idealist approach: a teacher's being in the classroom is being explained by his knowing. Theory was said to drive praxis rather than praxis providing the substance that a teacher theorizes. Sensuous objective activity is represented *as the consequence*, as the *external objectification of ideas*, plans, and concepts created by thought, rather than the other way around (Il'enkov 1977).

The emergence, proliferation, and perpetuation of practice teaching as a culminating experience outside of the university context created many contradictions. One contradiction arises from the division of labor associated with the split between university-based acquisition of theory and school-based acquisition of praxis. In schools, frequently untrained classroom teachers supervise them without receiving appropriate rewards. The future teachers often find themselves caught in the conflict between what their cooperating teachers tell them and the idealist recommendations made by university supervisors (whom they see much less frequently). As "student" teachers, they are reluctantly accepted into schools where they are often considered as lesser teachers.

Associated with the division of labor between schools and university relative to teacher education is the exacerbation of the dichotomy between theory and practice and the low regard school-based teachers and university educators (supervisors, methods teachers) hold for each other. University educators are said to be out of touch with the realities of teaching and their theories are said to have little value to practice. Practicing teachers are said to be unreflective and driven by seemingly immediate demands of schooling and reproduction of knowledge rather than education and understanding. Such opposition and hostility arises as a result of the division of labor between "active members" and "thinkers," who make up illusions and ideas about active members (Marx and Engels 1970). These difficulties are commonly heard in student critiques of teacher education programs as well as nationwide evaluations of teacher education. Prospective teachers often express frustration about being in schools where pedagogical and curricular principles contradict those espoused in the university courses.

Hand in hand with the separation of theory and practice came the increasing control over teaching by school (board) administrators and legislators. Curriculum content has become increasingly specified. Teachers have become executioners of highly specified plans. In some districts, teachers have to synchronize their activities so that competence tests can be administered simultaneously to students across the school board. It is well known that such rationalized work leads to alienation, which manifests itself in low levels of motivation or in drop out from the profession (Kuutti 1999).

The separation of theory and practice has led to two forms of mastery. There is symbolic mastery over the object, such as when teachers and university professors talk about teaching outside of teaching itself. But symbolic mastery is not mastery of the thing, teaching, and given the complaints teachers have about the theory-praxis gap, there may be little in common between symbolic mastery and real mastery of teaching. Individuals who master practice only formally, in terms of a rigid pattern and sequence of operations, without understanding its origins and links with real activity, are incapable of bringing about changes in the way curriculum is enacted. The conflation of real and symbolic mastery makes it possible to slur over the fundamental, philosophical, epistemological difference between material activity and the activity of the theoretician and ideologist who directly alters only the verbal, token objectification of the ideal image. In addition to the separation is the work in which each side of the debate declares its knowledge superior to that of the other.

In the final analysis, the contradictory nature of problems in teaching and teacher development can be reduced to contradictions that exist in an economically founded, bourgeois society and its lifeform. For example, despite the obvious benefits of coteaching or smaller student-teacher ratios to learning and professional satisfaction, costs are always cited as insurmountable for changing educational praxis in this way. The shortcomings and costs of such policies are ultimately born by the children and burned-out teachers.

Despite considerable work over the past several decades, education remains stuck in the theory-praxis gap. Both approaches to teacher education, praxis before theory and theory before praxis, have the same historical roots in an idealist epistemology that splits theory and praxis. Despite their contradictory form, they are both concrete embodiments of the same ideology. Any usable attempt to overcome the gap between theory and practice needs to analyze and theorize the relationship between concrete (i.e., available to lived experience) conditions of praxis and the actions that pertain to them. Theories that do not account for this connection are doomed to fail to pass the ultimate test—the tension between lived experience and categories of understanding it. To theorize praxis means to establish the structural relationship between the local contexts and concrete actions that these afford to practitioners. Research that attempts to understand praxis, by closely attending to the social and material contexts that situate this praxis, is likely to develop descriptions that are directly useful in that practice. However one approaches it, the dichotomy of theory and praxis is an idealist pit from which there is no escape. Only a dialectical logic allows an escape from this quandary. In a dialectic logic, contradictory pairs of concepts are not only accepted as single conceptual units but contradictions actually drive development. Contradictions, rather than being problems, are the real growth points in human activities such as teaching.

THEORY AND PRACTICE

In the sciences, the precise correspondence between measurements and their objective referents are taken for granted. That is, there is a fundamental isomorphism between theories and the world that they describe. This isomorphism implies that any operation accomplished in one domain, for example in theory, has a corresponding phenomenon in the other domain. In popular discourse, one can often hear comments on an action to be taken, "In theory, this should work."

Based on the model of the natural sciences, psychological theory was often constructed in terms of the relationship between measures of different psychosocial constructs, which are defined in terms of the relationship between operationally defined variables. Typically, research then finds correlations and causal relations between pairs of variables—individually or in complex structurally related sets of variables. As a result, researchers make statements such as "[The] classroom and school environment was found to be a strong predictor of both achievement and attitudes even when a comprehensive list of other factors was held constant" (Fraser 1998: 544). That is, individual actions are understood as being determined by environment, attitudes, intelligence, and so on. In these models, individual human beings are no longer in control of their actions, and therefore their lives, but whatever they do—barring "error" variation—is predetermined. Subjectivity is the main source of extraneous variation, which investigators have to limit by means of experimental control. Even in single-subject designs, "it is not 'I' as I experience myself and my world here and now that is represented; rather, values are calculated from my life situations and translated into distributional characteristics in order to make them amenable to statistical evaluation" (Holzkamp 1991b: 70). The very human feature that enables us to go this or that way (e.g., as articulated by Robert Frost in the poem, "The Road not Taken") is eliminated and becomes error variance. Although most teachers have not articulated critiques of such approaches to understanding the complexity of teaching, they are nevertheless opposed to such research. I do not want to engage in a critique of this approach to theorizing teachers and teaching. Suffice it to say that such approaches eliminate the object-relatedness of human activity and the possibility that the individual subject acts in a conscious way with respect to the objects of its activity.

There are two main problems in the existing theory-practice relationship. First, in the idealist tradition, real human life activity takes its particular form because humans are said to think and act in accordance with specific schemata (or worse, to be predetermined in the way correlational and causal models predict). Human beings are said to implement intentions and plans, which are said to be predictable to a great extent. In this model, human beings are cultural dopes whose behavior is pre-determined. This approach to human actions as determined by contextual factors is most clearly implemented in statistical models of social and psychological theories. Although others have critiqued this relation between plans and (situated) actions before, ethnomethodologists have repeatedly made the point that human beings are not cultural dopes who blindly implement plans and societal rules. The second problem is that theory, defined in terms of the intersection of common attributes, does not recognize underlying commonalities based on different criteria of universality.

The relationship between theory and praxis in formalist and dialectical framework was analyzed by the Russian philosopher Ewald Il'enkov (1982) in terms of the equivalent relationship between the general (universal) and the particular. In traditional thought, the general (concept) is based on common, general features of concrete objects (particulars); that is, the (set-theoretic) intersection of concrete objects constitute the general. (Many so-called "intelligence tests" include items that ask individuals to detect the similarities and differences in some set of items.) Family resemblance therefore characterizes the idea of the general, which is made up of abstract *attributes*. The characteristics common to different particulars are by definition "abstract" (Lat., *abstrahere, ab-*, "away" and *trahere*, "draw"), that is, drawn away and independent of the particular. The general is therefore completely isolated and separate from the particular—the general really ceases to be the theoretical expression of the concrete.

Universality can also be defined on genetic grounds so that a category may include rather dissimilar individual items. Different items are in the same category because of their common material historical origins, that is, by virtue of their common ancestors. Despite apparent differences between the particulars of dog, wolf, fox, and coyote, all are part of the *Canidae* family; in evolutionary terms, they have the same common ancestor. The genetic formulation has the advantage that the universal and particular are embodied in the same individual. The general is not formulated in abstract attributes, removed from concrete world, but is made of the same concrete material as the particular is. Understood in this way, universality does not mean silent and generic sameness of individuals. Rather, universality is "reality repeatedly and diversely broken up within itself into particular (separate) spheres mutually complementing each other and in essence mutually dependent on each other and therefore linked together by bonds of community of origin . . ." (Il'enkov 1977: Chapter 11).

Differences between individuals can therefore be attributed to the different conditions that—speaking in evolutionary terms—gave form to different phenotypic expression of a common form. Different subjective experiences in the same classroom can be theoretically grounded in common psychosocial categories that are expressed in different ways due to differences in socio-historical locations of the individuals. The general in human beings expresses itself in the concrete form of their interaction, as an intersubjectivity that predates (and is constitutive of) individual human subjectivity. The general includes and embodies in itself the wealth of details, not just in the form of ideas but as real and particular phenomena. In the tension that exists between the general and the particular within each individual human being also lies, as in all dialectic units, the necessity (rather than opportunity) for its self-development.

Materialist (evolutionary) approaches recognize that praxis precedes, from a cultural-historical perspective, the theory that is used to describe and explain it. Theory needs to be a function of practice, and in turn, needs to serve practice. Thus, social practice is the test bed of theory, which itself is created out of practice (articulation of praxis). Only those who participate in a social practice truly can understand it. Thus, ethnomethodologists point out time and again that investigators do not inductively generate knowledge about some situation but their existing knowledge about the situation makes them select what becomes data and lets them interpret whatever they collected.

To know something, one must personally participate in the practical struggle to change reality, to change that something, for it is only through participation in the practical struggle to change reality that you can uncover the essence of that thing and comprehend it. Members of society have (mundane) theories of reality that allow them to navigate the complexities of everyday life. Since their theories have not been constructed according to agreed-upon rules valid in the scientific community, these theories were at best counted as merely subjective but usually more as "misconceptions," "naïve theories," or "alternative theories." The conflict between academic and mundane conceptions of social reality is normally resolved in the theorists' favor. In this viewpoint developed by critical psychologists and ethnomethodologists, the relationship between theory and practice is different. Theory (of the hermeneutic kind that we discuss below) is thereby a resource for future action rather than determining it. The social actor is a practical actor who uses what he finds to navigate the contingencies of everyday life and work. The degree of fit between situated action and theory-based plan is thereby always a matter of a posteriori analysis rather than a matter of prediction. To be useful in praxis, theory therefore has to become a resource that allows individual human beings to increase the range of actions available. That is, theory has to be judged in terms of the increase in Spielraum that it provides the individual actor. Coteaching is a way of developing understanding of practice through participation in the praxis of teaching. Coteaching is not merely a way to generate understanding but is an explicit contribution to the task of teaching—facilitating the learning of students.

Spielraum, room to maneuver, as a praxeological concept arises from agency, itself a fundamental psychosocial category in critical psychology constructed through a historical analysis of hominid evolution to the emergence of society and culture (Holzkamp 1983). It encapsulates my experience of having an increasing number of possibilities to act, an increasing amount of room to maneuver, as I was teaching. I noticed that other teachers, too, described similar experiences whereby they "could go this way or that way" in particular classroom situations. Spielraum therefore characterizes teacher experiences as we move through our first years of teaching, is an experientially real category, which, upon reflection, assists teachers in making salient those resources that help them to increase their agency. Spielraum develops in response to the tension between the demands of the situation and our limitations in coping with them. Although Spielraum has turned out to be a viable category for understanding teacher development, it still does not take us far enough. We still lack the "engine" that drives (lifelong) teacher development. This driving force arises from the contradictions residing in dialectically related modes of knowing in teaching and knowing about teaching.

DIALECTICAL LOGIC

Georg Friedrich Hegel (1969) developed dialectics as method of reasoning in its modern form. Dialectics aims to understand phenomena concretely, in all their movement, change and interconnection, with opposite and contradictory sides as constitutive parts of the same unit. In the idea of the unity of opposites, dialectical logic recognizes that all processes and phenomena of the social and natural world embody contradictory, mutually exclusive and opposite tendencies. In dialectical logic, contradictions are not evils but the engine of development. That is, development arises from the resolution of contradictions and conflict.

Hegel recognized that human beings have the capacity to look at themselves, from the outside so to speak, as something "other" or a special object. This capacity also entails the possibility to change forms of activity and the context in which activity occurs. This capacity is made possible because humans also relate to the world in societally mediated ways rather than in the immediate ways animals do.

Up to a certain point, man is able to change the form of his activity . . . without touching the thing itself, but only because he can separate the ideal image from himself, objectify it, and operate with it as with an object existing outside him. (Il'enkov 1977: Chapter 8)

That is, humans have the capacity to transform the schemas of their own activity into object of their own. This capacity arises from the fact that humans do not simply enter immediate relationships with the objects of their inquiry, but the tools (e.g., language, material tools) that society bequeaths them with from the beginning mediate subject-object relationships. In a division of labor, where knowledge of an activity and knowledge about the activity are no longer in the same person, this capacity is institutionalized. Thus, some individuals are the productive subjects in some activity system, whereas other individuals take this activity system as an object of inquiry. That is, the latter individuals are themselves subjects but, because the objects in their productive activity are different, are so in a different—though neighboring—activity system. Problems arise when the subjects in one activity system, teaching, feel that the subjects in another activity system objectified them, for example, researchers or university-

based supervisors of new teachers. My interest in coteaching/cogenerative dialoguing is partially related to the new roles that are made possible for researchers, supervisors, methods teachers, and evaluators. Individuals in these roles no
longer have to stand on the sidelines, objectifying students, teachers, and their
lifeworlds, but participate in the activity to enhance student learning. At the
same time, they view teaching from the inside, granted that they take part in the
collective responsibility for scaffolding student learning. From this perspective,
in praxis, they can appreciate and understand the particular practical constraints
that are characteristic of teaching praxis.

A dialectic approach to the praxis of teaching has the advantage that development (of praxis and practitioner) automatically becomes an inherent feature.
Practical knowledge and praxeology are two forms of knowledge that stand in a
dialectical relationship because praxeology, an articulation of praxis, is always
partial, never quite able to catch up with praxis. In our work, praxeology is formulated based on praxis and praxis is enacted through praxeology. One does not
precede the other, if one exists both must exist. Praxeology separated from
praxis is anti-social and anti-realist. Contradictions are the driving force of development and evolution of activity systems. The dialectical tension between
the mutually contradictory elements in the praxis/praxeology unit gives rise to
development and evolution. Rather than focusing on teaching as being-in the
world, we therefore rethink teaching in the form of the praxis/praxeology unit as
a becoming-in the world of the classroom.

Hermeneutic phenomenology is an analytic methodology that goes well
with coteaching/cogenerative dialoguing because it is also based on a dialectical
relationship: understanding, which comes from lived experience, and explanation, which comes from and involves reflexive critical (hermeneutic) analysis.
The relationship between embodied understanding and explanation is dialectical
and mutually constitutive: explanation always requires understanding as a pre-
requisite, but explanation develops understanding in an analytic way, and is
grounded in the history of the discipline. That is, explanation is enveloped (preceded, accompanied, and concluded) by understanding which arises from our
practical engagement in the world of teaching. However, understanding also requires explanation to be further developed lest we become trapped in understandings that take the forms of ideology—we therefore have to be suspicious of ideology and radically doubtful regarding immediate understandings. Explanation-
seeking efforts are not simply based on common sense, or folk knowledge, but
draw on everything that the history of thought on the subject has produced. Local knowledge and research/theoretical knowledge interplay, which enriches and
develops both forms of knowledge.

The generation of knowledge through hermeneutic elaboration of primary
understanding does not stop there. Knowledge begins with practice, and theoretical knowledge is acquired through practice, but must return to practice. The
problem of whether theory corresponds to practice cannot be solved in the induc-
tive movement from praxis to praxeology. Rather, the only way to solve the

problem of relevance is to redirect the knowledge constructed through critical hermeneutic analysis to social practice. It is only when theory allows us to achieve the objectives we have in mind that it shows its usefulness. But if social practice is changed, further research is required for understanding. Social practice paired with cogenerative dialogue is a continuously evolving becoming. We therefore arrive at a framework that includes multiple parallel levels of conceptualization. The two concepts in each pair are mutually exclusive; one cannot be the same as the other. Even teacher-generated praxeology is about praxis rather than praxis itself.

PRAXIS/PRAXEOLOGY AS DIALECTICAL UNIT

"Schools institutionalize, and are predicated on, widespread beliefs about learning that are called in questions by views of learning as situated activity" (Lave 1997: 127). Teacher education practices are aimed a transforming participation in schools, settings other than the university classroom; to understand the relation between the two, we must investigate ongoing practices in both, and how each is in part created in the other. I extend this criticism to university-based teacher education programs. The traditional approach to teacher education, built on the separation of theory and praxis, led to the idea that learning and development stopped once an individual had receive the university diploma. I propose a dialectical approach, because it builds continuous learning and development into the very definition and praxis of teaching. As a result of conceptualizing teaching in terms of the praxis/praxeology unit, becoming in the classroom is an ongoing project that does not have a defined starting point and ends when a teacher withdraws from active service. As a dialectical unit, praxis/praxeology aligns itself with the other dialectical units discussed in the literature (Table 9.1).

The driving force for change is the fact that praxis and praxeology can never be the same: praxeology is always talk *about* praxis, generated in an activity with different though related central motives than praxis itself.

Discussions about the relationship between theory and praxis in terms of their separation by a gap go hand in hand with chicken-and-egg–type discussion about the temporal order of practice teaching and theory courses. One has to acknowledge the impossibility of engaging in a practice and simultaneously making this practice an object of reflection. There will therefore always have to be at least a temporal shift in the praxis of teaching and the praxis of reflecting on this teaching. At the same time, if we are interested in the continuing development of teachers then articulating the induction of teacher in terms of the dialectical praxis/praxeology unit requires an engagement in both types of activities. On the on hand, there is the lived experience of teaching praxis. On the other hand, there is the hermeneutic experience of analyzing teaching with others in cogenerative fashion, a process from which grows conceptual understandings *about* praxis.

Table 9.1
Dialectical Pairs of Concepts Relating to Theory-Practice

Dialectical Unit		Source
Lived experience	Hermeneutic experience	
Praxis	Theory	Marx and Engels 1970
World	Language	Latour 1993
Understanding	Explaining	Ricœur 1991
Praxis	Praxeology	Roth, Lawless, and Tobin 2001
Coteaching	Cogenerative dialoguing	Roth and Tobin 2001b

Approaches to psychology consistent with the dialectic approach situate (local) theory building in practice and through the eyes of the practitioner. I am not advocating here that theory building should be abandoned altogether. Rather, I suggest that we generalize descriptions of praxis but do so grounded in experience and in ways understandable to practitioners, who thereby are empowered by having available new possibilities for action. These explanations of praxis, grounded in and developed out of praxis, constitute praxeology, (principled) talk about praxis. The potential danger of describing practice from the position of the practitioner is one where we might submit to a primacy of primary experience and the understanding associated with it. But this is not my intent. Rather, these primary understandings, while they constitute a crucial element have to be developed through reflexive critical hermeneutic analysis. Critical hermeneutic analysis takes the attitudes of "radical doubt" and "suspicion of ideology" toward the primary understanding—lest we are to end up in ideological (uncritical and unreflexive) understandings. However, critical hermeneutic analysis presupposes primary understanding such that it really is a hermeneutic phenomenological analysis.

REVISING PRACTICAL KNOWLEDGE

Practitioners have experiences that they, as all human beings, reflect upon. However, in most instances, these reflections are in terms of immediate understandings arising from the lifeworld to be described. These reflections will remain limited because they neglect to account for lived experience as mediated by society (including rules, community, division of labor, and tools). Received forms of describing concrete praxis are unreliable and have to be developed by means of yet-to-be developed instruments of description. The necessary culture of representation has yet to be created. Such personal reflections can rarely be represented in collective forms and therefore be subjected to discussion and used by others. As a result, there are differences not only in content but also in the forms of representing praxis. Differences in opinion, power relationships, and interpersonal conflicts remain outside of the understanding of praxis, whereas structural analysis would attempt to articulate such differences in terms of the personal histories, societally mediated location of individuals, and so forth. Research in praxis needs to be concerned with generalizable aspects of concrete action contexts that make recognizable typical structures and possibilities for change, which are tested by those concerned in and as of exemplary praxis. The analysis of experience is rooted in assumptions about the categorical nature of praxis (i.e., its ontology); these categories determine what is salient in the reality of praxis and what can be learned from experience.

Let us return to the cogenerative-dialoguing session featured in the previous chapter (pp. 154–155), in which the students Sally and Sandy make suggestions about organizing their science class that were different from what their teacher, Tony, was doing. In this situation, the point of discussion concerns the best way of organizing the class given that there are at least three teachers available. Tony suggests that small groups working in separate physical locations are preferable from his perspective because that would allow him to give more attention to individual students. However, without feeling threatened that Tony was a senior teacher in the school, they disagreed with him. First, Sandy articulated the objection that the teacher-student ratio remained the same whether the class was broken into three groups, each with one teacher, or the whole class stayed together with all three teachers present. Peter added that in this case, the teachers would be available as learning resources to those students who needed their expertise the most, and students could also become teachers thereby increasing the learning resources in the class. At this point, the group did not analyze whether these student preferences were also related to cultural patterns. Throughout the session, however, students repeatedly voiced their preferences to remain together as a whole class and to divide the teacher resources within the large class.

In this excerpt, there are not only teachers coming to new understandings about teaching but also students who learn to theorize the teaching-learning situation. Students do not just help others, but become "wandering experts" and teachers "resources" to learning.

In this case, the subjects involved in the praxis of teaching and learning cogeneratively develop theory of teaching (and learning) that pertains to this class in this school. The understandings and solutions created in these meetings were immediately tested in the classroom leading to changes in practice and increasing affordance for learning and teacher development. This and other conceptual understandings therefore led to theory that was subsequently tested in practice and further developed. This was possible because of the direct involvement of those who were most concerned. The purpose of these cogenerative-dialoguing sessions was not to create some abstract theory that might hold across many situations in the country, but to change local practice. However, even if the theory was local, it has the potential to inform praxeological understandings in other situations, with other teacher and student collectives working on improving their praxis. Outsider perspectives lead to theory given prior to praxis and professional action; they lead to understandings of practical actions as controllable and externally determined. This therefore excludes the manifold possibilities for the concrete realization and rationalization of action by the practitioner. Practical concepts, on the other hand, are not recipes but resources for the articulation of concrete action possibilities in setting. Teaching praxis becomes the locus of a practical deconstruction of praxeology, knowledge about teaching; cogenerative dialogue becomes the locus of a critical deconstruction of praxis, knowledge of teaching.

Having all participants (or their representatives) involved in the praxis of teaching and learning also take part in the cogenerative dialogue sessions mediates the possibility for one stakeholder (group) to get trapped in ideology. If teachers were to reflect on their teaching individually, they might easily get stuck with their descriptions that have arisen from the lived experience in the classroom. In coteaching, collective reflection substitutes individual reflection, introducing potential differences between the lived experiences of differently located coteachers (e.g., supervisor, experienced teacher, and new teacher). When the group attempts to understand these differences in terms of the different locations and developmental trajectories, there emerges the potential for a critical hermeneutic analysis of the societal mediation of the teaching practice. The addition of students brings yet another dimension to the collective analysis. Now, all members are part of the effort to understand not only their own experiences but also those of the other parties in terms of societal mediation. Differences and contradictions are not to be explained away. Rather, they are used as the driving forces for changes of practice, which are subsequently tested on the spot by all participants.

In the excerpt from the cogenerative-dialoguing session, the seasoned teacher, Tony, articulated his rationale for breaking the class into two or three parts, each being taught by one of the resident teachers. Small class sizes allowed more attention to individual students; there is also a brought-based teacher experience that small class sizes make teaching (i.e., "control") easier. Both new teachers who cotaught with Tony had found themselves in agreement with this rationale and, for a considerable period of time, taught smaller sections of the class on their own. (For this reason, the other new teacher was not present in this meeting.) In this session, however, both students were quite explicit about the fact that they and their peers preferred a different arrangement. Although the teachers' rationale had made sense to them and to the researcher and university supervisor present, Peter, it became clear that student needs were not addressed in this way.

The coteaching/cogenerative-dialoguing unit is a dialectical one (Table 9.1): contradiction and difference are built into the new form of cultural practice brought into being. This new form of collective activity is associated with new opportunities for knowing and acting that do not exist when teachers work on their own. This is because the difference between individual action and new, collective activity spans a zone of proximal development in which culturally more advanced practices are possible than in non-collective situations (Engeström 1987). Whatever the lived experience of teaching—a good lesson, a lesson in which we feel to have achieved some objectives—there is always the possibility that others, coteachers and students, had a different experience. Cogenerative dialogue, with its intention to produce explanations through critical hermeneutic inquiry, has the potential to develop new ways of framing praxeology, which can be tested as soon as the participants are back in the classroom. Theoretical framing and solutions that do not bring about expected changes lead to new tensions between praxeology and praxis, providing the contradictions that drive further development. Local theory-focused activity, which leads to praxeology, is therefore inherently an emancipatory activity, rather than an activity that stops at understanding (isolated from practice), or worse, is in the service of the ruling ideas that are associated with institutionalized forms of power.

TEACHER DEVELOPMENT

Lifeworld articulations are directly related to the actions that each lifeworld affords; that is, forms of practice determine forms of thought. Thus, the distinctions between "teacher training" and "student teacher," on the one hand, and "teaching" and "teacher," on the other, frame an individual's trajectory in terms of stages, with definite boundaries sometimes marked by diplomas (and associated rites of passage). As he or she receives the university diploma and teaching certificate, the individual changes status. Individual trajectories are in this way marked in terms of stages. Associated with these stages are also notions that "learning" is tied to institutions and times. My research with other coteachers, involving newcomers (previously student teachers) and old-timers convinced me of the need to articulate teaching (praxis) and teacher learning in new and different ways; new forms practice allowed us to change our existing thoughts. Individual qualification should not be understood as the enculturation into specific and unchanging work contexts or independent of the cultural-historical developments of the praxis. Rather, individual qualification and professional development have to be understood as production and reproduction of the action Spielraum necessary in and characteristic of praxis. (In this, the development of the action potential as a practitioner is structurally equivalent to the development of the action potential of the individual subject more generally.) By framing teacher knowledge in the form of praxis/praxeology, learning and development become endemic to teaching practice and an integral part of the trajectory of becoming a teacher. Becoming a teacher is therefore a never-ending process. My comments on teacher development pertain to the experiences teachers might have anywhere in their career; my notion of "professional development" pertains to periods previously referred to as teacher training (at the university) and professional praxis (out in the schools). Because the meaning of professional development is most of all practical it has to be *built into* the context of each individual's everyday work. Otherwise, professional development remains without relevance and is, at best, episodic. To make professional development worth its while, it has to be build on a variety of forms of collective exchange, collective elaboration of experience and change of praxis. Most importantly, professional development has to deal with the professional isolation teachers generally experience.

Central to our conception of the praxis/praxeology dialectic is the double work of teachers: they come to an understanding of students as subjects in the teaching-learning situation and to an understanding of themselves as subjects involved in the same situation. This double task is not possible simultaneously but is accomplished in the temporal delay between the practice of teaching and the praxis of reflection. All individuals involved in the first are also involved in the second form of praxis. Cogenerative dialoguing will therefore always be temporally (and frequently spatially) shifted with respect to coteaching. The intervening temporal and spatial distance parallels (is analogous to) the distance between practical mastery and symbolic mastery characteristic of the two settings, respectively. However, personal and spatial distance to work practice does not automatically guarantee sufficient and appropriate reflection on the context of work nor does it automatically increase the available room to maneuver. That is, personal, spatial, and temporal shifts do not guarantee the objectivity of an outside look at our practices.

Professional development should always pertain to everyday work and be evident in the workplace. It consists of subjects' realization of objectively available action Spielraum and participation in its enlargement. Professional development pertains to the increase of the action possibilities subjectively available to the individual. Practical actions cannot be reduced to simple routines. Their meaning can only be determined out of the concrete relationships given in praxis (to the practitioner rather than the detached observer). Spielraum encompasses all practical actions immediately available to the practitioner, that is, all practical actions that are given to him or her without reflection. For professional development (beginning or experienced teachers) to be meaningful, one has to take into account its concrete meaning for participants and their subjective grounds to participate in it and use it for their work. But one can only take into account the meaning of professional development if it occurs out of the concrete relations that characterize the work situation and if it becomes a considerable aspect of professional development praxis. That is, the meaning of activity has to be determined out of the reality of lived experience rather than from the outside. Professional development is not an external condition that determines work praxis but in its special quality and theoretical-practical relevance is to be understood as concrete aspect of each individual's professional praxis.

When I speak of bringing together research and praxis, I do not mean research that becomes detached from the practical situation. Rather, I think about research that has as its focus the systematic analysis of professional experience for the determination of action possibilities and developmental trajectories. Research is, in this way, tightly related to the potential for bring about change in praxis.

In the traditional way of considering teaching and teacher training, individuals are left on their own in finding relationships between theory and praxis. Teachers, whether they are just beginning or interested in professional development, find themselves facing the task of clarifying the relationship between the theoretical discourse and work, and are ultimately responsible individually for making relevant connections. Professional development is thus left to the individual rather than making it a collective responsibility. I propose coteaching/cogenerative dialoguing as a model for professional development to overcome the problems in the traditional teacher education model, embodies the theory-practice gap.

CONCLUSION

The problematic relationship between theory and professional praxis is not particular to education—historical rifts and gaps between initial training and praxis exist in many fields. However, as educators of educators we are particularly concerned with this relationship because it pertains to our daily practice in schools and universities. We therefore need to continue building our theoretical tools to help us understand teachers as they are engaged in meaningful practices. Our understanding needs to acknowledge and build human values contained in those practices; and our understanding has to have the potential to become part of practice.

In the past, educators have come to elaborate on the gap between theory and practice in many different ways. Some strove to narrow it others to eliminate it and again others promoted one entity over the other. I do not pretend that there is no gap but rather emphasize that it is a true and constitutive aspect of the praxis/praxeology relationship. I attempt to show that rather than to wish this gap away, we should embrace it in true dialectical fashion in such a way that we draw the maximum benefit of the driving force that such contradictions embody. Out of the dialectic of praxis and praxeology, and the parallel dialectic of immediate understanding and explanation, we can develop a new understanding of teaching as praxis and what to do to bring new members to the profession.

Fred Newman and Lois Holzman (1997) launched a critique of all epistemologies that conceive of knowledge as separate from praxis. They articulate the breakdown of the modernist enterprise of reconciling formal knowledge and the world and propose instead a "practice of method" as an attempt to achieve a unity, knowing in praxis, a move that makes epistemology altogether obsolete. In practice, there are no "things" and no "knowledge." It is in interactions with others we perform what we know and change both what we know and the relationships where knowing is performed and constituted. In my view, such a move leads to an "absolute monopolization of experience" at the expense of theory or, as what I prefer, of praxeology. There lies a danger in the approach proposed by Newman and Holzman: the lack of contradiction leads directly into stagnation and ideology. I do not think that doing away with theorizing, in the way it occurs in cogenerative-dialogue sessions to produce praxeology, should be abandoned.

In the dialectic approach, praxis and praxeology are mutually exclusive poles. But because we think these poles as part of a unity, there always remains the tension that the concepts (even though developed by the copractitioners) never capture praxis in its totality. They will always only deal with some aspects that become salient against a non-thematic background. At the same time, praxis will always remain open, where we achieve previously stated plans and goals only in a proximal way, the match being assessable only after the fact, and in a process of reflection on action. Thus, "theory and practice, then, being vanishing moments in an ever ongoing, self-contradictory or circular movement, tend to slip through our fingers as objects when we come close enough to them" (Nissen 1998: 83). In coteaching, with its constitutive parts of teaching and cogenerative dialoguing, we establish a dialectical process, as a core element of praxis. As we enact teaching, there is theory in practice; as we develop our understanding through hermeneutic critique of primary experience and understanding, we enact theory-making praxis.

Development is a central aspect in the conception of the dialectical unit of praxis/praxeology and the situations of coteaching/cogenerative dialoguing, where they are produced. Praxis/praxeology as a unit of inherently contradictory forms of knowledge, is continuously produced and reproduced, in situation, and therefore constitutes learning in and as practice. In this, my conception is consistent with the notion of knowledgeability. In coteaching, we no longer make a distinction between teacher training and development but see both in terms of developments involving differently located individuals. This is consistent with the practice of thinking of new teachers rather than "student teachers," a term that draws a priori distinctions that interfere with professional integration and legitimate peripheral participation from early on. Individuals, once they make a decision for teaching, begin a trajectory of legitimate peripheral participation. Even as complete newcomers, their contribution to teaching is welcomed and appreciated, as these are additional and valuable resources in the societal project of working on its own survival. No longer are there mere university students, recipients of academic knowledge about teaching. No longer are there "student" teachers, whose lesser status is being constructed and exploited by school students and teachers alike. There are only individuals who contribute, at whatever stage they currently are, to the overall project of educating future generations.

Appendix

The following, common transcription conventions are used throughout the book:

(3.2)   Pauses in seconds, one-tenth of a second accuracy;
-           hyphen at the end of word marks a sudden stop in an utterance
=   Equal sign indicates "latching," meaning that the normal period of silence between the end of one speaking turn and the beginning of the next does not exist;
that   italics indicate a greater emphasis on a word or syllable;
(*points*) italics in parentheses indicate actions;
OUT   capitals to indicate louder than normal speech;
[square bracket to indicate overlap of speakers and activities with respect to ongoing talk; and
?!.   punctuation marks note speech patterns such as questions, exclamations, stops, and full stops, rather than grammatical units.

References

Bakhtin, M. M. (1993). *Toward a philosophy of the act*. Austin: University of Texas Press.

Bourdieu, P. (1980). *Le sens pratique*. Paris: Les Éditions de Minuit. (Translated as: P. Bourdieu, *The logic of practice*. Cambridge: Polity Press, 1990)

Bourdieu, P. (1992). The practice of reflexive sociology (The Paris workshop). In P. Bourdieu and L.J.D. Wacquant, *An invitation to reflexive sociology* (pp. 216–260). Chicago: University of Chicago Press.

Bourdieu, P. (1997). *Méditations pascaliennes* [Pascalian meditations]. Paris: Seuil.

Bourdieu, P., and Wacquant, L.J.D. (1992). *An invitation to reflexive sociology*. Chicago: University of Chicago Press.

Chaiklin, S. (1993). Understanding the social scientific practice of *Understanding practice*. In S. Chaiklin and J. Lave (Eds.), *Understanding practice: Perspectives on activity and context* (pp. 377–401). Cambridge: Cambridge University Press.

Cochran-Smith, M. (1994). Teacher research in teacher education. In S. Hollingsworth and H. Sockett (Eds.), *Teacher researcher and educational reform: Ninety-third yearbook of the National Society for the Study of Education* (pp. 142–165). Chicago: University of Chicago Press.

Dreyfus, H. L. (1991). *Being-in-the-world*: A commentary on Heidegger's "Being and Time," division I. Cambridge, MA: MIT Press.

Dreyfus, H. L., and Dreyfus, S. E. (1986). *Mind over machine: The power of human intuition and expertise in the era of the computer*. New York: Free Press.

Engels, F. (1970). *Socialism: Utopian and scientific*. Moskow: Progress Publishers. Available on-line: Marx/Engels Internet Archive: http://www.marxists.org, 1999

Engeström, Y. (1987). *Learning by expanding: An activity-theoretical approach to developmental research*. Helsinki, Finland: Orienta-Konsultit.

Feynman, R. P. Leighton, R. B., and Sands, M. (1989). *The Feynman lectures on physics*. Redwood City, CA: Addison-Wesley.

Fraser, B. J. (1998). Science learning environments: Assessment, effects and determinants. In B. J. Fraser and K. G. Tobin (Eds.), *International handbook of science education* (pp. 527–564). Dordrecht, The Netherlands: Kluwer Academic Press.

Freire, P. (1972). *Pedagogy of the oppressed*. Harmondsworth, England: Penguin.

Garfinkel, H. (1967). *Studies in ethnomethodology*. Englewood Cliffs, NJ: Prentice-Hall.

Haber-Schaim, U., Cutting, R., Kirksey, H. G., and Pratt, H. (1994). *Introductory physical science*. Belmont, MA: Science Curriculum Inc.

Hegel, G. F. (1969). *The science of logic* (A. V. Miller, Trans.). London: Allen and Unwin. Available on-line: at http://www.marxists.org.uk/reference/archive/-hegel/index.htm

Heidegger, M. (1977). *Sein und Zeit*. Tübingen, Germany: Max Niemeyer. (Consulted in English as *Being and time*, J. Stambaugh, Trans., Albany: State University of New York, 1996)

Holzkamp, K. (1983). *Grundlegung der Psychologie* [Foundations of psychology]. Frankfurt, Germany: Campus.

Holzkamp, K. (1991a). Experience of self and scientific objectivity. In C. W. Tolman and W. Maiers (Eds.), *Critical psychology: Contributions to an historical science of the subject* (pp. 65–80). Cambridge: Cambridge University Press.

Holzkamp, K. (1991b). Societal and individual life processes. In C. W. Tolman and W. Maiers (Eds.), *Critical psychology: Contributions to an historical science of the subject* (pp. 50–64). Cambridge: Cambridge University Press.

Il'enkov, E. V. (1977). *Dialectical logic: Essays in its history and theory*. Moskow: Progress.

Il'enkov, E. V. (1982). *Dialectics of the abstract and the concrete in Marx's Capital* (Sergei Kuzyakov, Transl.). Moskow: Progress.

Jordan, B. (1989). Cosmopolitical obstetrics: Some insights from the training of traditional midwives. *Social Science in Medicine, 28,* 925–944.

Kuutti, K. (1999). Activity theory, transformation of work, and information systems design. In Y. Engeström, R. Miettinen, and R.-L. Punamäki (Eds.), *Perspectives on activity theory* (pp. 360–376). Cambridge: Cambridge University Press.

Latour, B., and Woolgar, S. (1979). *Laboratory life: The social construction of scientific facts*. Beverly Hills, CA: Sage Publications.

Lave, J. (1988). *Cognition in practice: Mind, mathematics and culture in everyday life*. Cambridge: Cambridge University Press.

Lave, J. (1990). Views of the classroom: Implications for math and science learning research. In M. Gardner, J. G. Greeno, F. Reif, A. H. Schoenfeld, A. diSessa, and E. Stage (Eds.), *Toward a scientific practice of science education* (pp. 251–263). Hillsdale, NJ: Lawrence Erlbaum.

Lave, J. (1991). Situating learning in communities of practice. In L. Resnick, J. Levine, and S. D. Teasley (Eds.), *Perspectives on socially shared cognition* (pp. 63–82). Washington, DC: APA Press.

Lave, J. (1993). The practice of learning. In S. Chaiklin and J. Lave (Eds.), *Understanding practice: Perspectives on activity and context* (pp. 3–32). Cambridge: Cambridge University Press.

Lave, J. (1996). Teaching, as learning, in practice. *Mind, Culture, and Activity, 3,* 149–164.

Lave, J. (1997). On learning. *Forum Kritische Psychologie, 38,* 120–135.

Lave, J., and Wenger, E. (1991). *Situated learning: Legitimate peripheral participation*. Cambridge: Cambridge University Press.

Leont'ev, A. N. (1978). *Activity, consciousness and personality*. Englewood Cliffs, NJ: Prentice Hall.

Marx, K., and Engels, F. (1970). *The German ideology* (C. J. Arthur, Ed.; W. Lough, C. Dutt, and C. P. Magill, Trans.). New York: International.

Merleau-Ponty, M. (1945). *Phénoménologie de la perception*. Paris: Gallimard.

Müller, A.M.K. (1973). Naturgesetz, Wirklichkeit, Zeitlichkeit [Natural law, reality, and the structure of time]. In E. von Weizsäcker (Ed.), *Offene Systeme I* (pp. 303–358). Stuttgart, Germany: Klett.

Munby, H., and Russell, T. (1992). Transforming chemistry research into chemistry teaching: The complexities of adopting new frames for experience. In T. Russell and H. Munby (Eds.), *Teachers and teaching: From classroom to reflection* (pp. 90–108). London, England: The Falmer Press.

Newman, F., and Holzman, L. (1997). *The end of knowing: A developmental way of learning*. New York: Routledge.

Nissen, M. (1998). Theory and practice: Happy Marriage or passionate love affair? *Nordiske Udkast, 26,* 79–84.

Ricœur, P. (1984). *Time and narrative, Vol. 1* (K. McLaughlin and D. Pellauer, Trans.). Chicago: University of Chicago Press.

Ricœur, P. (1985). *Time and narrative, Vol. 2* (K. McLaughlin and D. Pellauer, Trans.). Chicago: University of Chicago Press.

Ricœur, P. (1988). *Time and narrative, Vol. 3* (K. Blamey and D. Pellauer, Trans.). Chicago: University of Chicago Press.

Ricœur, P. (1990). *Soi-même comme un autre*. Paris: Seuil. (Consulted in English as *Onself as another*, K. Blamey, Transl., Chicago: Chicago University Press, 1992)

Ricœur, P. (1991). *From text to action: Essays in hermeneutics, II*. Evanston, IL: Northwestern University Press.

Roth, W.-M. (1990). Neo-Piagetian predictors of achievement in physical science. *Journal of Research in Science Teaching, 27,* 509–521.

Roth, W.-M. (1991). The development of reasoning on the balance beam. *Journal of Research in Science Teaching, 28,* 631–645.

Roth, W.-M. (1993). Metaphors and conversational analysis as tools in reflection on teaching practice: Two perspectives on teacher-student interactions in open-inquiry science. *Science Education, 77,* 351–373.

Roth, W.-M. (1996). Teacher questioning in an open-inquiry learning environment: Interactions of context, content, and student responses. *Journal of Research in Science Teaching, 33,* 709–736.

Roth, W.-M. (1998a). *Designing communities*. Dordrecht, The Netherlands: Kluwer Academic Publishing.

Roth, W.-M. (1998b). Science teaching as knowledgeability: A case study of knowing and learning during coteaching. *Science Education, 82,* 357–377.

Roth, W.-M. (1998c). Teaching and learning as everyday activity. In B. J. Fraser and K. G. Tobin (Eds.), *International handbook of science education* (pp. 169–181). Dordrecht, The Netherlands: Kluwer Academic Publishers.

Roth, W.-M. (2000). Learning environments research, lifeworld analysis, and solidarity in practice. *Learning Environments Research, 2,* 225–247.

Roth, W.-M. (2001). Becoming-in-the-classroom: Learning to teach in/as praxis. In D. R. Lavoie and W.-M. Roth (Eds.), *Models for science teacher preparation: Bridging the gap between research and practice* (pp. 11–30). Dordrecht, The Netherlands: Kluwer Academic Publishers.

Roth, W.-M., Bowen, G. M., Boyd, N., and Boutonné, S. (1998). Coparticipation as mode for learning to teach science. In S. L. Gibbons and J. O. Anderson (Eds.), *Connections 98* (pp. 80–88). Victoria, BC: University of Victoria.

Roth, W.-M., and Boyd, N. (1999). Coteaching, as colearning, in practice. *Research in Science Education*, 29, 51–67.

Roth, W.-M., Masciotra, D., and Boyd, N. (1999). Becoming-in-the-classroom: a case study of teacher development through coteaching. *Teaching and Teacher Education*, 17, 771–784.

Roth, W.-M., McGinn, M. K., Woszczyna, C., and Boutonné, S. (1999). Differential participation during science conversations: The interaction of focal artifacts, social configuration, and physical arrangements. *The Journal of the Learning Sciences*, 8, 293–347.

Roth, W.-M., and Milkent, M. M. (1991). Factors in the development of proportional reasoning by concrete operational college students. *Journal of Research in Science Teaching*, 28, 553–566.

Roth, W.-M., and Lawless, D. (2001). *From temporality to action and morality: A reflection on the phenomenological structure of time in teaching.* Unpublished manuscript.

Roth, W.-M., Lawless, D., and Masciotra, D. (2001). Spielraum and teaching. *Curriculum Inquiry*, 31, 183–208.

Roth, W.-M., Lawless, D., and Tobin, K. (2000). Time to teach: Towards a praxeology of teaching. *Canadian Journal of Education*, 25, 1–15.

Roth, W.-M., and Tobin, K. (2001a). Learning to teach science as praxis. *Teaching and Teacher Education*, 17, 741–762.

Roth, W.-M., and Tobin, K. (2001b). The implications of coteaching/cogenerative dialogue for teacher evaluation: Learning from multiple perspectives of everyday practice. *Journal of Personnel Evaluation in Education*, 15, 7–29.

Roth, W.-M., and Tobin, K. (2002). *At the elbow of another: Learning to teach by coteaching.* New York: Peter Lang.

Roth, W.-M., and Tobin, K. (in press). Redesigning an "urban" teacher education program: An activity theory perspective. *Mind, Culture, and Activity.*

Roth, W.-M., Tobin, K., and Zimmermann, A. (in press). Coteaching: Learning environments research as aspect of classroom praxis. *Learning Environments Research*, 3.

Schön, D. A. (1983). *The reflective practitioner: How professionals think in action.* New York: Basic Books.

Schön, D. A. (1987). *Educating the reflective practitioner.* San Francisco: Jossey-Bass.

Shulman, L. S. (1987). Knowledge and teaching: Foundations of the new reform. *Harvard Educational Review*, 57, 1–22.

Suchman, L. A. (1987). *Plans and situated actions: The problem of human-machine communication.* Cambridge: Cambridge University Press.

Thorndike, E. L. (1912). *Education: A first book.* New York: The MacMillan Company.

Tobin, K. (2000). Becoming an urban science educator. *Research in Science Education*, 30, 89–106.

Tobin, K., Roth, W.-M., and Zimmermann, A. (2001). Learning to teach in urban schools. *Journal of Research in Science Teaching*, 38, 941–964.

van Manen, M. (1995). On the epistemology of reflective practice. *Teachers and Teaching: Theory and Practice*, 1, 33–50.

Index

About the Author

WOLFF-MICHAEL ROTH is Professor of Applied Cognitive Science at the University of Victoria, British Columbia. He taught science, mathematics, and computer science before beginning his current career in phenomenologically and sociologically oriented research.